HEILONG...   ...IA
                    • Khabarovsk

        • Harbin

    • Changchung   • Jilin

    JILIN PROVINCE   • Vladivostok
                        Tumen •
                        Yanji •   Khasan
        • Shenyang   Musan •
    LIAONING PROVINCE   Chongjin

                    NORTH KOREA

        Dandong • • Sinuiju
                    • Pyongyang
        • Dalian   DMZ

    • Beijing

                    Incheon • Seoul
        • Shandong
                    SOUTH KOREA
                        Daegu •
                                    JAPAN

                    • Shanghai

                        TAIWAN
    iangzhou •

    Hong Kong

Praise for *Escape from North Korea*

"Melanie Kirkpatrick is one of the finest newspaperwomen of her generation, and she has, in *Escape from North Korea*, brought in an astonishing scoop—a story that illuminates how America's own abolitionists, across the centuries and oceans, are inspiring a new underground railroad. Her account reminds us all of why Communist regimes so fear religion."

—Seth Lipsky, editor of the *New York Sun*

"*Escape from North Korea* is a troubling and inspiring story of both man's inhumanity to his fellow man and a testimony to the indomitable human spirit in the midst of horrific torture and privation. Melanie Kirkpatrick has done us all a great service by telling this compelling story."

—Richard Land, president of the
Ethics & Religious Liberty Commission

"Kirkpatrick puts the spotlight on one of the greatest tragedies of the postwar world: the transformation of an entire nation into a gulag. But despite the many horrors of North Korea, courage and the human spirit endure. Kirkpatrick's timely book should convince Koreans and Americans of the immediate need to end North Korea's totalitarian dictatorship and unify the peninsula under a free and democratic government."

—John Yoo, professor of law at the
University of California at Berkeley

ESCAPE FROM NORTH KOREA

THE UNTOLD STORY OF ASIA'S UNDERGROUND RAILROAD

Melanie Kirkpatrick

Encounter Books e New York • London

First American edition published in 2012 by Encounter Books,
an activity of Encounter for Culture and Education, Inc.,
a nonprofit, tax-exempt corporation.
Encounter Books website address: www.encounterbooks.com

Manufactured in the United States and printed on
acid-free paper. The paper used in this publication meets
the minimum requirements of ANSI/NISO Z39.48–1992
(R 1997) (*Permanence of Paper*).

FIRST AMERICAN EDITION

LIBRARY OF CONGRESS CATALOGING-IN-PUBLICATION DATA
Kirkpatrick, Melanie.
Escape from North Korea: The untold story of Asia's underground railroad/
by Melanie Kirkpatrick.
p. cm.
Includes bibliographical references and index.
ISBN 978-1-59403-633-0 (hardcover: alk. paper)—ISBN 978-1-59403-646-0
(ebook) 1. Korea (North)—Emigration and immigration. 2. Refugees—Korea
(North) 3. Refugees—Government policy—China. 4. Missionaries—Korea
(North) 5. Missionaries—China. 6. Church work with refugees—Korea (North)
7. Church work with refugees—China. 8. Illegal aliens—China.
9. Repatriation—Korea (North) 10. Repatriation—China. I. Title.
HV640.5.K67K63 2012
305.9'0691409513—dc23
2012007386

FOR JACK

CONTENTS

Contents

AUTHOR'S NOTE

This is a book about personal courage and the quest for liberty. These qualities are embodied in the North Koreans who
dare to escape from their slave-state of a nation to the neighboring,
but unwelcoming, country of China. They are embodied, too, in
Christian missionaries and other humanitarian workers who help
the North Korean runaways flee China and reach sanctuary in free
countries. They travel along a secret route known as the new underground railroad.

This is also a book about North Korea's future. Through the stories recounted in these pages, the reader will catch a glimpse of the
potential of the North Korean people, what they and their country
could become if they were liberated. The twenty-four thousand North
Koreans who have fled to safety in South Korea (or, in a few cases,
North America or Europe) constitute a tiny minority of the country's
twenty-four million people. Yet they are the change-makers. They are

a bridge to a free and unified Korea. Through their efforts to reach family and friends they have left behind, the fugitives are opening up their information-starved homeland, exposing their countrymen to liberal ideas, and helping to lay the intellectual groundwork for dissent. The escapees already are beginning to transform their country, and they may eventually replace the totalitarian regime that keeps their fellow citizens in chains.

Supreme Leader Kim Jong Eun, North Korea's young new dictator, understands the threat that the escapees pose to his rule. One of his first acts after succeeding his late father, Kim Jong Il, in December 2011, was to issue a shoot-to-kill order to guards along the Sino-Korean border. Anyone observed fleeing across the Tumen or Yalu River to China was to be stopped, he commanded. Kim Jong Eun reportedly also issued orders for the on-the-spot execution of any North Korean arrested in flight.

Through the North Korean escape stories, I also illustrate the effects that policy decisions made in Beijing, Washington, Seoul, and other world capitals have on the men, women, and children who flee North Korea. I pay particular attention to China, whose forced repatriation of the North Koreans living in China is both morally wrong and illegal under international agreements to which China is a party. Beijing deems the North Koreans "economic migrants," a status that conveniently ignores Pyongyang's savagery against its own people, including the use of economic repression, especially the withholding of essential food supplies, as a tool of political control. China's inhumane repatriation policy also ignores the harsh punishment inflicted upon the North Koreans it sends back against their will.

The principal characters of this narrative are the passengers and conductors on the new underground railroad—the secret network of safe houses and transit routes that crisscrosses China and transports North Koreans to refuge in bordering countries. The new underground railroad is operated by humanitarian workers, largely Christian, from the United States and South Korea, and it is supported by thousands of ordinary men and women in China, Christian and not, who are willing to break their country's laws and risk imprisonment to assist the North Koreans. Helping a North Korean—even so much as giving him a meal—is a crime in China, punishable by fines, jail sentences, and, in the case of foreigners, deportation after they have served their time in prison. The men and women who rescue North Koreans are acting on the dictum of the eighteenth-century British philosopher Edmund Burke, who warned, "Evil flourishes when good men do nothing." Enterprising business people—both honest and dishonest in their dealings—also are increasingly active along the new underground railroad, where North Koreans can purchase passage with cash or on credit.

My admiration for the North Koreans who escape and for those who help them is my motivation for writing their untold story, but I also cover areas where both groups fall short. In their zeal to spread their faith, religious workers are sometimes too quick to jeopardize their own lives and those of vulnerable North Koreans. In the United States, too many people in the Korean-American community avert their eyes from the depredations of the regime in Pyongyang and the plight of the North Koreans in China; they fail to use their political clout in Washington on behalf of their fellow Koreans. South Koreans too often treat the North Koreans who settle in their country as strangers rather than brothers.

As for the fugitives themselves, when North Koreans finally reach safety in a third country after surmounting great odds, they can have a difficult time learning to be free. The survival skills that characterize the refugee's life on the run do not necessarily translate into coping skills in an open, modern society. Even though many North Koreans succeed in their new homes, and some do so spectacularly, others are not up to the task.

I first came to this subject when I was a journalist at the *Wall Street Journal,* a newspaper whose editorial philosophy is summed up by its unofficial credo: free markets and free people. At the *Journal,* I

Author's Note

had the opportunity to interview many of the heroes of freedom in our time. They were men and women who fought the evils of totalitarianism at great personal risk. Among them were Natan Sharansky and Vladimir Bukovsky of the Soviet Union, the Dalai Lama of Tibet, Lech Walesa of Poland, Fang Lizhi of China, Mart Laar of Estonia, and Martin Lee of Hong Kong. These are figures of international prominence, people whose deeds have been in the headlines, who have written books, and, in a few cases, who became leaders of the countries they helped liberate.

In researching this book, I interviewed many North Koreans who fled their country, including, in 2006, members of the first tiny group of refugees to arrive in the United States. In contrast to the internationally prominent heroes of freedom mentioned above, the North Korean freedom-seekers and their rescuers are mostly invisible. This book is an effort to make their stories known and, in some cases, their names as well. I say "some" because many of the North Koreans I spoke to asked that their names and other identifying information be kept secret in order to protect loved ones back home. The regime in Pyongyang practices collective punishment. Fathers and mothers, brothers and sisters, aunts and uncles, sons and daughters are punished for the supposed crime of a relative.

Many of the Christians and humanitarian workers prefer anonymity, too, out of a concern that publicity would jeopardize their rescue work. A number of the government officials with whom I spoke also asked for confidentiality, in the belief that public statements could hamper their country's diplomatic efforts on behalf of the North Korean refugees. If anyone I interviewed asked me to keep his name confidential, I have honored that request. In the course of researching this book, I have interviewed more than two hundred people in South Korea, China, Japan, Southeast Asia, and the United States. They include dozens of North Koreans, as well as Christian missionaries, humanitarian workers, community leaders, military officers, government officials, and scholars.

x

North Koreans who reach South Korea go through a government-sponsored resettlement program at an institute outside Seoul called Hanawon. *Hanawon* is a hopeful name that translates into English as "house of unity" or, more poetically, "one country." The director of Hanawon meets with each class that passes through the institute's three-month training program. "You are the winners," she tells them. "You are the survivors. You are strong."

If there is one story that is missed in the extensive media coverage of North Korea, it is the story of these winners. Sixty years of political oppression have not dulled North Koreans' appetite for freedom. The Christians and humanitarian workers devoted to this cause see their mission as the liberation of North Korea, one person at a time.

All the North Koreans I interviewed want to return to their home country one day. Their personal experiences of life in modern, free countries are preparing them for future leadership roles in the North. The bravery, enterprise, and persistence necessary for their perilous journey on the new underground railroad will serve them and their country well in years to come, when North Korea is finally free.

INTRODUCTION:
"I AM A MAN AMONG MEN"

In the spring of 1857, the antislavery Vigilance Committee of Philadelphia copied into its confidential *Underground Railroad Record* an excerpt from a letter it had received from Abram Harris, a former slave who had escaped from his master in Charles County, Maryland.

Some weeks earlier, Harris had reached the Philadelphia station along the Underground Railroad that transported fugitive American slaves to safety in Canada. He traveled by night, barely eluding the slave catchers who were hot on his heels. The friend with whom he fled was not so lucky. He died along the journey, "the first instance of death on the Underground Rail Road in this region," the *Record* states.

The Vigilance Committee kept meticulous notes on the slaves who passed through its territory and what happened to them after they departed Philadelphia. Harris, the *Record* notes, was "a man of medium size, tall, dark chestnut color." He "could read and write a little and was very intelligent." The Committee recorded that it fed and housed Harris before handing him over to another conductor and dispatching him farther north to the next depot on the Underground Railroad.

The *Record* doesn't say how Harris reached his final destination in Canada. He could have hidden in a boat that sailed from the young metropolis of Buffalo, New York, across Lake Erie to a private dock on the Canadian shore. Or perhaps a New England abolitionist guided him at night over the sparsely guarded, wooded border in Vermont. However he achieved his freedom, Abram Harris expressed his relief and happiness. Written from the newfound safety of Canada, the former slave's letter sings with joy.

"Give my love to Mr. _____ and family," he writes—the name of the Philadelphian who helped him was redacted in case the *Record* fell into the wrong hands. "And tell them I am in a land of liberty! I am a man among men!"[1]

Now, fast-forward 150 years and consider the story of a young woman who escaped from the slave-state of North Korea. "Hannah" is a modern-day Abram Harris. She rode the new underground railroad across China to temporary refuge in Southeast Asia and eventually to a permanent home in the United States. I interviewed her in 2006 in Elizabeth, New Jersey, a few days after she arrived in her new country. She was among the first group of North Koreans to be granted political asylum in America. We spent an afternoon together, closeted in the windowless conference room of a New Jersey hotel not far from Newark Liberty International Airport.

Hannah used her English name—call it a *nom de liberté*—given to her by the Christian pastor who helped her get out of China.

Her escape route along the new underground railroad took her from a rural village in northeast China more than two thousand miles across the country to the southwestern city of Kunming. From there, she slipped into Laos and then Thailand before finally going on to the United States.

Hannah asked me to use her new first name. Her real name, she feared, might attract the notice of the regime in North Korea. According to a dictate laid down by the late Kim Il Sung, founding father of the Democratic People's Republic of Korea and its Eternal President, the crimes of an individual are paid for by three generations of his family. It is against the law for a citizen to leave North Korea without government approval. The relatives of escaped North Koreans who come to the attention of Pyongyang have been known to disappear into the country's vast prison system or suffer unfortunate "accidents." Hannah's husband and daughter still live in North Korea.

Like that of the former slave American slave Abram Harris, Hannah's mood was euphoric. We had reached the end of the interview; she had recounted some of the horrors she experienced in North Korea and then in China, where she had been sold as a bride to a farmer. Like every trafficked bride I've interviewed, Hannah remembered the price for which she was sold. She fetched 20,000 Chinese yuan, she recalled, roughly $2,400. Her new "husband" threatened to beat her to death if she didn't submit to him. "North Koreans like you are easier to kill than a chicken," he told her.

My notebook closed, I asked Hannah how she felt about being in the United States. She smiled—the first time she'd done so in our four hours together. Her words echoed those of Abram Harris more than a century and a half earlier.

"My heart feels free," she said.

More than twenty years after the collapse of the Soviet Union and the fall of the Berlin Wall, North Korea remains the world's last closed totalitarian state, intent on keeping foreigners out and its own citizens in. It is a modern-day Hermit Kingdom, a throwback to the eighteenth and nineteenth centuries and the isolationist policies of the Chosun Dynasty, which sealed Korea's borders to every nation except China and decreed it a capital crime to leave the country. The rulers feared outside influence. Koreans who left the country and then dared to return were executed.

Today it is hard to overstate the isolation that North Koreans endure. Radios are fixed by law to government-run stations, and listening to foreign radio broadcasts is a crime. Cellphone use is limited to calls within the country. The Internet is forbidden to all but a chosen few, among them the late dictator Kim Jong Il, who in 2000 famously asked visiting American Secretary of State Madeleine Albright for her email address. Only twenty-three countries have embassies in Pyongyang.[2]

The darkness in which the Kim family regime keeps the country is more than metaphorical. It is not only an information blackout. It is a literal blackout. Nowhere is this more evident than in the Chinese border city of Dandong, situated on the Yalu River directly across the water from the North Korean trading port of Sinuiju. The Chinese city's brightness stands in dramatic contrast to the North Korean side of the river. At night, Dandong's waterfront sparkles like a carnival. The high-rise apartment buildings that line the shoreline drive are outlined in neon. Downtown, signs for hotels, seafood restaurants, and trading companies flash brightly. The riverside park is studded every few yards with street lamps that cast a soft, golden glow. The most prominent feature of Dandong after dark is the Friendship Bridge that connects the two cities across the Yalu. The bridge's silhouette is traced in running lights that cycle from blue to red to green to yellow every few minutes.

And on the North Korean side of the river? If there is a moon and the night is clear, you might be able to see a dim light or two in a low building. On a moonless night, the opposite shore is black. No one standing in Dandong would be able to tell that there was a city of 360,000 people on the other side of the Friendship Bridge. North Korea is so short of electricity that much of the country is switched off in the early evening. Like medieval peasants, North Koreans go to bed with the sun. So accustomed are North Koreans to the lack of light that when I asked a North Korean who had settled in an American city if there was anything she missed from home, she replied, "the darkness."[3]

In October 2006, shortly after North Korea conducted a nuclear test, Secretary of Defense Donald Rumsfeld unveiled to the press a striking satellite image of the Korean Peninsula at night. The photograph showed the northern half of the peninsula completely in the dark except for a speck of light, which indicated the location of the capital, Pyongyang. South Korea's portion of the peninsula, in contrast, was aglow, its myriad cities alive with light.

South Korea's luminosity is a shining testimony to its advanced economy. In 2010, the World Bank reported that it was the world's fourteenth-largest economy, with a gross domestic product of $1.45 trillion and a per-capita income of nearly $20,000.[4] Reliable statistics from North Korea have proven so elusive that the World Bank refuses even to estimate the size of its paltry economy. The satellite photo "says it all," Rumsfeld commented. "There's the South, the same people as the North, the same resources, North and South, and the big difference is in the South, it's a free political system and a free economic system."[5]

North Korea ranks at the bottom of every international measure of freedom. It is dead last, after Cuba and Zimbabwe, in the Heritage Foundation/Wall Street Journal Index of Economic Freedom.[6] Freedom House's annual survey of political rights and civil liberties categorizes it as "not free."[7] North Korea is the world's worst persecutor of Christians, according to Open Doors International, which evaluates religious liberty worldwide.[8] North Korea is also the world's worst abuser of human rights. The United Nations' special rapporteur on human rights in North Korea has called the country's record "abysmal," citing food shortages, public executions, and torture.[9]

According to South Korea's National Human Rights Commission, two hundred thousand men, women, and children—almost 1 percent of the population—are locked up in gulag-style political prisons known as *kwan li so,* which are located in remote mountainous regions. The inmates' ideological crimes include offenses such as possessing a Bible or disrespecting photographs of Kim Il Sung, the late founder of the Democratic People's Republic, or Kim Jong Il, his son and, until his death in 2011, successor as the country's dictator. "The inmates are suffering starvation, torture, forced labor, rape, and executions out of [the eye of] global attention," the report from Seoul said.[10] Some sections of the political prison camps are designated "total control zones." They house "enemies of the people" who are deemed incorrigible and are serving life sentences with no possibility of release. Several hundred thousand North Koreans have died in the political prison camps from torture, starvation, disease, and execution, according to the Washington-based Committee for Human Rights in North Korea.[11] The total number of dead may be as high as one million, according to the human-rights group Christian Solidarity Worldwide.[12]

Food might be scarce in North Korea, but if there is one thing the country has an abundance of, it is jails. In addition to those being held in political prison camps, thousands of North Koreans are imprisoned in another type of prison called labor-through-reeducation camps. The sentences at the labor camps are usually shorter than those in the *kwan li so*—that is, there is a chance that the authorities will eventually permit an inmate to go home—but the living conditions are equally bad. In both types of prisons, the inmates are overworked, underfed, and subjected to extraordinary degrees of violence. Many don't survive the experience. Pyongyang bars the International Red Cross from inspecting any of the prison camps.

Beyond the *kwan li so* and the labor camps is a hierarchy of well-used local detention centers. Economist Marcus Noland reported that an astonishing 100 percent of the North Korean refugees he interviewed in China said they had had the experience of being detained by police in North Korea. "They could be walking down the street and hauled off to the police station to be interviewed for four or five hours," he said. In many cases, a well-placed bribe secured their release. Only 12.5 percent of the refugees Noland interviewed enjoyed any legal process. His most striking finding, however, had to do with the treatment of people while in custody. "While detained, they were subjected to an extraordinary degree of brutality," Noland said. "The political prisons [*kwan li so*] are only a mild escalation in brutality."[13]

In short, North Korea is hell on earth. Refugees' stories of life in North Korea's prisons recall *The Triumph of Death*, the sixteenth-century painting by Flemish artist Pieter Bruegel the Elder. In Bruegel's images, armies of skeletons kill men, women, and children in a variety of gruesome ways—slitting throats, drowning, hanging, beheading, slaughtering with scythes. A starving dog nibbles on the face of a child.

From North Koreans who have fled, I have heard accounts of tortures that rival Bruegel's images. They speak of beatings, public hangings, firing squads, and forced abortions. At a press conference in Washington, D.C., I listened to a young man describe an episode he had witnessed at the prison camp where he had been incarcerated after being captured in China and repatriated to North Korea. One morning at roll call, he recounted, an inmate who had been badly beaten during the night was too sick to get out of bed. The guards ordered his fellow prisoners to carry the injured man into the woods and bury him alive. "I keep thinking, maybe he would still be alive if we hadn't buried him," the young man told the reporters in Washington. He didn't want his name used, for fear of retribution against his family in North Korea. But he told us the name of the man he buried, and I record it here: Kim Young-jin.

"I am very glad to be here and tell the people in America how life in North Korea really is,"[14] the man who escaped told reporters.

For North Koreans who flee to China, there is another circle of hell: life on the run. North Koreans hiding in China eke out a precarious and secretive existence, forced underground by China's policy of repatriation. The policy, in contravention of international law, is to send the refugees back to North Korea, where they face savage treatment for the crime of leaving the country without permission. China refuses to let the United Nations Office of the High Commissioner for Refugees or any other international aid group help the North Koreans. The plight of the North Koreans hiding in China is a humanitarian disaster. Yet most of the world has never heard about it.

I have interviewed dozens of North Koreans who have reached freedom in South Korea, the United States, or elsewhere and heard what most prefer to call their "testimonies." It is an apt word. In speaking out, the North Koreans are presenting evidence against the immoral regime they fled. They are putting their stories on the record for the day when the Kim family regime and the vicious elite who run the country are gone. Their stories are also an indictment of China.

The majority of North Koreans in China are women, many of whom are victims of human trafficking. Some work in brothels or in the online pornography business. A high percentage are sold, or sell themselves, as brides to Chinese men, especially in rural areas, where men are desperate for wives. North Korean men who flee to China work as loggers or laborers. They routinely are exploited by employers who threaten to turn them over to the Chinese authorities. North Korean children who have become separated from their parents in China roam the streets or take refuge in train stations until they are noticed by the police, rounded up, and sent back to the North. The children of Chinese men and North Korean women also fare badly, effectively denied citizenship by the governments of both countries, neither of which wants to acknowledge the children of "impure" blood. Providing shelters for these half-Chinese, half-Korean children is a growth industry for Christian missionaries in northeast China.

This book is the story of the new underground railroad that a few courageous North Koreans ride across China to freedom in South Korea or the West. It is the story of the small number of North Koreans who dare to flee. It records how they do so and describes the challenges they face in learning to be free in their new homes. It records, too, what happens to those who fail.

The new underground railroad begins in northeast China, near the 880-mile border that China shares with North Korea. This is the region that used to be known as Manchuria after the Manchu invaders, who ruled China during the 1644–1911 Qing Dynasty. Today it is called *Dongbei* in Chinese, which translates into English as "the Northeast." The vast region stretches from just north of Beijing to the border of Siberia and the Russian Far East. Dongbei encompasses the provinces of Heilongjiang, Jilin, and Liaoning and is home to approximately two million Chinese of Korean descent. The Korean-Chinese in northeast China constitute one of China's fifty-five official ethnic minorities. Most are bilingual, fluent in both Mandarin Chinese and Korean. Many have relatives in the northern reaches of North Korea. The Tumen and Yalu Rivers define the border separating the two countries.

The route of the new underground railroad varies. Sometimes it goes north to Mongolia or Russia. Most often it passes through the Golden Triangle area of Southeast Asia. After traveling thousands of miles across China, the passengers on the new underground railroad cross clandestinely into a third country, where they wait for months or occasionally even years for permission to settle in South Korea or the West. Vietnam, Thailand, Laos, Cambodia, and Burma all provide sanctuaries for the North Koreans, although none wishes to advertise it out of concern for antagonizing their muscular neighbor, China.

Like the Underground Railroad of pre–Civil War America, the new underground railroad across China is an ever-shifting network of secret routes and safe houses. It is run by small groups of rescuers, both humanitarians and brokers, who work mostly independently. Even within a single cell, it is rare for an individual rescuer to know every detail of every escape route. There is safety in limiting operational knowledge. If one person is arrested and interrogated, he won't endanger the entire network.

Some of the rescuers staff the shelters where North Koreans are fed, housed, and prepared for their journey if they decide to flee. To get out of China without being caught, the fugitives need new clothes to help them blend in. Depending on what role they are playing—South Korean businessman? Korean-American tourist? Chinese citizen?—they also need instruction in how to behave on their journey so they won't call attention to themselves. North Koreans stick out in China, even in the northeast region that is home to so many ethnic Koreans. One giveaway is their physical condition. Chronic malnutrition has made North Koreans shorter and thinner than the average Chinese person. "You can tell by their hair," one North Korean woman who settled in South Korea told me. "A North Korean's hair is dull and full of split ends. Chinese are well fed, and their hair is shiny."[15]

Still other rescuers do the dangerous work of guiding, accompanying the refugees along a portion of their journey or throughout the entire route. The rescuers' presence provides camouflage, and their Chinese-language skills can be critical in interacting with the public. Other rescuers act as liaisons. The humanitarians often work with brokers, for whom the transportation of people on the new underground railroad is a growing business. Or rescuers interact with the local Chinese Christian community; the activities of these Christians are closely monitored by the government, so they can provide only minimal support to the refugees.

Like the fugitive slaves of the American South, North Koreans must begin their journey unaided. Escaping the slave master—getting out of North Korea—is the dangerous first step. A failed attempt brings dire consequences. If a runaway is spotted by border guards on the Korean side of the frontier, he can be shot on the spot. If he is taken alive, he is hauled off to one of the North's detention centers or prison camps. Incarceration is also the fate of those who are captured on the Chinese side of the border and returned to the North. Runaways in China who are forced to return and whom North Korea suspects of having come into contact with Americans, South Koreans, or Christians fare worst of all. They are treated as traitors and dispatched to the *kwan li so.*

In early 2012, news organizations with sources in North Korea reported a sharp crackdown on border crossings, following the personal orders of the country's new leader, Kim Jong Eun. Free North Korea Radio, run by North Korean defectors in Seoul, said that North Korea was planting landmines on its side of the border to deter would-be crossers. The Daily NK, a defector-run Web journal, reported that North Korea had placed nail-studded boards on the banks of the rivers that separated North Korea from China. According to the South Korean *JoongAng Daily*, Kim Jong Eun issued shoot-to-kill orders to the border guards and also ordered the immediate executions of North Koreans arrested trying to cross the border. The U.S.-based Radio Free Asia reported that North Korean security guards shot three North Koreans who were trying to cross the Yalu River on New Year's Eve, 2011.

In the decades prior to the American Civil War, the Underground Railroad helped speed an estimated one hundred thousand fugitive slaves to liberty in a free state or in Canada. Upper Canada (the modern-day province of Ontario) had abolished slavery in 1793—the first overseas territory of the British Empire to do so. In 1833, the British Parliament abolished slavery in most of the British Empire.

The word "railroad" was a useful metaphor for the rescue operations run by antislavery activists, with its connotations of moving people quickly, efficiently, and anonymously. The rescuers used railroad nomenclature to describe what they did. The guides were known as "conductors," and the escaped slaves were "passengers" with "tickets." Safe houses were "depots" run by "station masters." In public, runaways were sometimes referred to as "freight" or "baggage" or "packages" in order to deflect attention from the rescue operations. The "branch lines" of the Underground Railroad zigzagged deliberately in order to confuse bounty hunters who were pursuing the fugitive slaves.

It was dangerous work for both passenger and conductor. Captured slaves faced harsh treatment when they were returned to their owners. To discourage others from taking flight, returnees might be whipped in front of their fellow slaves or sometimes even killed. If they had worked at light labor, their masters might sell them as field hands into the Deep South, where they had less chance of escaping again. Owners sometimes took retribution on the escaped slave's family.

Rescuers who were caught also faced retribution—financial and worse. In the South, anyone caught helping slaves escape could expect to lose his life. If he wasn't strung up by locals practicing vigilante justice, he could be hanged after being convicted in a court of law. William Still's *Underground Railroad Record* records the fate of one rescuer, a white man who was arrested while helping a family of five slaves escape. He was last seen alive near the Cumberland River in Kentucky. He was later found "drowned, with his hands and feet in chains and his skull fractured."[16]

Throughout the United States—South *and* North—anyone caught providing food or shelter to runaway slaves was subject to six months in prison and a fine of $1,000 under the onerous provisions of the federal Fugitive Slave Act.[17] That legislation stiffened earlier penalties for helping escaped slaves. It was passed as part of the Compromise of 1850 and signed into law by President Millard Fillmore, who hoped to ward off war between the Southern slave-holding states and the Northern free states. Abolitionists nicknamed it the "bloodhound law," for the dogs they said were used to track down runaway slaves.

In *Uncle Tom's Cabin*, Harriet Beecher Stowe's searing antislavery novel, published in 1852, one character expresses the widely held Northern view of the Fugitive Slave Act: "It's a shameful, wicked, abominable law, and I'll break it, for one, the first time I get a chance; and I hope I shall have a chance, I do!" she exclaims. "Things have got to a pretty pass, if a woman can't give a warm supper and a bed to poor, starving creatures, just because they are slaves, and have been abused and oppressed all their lives, poor things!"[18] *Uncle Tom's Cabin* was the best-selling book of the nineteenth century after the Bible, and it is one of the best-selling books of all time. Its political impact is hard to overstate. When Abraham Lincoln met Harriet Beecher Stowe in 1862, he is reported to have said, "So this is the little lady who started this great war."[19]

The number of slaves who traveled the Underground Railroad in nineteenth-century America is small when compared with the three and a half million African-Americans still in bondage in 1860 on the eve of the Civil War. But the fugitives' impact on public opinion in the North was enormous. Their escape stories—told in personal narratives, in abolitionist newspapers, in public meetings, and from church pulpits—brought home the evils of slavery to Northerners, who no longer had the option of averting their eyes or accepting pro-slavery arguments that slaves were happy and well treated. The graphic tales of deprivation and violence, sexual abuse, and family separation did much to strengthen the abolitionist cause in the North.

The slaves' escape narratives were inspirational stories of bravery, enterprise, and self-assertion. As such, they helped erode a popular image of the black man as subservient, unable to take care of himself, and unworthy of freedom. In their own accounts and in the accounts of others, the men and women who rode the Underground Railroad to freedom emerged as fully worthy of respect. The same was true of their conductors, who were often free blacks.

In the course of research for this book, I have interviewed numerous Americans who conduct North Korean refugees along the new underground railroad. Among them were a businessman from Long Island, New York, who spent four years in a Chinese prison for the crime of feeding and sheltering North Korean refugees in safe houses in China; a student who dropped out of Yale University to form an organization that guides North Koreans to safety in third countries; a retired couple from the Midwest who oversee orphanages for abandoned Chinese-Korean children in China; a pastor from Seattle who was arrested and jailed in China after he helped more than one hundred refugees escape; a woman who left a glamorous job in the public-relations industry in Manhattan to head a California-based organization that helps North Koreans escape from China.

Like the Underground Railroad of yore, the new underground railroad is supported in part by a network of benefactors. The original Underground Railroad referred to its funders as "stockholders." Then, as now, these people put up the money to keep the underground railroad running. Many of the donations supporting the new underground railroad are small, offered by church members moved to give by the stories they hear from missionaries working with refugees. Brokers who work on the new underground railroad often take IOUs from refugees, who promise to pay for their passage out of the resettlement money they receive from the South Korean government once they reach Seoul.

The new underground railroad also has ideological stockholders. In Washington, a core group of congressmen and senators keeps the issue alive on Capitol Hill. They work with a small number of dedicated activists who raise awareness and money through small nonprofit organizations. There are nearly two million Americans of Korean heritage. Like free blacks of the pre–Civil War North who helped runaway slaves, many of the conductors, benefactors, and activists along the new underground railroad are Korean-American.

Meanwhile, the world remains silent. While Pyongyang bears the ultimate responsibility for the plight of the North Korean fugitives, Beijing acts as a facilitator; Seoul until recently has turned a blind eye; Washington is usually quiet; and the United Nations, led by a South Korean Secretary-General, Ban Ki-moon, has refused to take effective action.

The number of North Koreans who have escaped so far on the new underground railroad is small. In the more than fifty years since the end of the 1950–53 Korean War, fewer than twenty-five thousand North Koreans have reached safety in South Korea. Since 2004, when Congress enacted legislation welcoming North Korean refugees, the United States has accepted 128, as of early 2012. More than one thousand are making new lives in Britain and Europe. Japan has welcomed about two hundred. Canada has given refuge to more than one hundred. These numbers are a drop in the bucket compared with the tens of thousands of North Koreans still hiding in China, much less the twenty-four million people still enslaved in North Korea.

Yet the North Korean fugitives may hold the key to regime change in North Korea and, by extension, to halting the North's nuclear and missile programs. Help one man or woman escape, and that person will get word to his family back home about the freedom that awaits outside their prison state. Others will follow, especially if they know the world will welcome them. A sip of freedom, even the limited kind available in China to refugees on the run, is intoxicating. This is already happening.

Knowledge is power. The more that North Koreans learn about the world outside their borders, the better educated they will be about their own country. The mantra of the Kim family regime—that they live in the greatest, most prosperous nation on earth and that North Koreans are the world's happiest people—will be exposed for the lie it is.

In the 1850s—the exact date is not noted—the *Underground Railroad Record* copied into its pages the words of John Thompson, a fugitive slave who had reached the city of Syracuse in central New York state. From there, Thompson wrote the Philadelphia Vigilance Committee, asking for help in getting a letter to his mother in Virginia. The letter is set down in the *Record* exactly as Thompson wrote it, including idiosyncrasies in capitalization as well as spelling and grammatical mistakes.

"MY DEAR MOTHER," he wrote. "I think highly of Freedom and would not exchange it for nothing that is offered me for it. . . . . Say to Miss Rosa that I am as Free as she is & more happier."[20]

In October 2009, a similar letter arrived via email in the in-box of 318 Partners, a Long Island–based charitable organization dedicated to rescuing North Korean refugees from China. With the help of 318 Partners, the writer, a young woman, had arrived safely in South Korea a few months earlier.

"Hello. How are you?" the email began. "My name is Lee Sun-hua. I used to live in China. I am truly thankful to you for all your help in enabling me to live in South Korea. I was sold by human traffickers in China . . . and I lived a very difficult life there."

She went on: "Right now living in South Korea is like living in heaven. It's still like a dream to me."[21]

Lee Sun-hua is not alone. Her sentiments mirror those of other North Koreans who have made it out of their homeland, to China and on to safety in third countries. Sixty years of oppression have not extinguished the spirit of these North Koreans. As they ride the new underground railroad to freedom, they are signaling the brighter future that is possible for their countrymen. There is no happy ending, as yet, to their country's story. But there is hope—and there is inspiration from their testimonies.

PART
I

ESCAPE

Anthony had fully made up his mind that when the last day of December ended, his bondage should end also, even if he should have to accept death as a substitute. He then began to think of the Underground Rail Road and of Canada; but who the agents were, or how to find the depot, was a serious puzzle to him.

—THE UNDERGROUND RAILROAD RECORD
NOVEMBER 1854

CROSSING THE RIVER

Under the terms of the armistice that suspended the Korean War in 1953, a narrow strip of land, two and a half miles wide and 155 miles long, divides the country of Korea along the thirty-eighth parallel north. Since that time, that strip of land, called the Demilitarized Zone, has served as a buffer between the Republic of Korea in the south and the Democratic People's Republic of Korea in the north. It also has served another purpose: It has kept the people of North Korea from running away.

For more than half a century, the DMZ has been virtually impenetrable. It is seeded with land mines, surrounded by fences, barbed wire, and watchtowers, and patrolled on both sides by heavily armed soldiers. North Korea's million-man army faces South Korea's six hundred thousand troops, who are backed by twenty-eight thousand American ground forces. For good reason, the DMZ is often called the most militarized border in the world.

In the nearly sixty years since its creation, the DMZ has seen so little human activity that it has reverted to a natural state. It is home today to the Asiatic black bear, Eurasian lynx, red-crowned crane, and other exotic species that have fled the development accompanying East Asia's newfound prosperity. More than one thousand plant and animal species coexist in this accidental nature preserve. Even the extremely rare Siberian tiger, the largest of its species, is said to prowl the DMZ.[1]

The last human beings to cross the thirty-eighth parallel in any number were Korean War refugees. At the time war broke out on June 25, 1950, an estimated one million men, women, and children living in North Korea fled south in advance of the Communist forces led by Kim Il Sung. Since the war, the only North Koreans to have crossed the line have been regime officials en route to discussions in Seoul, infiltrators bent on assassination or other mayhem in South Korea, and a few soldier-defectors familiar with the pathways that routed them safely past the million land mines buried there. As every North Korean knows, to reach South Korea, you cannot go south. You must first go north, to China. You must cross the river.

North Korea's boundary with China stretches 880 miles and is delineated by two rivers, the Yalu and the Tumen. The source of both rivers is on Mount Paektu, the volcanic mountain sacred to Koreans as the ancestral home of the Korean people and the location of Korea's first kingdom some four millennia ago. The Yalu River runs along North Korea's northwest border and empties into the Yellow Sea near the Chinese port of Dandong and the North Korean city of Sinuiju. The Tumen River separates the two countries in the Northeast. For its last eleven miles, it runs along the frontier between North Korea and Russia before finally flowing into the Sea of Japan, the body of water that the people of both Koreas prefer to call the East Sea, a rare show of cross-border unanimity in their shared detestation of the name imposed by their former colonial masters.

For North Koreans seeking to escape from their country, the Tumen River is usually the preferred crossing point. Unlike the Yalu, which is swift and wide and can defeat even expert swimmers, the Tumen is shallow and narrow. In winter, it is possible to walk across the frozen Tumen. In summer, it is easy to swim across or even wade, and there are sections where the riverbed dries up altogether.

The Christian missionaries and humanitarian organizations that assist North Koreans in China and help them navigate the new underground railroad out of that country rarely operate within North Korea itself. North Koreans who cross the river into China do so on their own initiative or with help from family members, friends, or paid professional guides. One survey of North Koreans hiding in China showed that even though a high number received assistance from Christians once they arrived in that country, barely 1 percent received any such assistance in exiting North Korea.[2]

Crossing the river requires an abundance of two things that are in short supply in North Korea: luck and money. A fugitive needs luck to evade border guards who think nothing of shooting a fleeing man in the back.[3] Luck will also help him stay clear of the primitive but effective man-traps that are dug into the riverbanks for the purpose of snaring North Koreans who are about to cross the river to China.

Money is essential for bribing border guards to look the other way when a traveler wants to cross the river. So, too, it is needed for hiring a guide to lead the way and pay off the relevant officials. But money isn't always enough. Some guides don't think twice about absconding with a client's down payment and leaving him to his fate. Nor can the border police always be trusted to live up to their promises even when their palms have been well greased. Police can play a double game. Timing is everything, and the price of crossing the river can range from one hundred dollars to $1,000 during one of Pyongyang's periodic crackdowns, when a border guard would be risking his life if he defied orders to prevent crossings.

Some North Koreans wait for years before they accumulate the resources and summon the courage to flee. For others, the insecurity of their situation in North Korea leaves them little choice. Crossing the river is the only way to survive. It means the difference between life and death.

"If I hadn't gone to China," the boy said, "I would have died."[4]

Joseph Gwang-jin Kim and I were sitting at a table in the restaurant of a hotel in Washington, D.C. It was Saturday morning, and the restaurant was doing a brisk business with the weekend brunch crowd. Joseph and his foster mother had gotten up in the early hours of the morning to drive to the capital for our interview, and they were hungry. I had offered to meet them earlier in the week at a time that might be more convenient for them, but Joseph did not want to miss a day of school, so we settled on Saturday.

Joseph looked like an ordinary American teenager. His hair was short and spiky, his jeans were skinny, and the three-quarter-length black jacket he wore over his T-shirt was the essence of cool. His look fit right in with the hotel's chic glass-and-chrome decor. The last thing he looked like was what he in fact was: a refugee who had been granted political asylum in the United States. Joseph escaped from North Korea in 2005 and hid out in China for more than a year. In 2006, with the help of an American aid organization, he decided to flee China and go to the United States. He walked past the Chinese guards and into the United States Consulate in the city of Shenyang in northeast China and asked for sanctuary. He was fourteen years old when he left North Korea. When he finally reached the United States in 2007, he was sixteen years old. As a minor, he was assigned to live with a foster family in a small Southern city.

From where Joseph and I sat in the dining room, we could glimpse the brunch buffet in an adjacent alcove. Hotel guests passed our table carrying plates piled high with the usual American breakfast favorites: eggs, pancakes, bagels and lox, fresh fruit. This abundance sparked chitchat about food. Joseph chatted about his after-school job at a sushi restaurant. He explained that he had memorized the English, Korean, and Japanese names of dozens of kinds of fish he had never heard of, much less tasted, before he arrived in the United States. After our own trip to the buffet, we began the interview. The subject of our conversation was starvation.

Joseph was explaining his decision to leave North Korea. The famine that killed at least one million people in the 1990s had ended, but food shortages persisted and Joseph was among the many North Koreans who were still starving. Children were especially at risk. In 2006, the year after Joseph fled, UNICEF reported that almost one-quarter of North Korean children were underweight due to lack of food and poor nutrition.[5] UNICEF also noted that child malnutrition was especially severe in the northern provinces, which included the city of Hoeryong, where Joseph lived.

That section of the country is home to many citizens who belong to the unfortunate "hostile" class, the bottom ranking in the caste system created by the regime and to which every North Korean is assigned. The caste system is based on family background and loyalty to the regime. It is a key factor in determining where a citizen may live, whether he can go to university, and what kind of job he can obtain.[6] It can determine, too, whether he has access to food.

Joseph was a *kotjebi*, or "fluttering swallow." *Kotjebi* is the North Korean nickname for homeless children who wander the streets, "fluttering" from place to place and begging for food. *Kotjebi* are usually orphans whose parents have died of starvation or abandoned them and fled to China. *Kotjebi* often hang out in groups. They loiter around markets during the day and sleep in train stations or other public places at night. At the markets, they take up positions a few steps away from a noodle stand or a vegetable seller, heads bowed in supplication and plastic bags held open. They wait for hours for a customer to take pity on them and dump some leftovers into their bag. Or they take matters into their own hands and snatch a bun from a customer's hands before he has a chance to take a bite.

Joseph became a *kotjebi* at the age of twelve, after his father starved to death. Joseph admired his father and insisted on telling me about him, although I had not inquired. It was a sensitive subject, I inferred, so I focused on listening and not asking too many questions. I had the impression that he was still trying to come to terms with his father's death, which started a train of events that destroyed his family and almost killed him, too.

"My father was very conventional and traditional," he said. "What I mean is that he was a very honest person and a person with integrity." These Confucian virtues were responsible for his death, in Joseph's view. His father refused to beg, he would not steal, and he did not reject his country and go to China. "If you want to survive in a society like North Korea, you have to be able to deceive yourself and others," Joseph told me. His father was unable, or unwilling, to do that.

After his father died, Joseph made a resolution: He would survive. His mother had no job and could not support him, and his beloved older sister had disappeared into China, where Joseph believed she was sold as a bride. His sister was nineteen years old when she left. She had promised Joseph that she would come back in two months, bringing food. She told him to wait for her, but she never reappeared. Once Joseph gave up hope of seeing her again, he left home and took to the streets. He begged for food during the day and slept under a bridge at night. Sometimes he was so hungry that he would resort to theft. Once in a while he would go home to see his mother and sleep in his old bed for a night.

At twelve years old, Joseph was nearly a teenager, but malnutrition had stunted his growth, and he looked much younger. He was a preteen trapped in the body of an eight-year-old. In addition to being small, he lacked street smarts, and before long he was picked up by the police and incarcerated in a youth detention center. The government set up youth detention centers during the famine years of the 1990s with the ostensible purpose of providing for orphans. Cynics said the government's real objective was to force dying children off the streets and out of sight. Joseph was worked hard at the center. Sometimes he would be sent to the countryside to pick corn; other days he was assigned to a construction gang. At least he got fed, but the twice-a-day meals were rarely more than a watery gruel made of corn. The food was enough to keep his hunger at bay, and Joseph ate it, but he told himself as he swallowed that pigs and cows ate better than he did.

After two and a half months, he escaped. The warden liked to watch the children fight, and he came to Joseph with a proposal. Defeat the older, bigger boy who was the supervisor of the dorm, and Joseph could take his place. The job came with better food and more privileges, and Joseph jumped at the chance to improve his lot. He won the fight, although not without cuts and bruises. One evening when the warden had left him in charge, he deserted his post and slipped out into the night.

"Did you go home?" I asked the obvious question.

There was a pause, as Joseph considered his answer. Yes, he finally said. But no one was there. Neighbors told him that his mother had been looking for him for a while but then gave up and left; no one knew where she had gone. He paused again. "It seems she thought I had died." I couldn't tell whether Joseph really believed this interpretation of his mother's disappearance or whether he found it simply too painful to consider that she might have abandoned him. He never saw her again.

Joseph spent another year on the street before he made the decision to go to China. "Many people would think that I left North

Korea because I hated the government or because I hated my hometown," he said. "But that was not the reason why. I was just hungry, and I was willing to risk my life to get out of there. I didn't know how to make a living." He repeated: "I was just hungry."

He chalked up his escape to survival skills his father never had.

The flow of people across the Sino–North Korean border did not become a problem until the early 1990s. Before then, it wasn't worth the risk for a North Korean to leave without permission; the potential rewards weren't big enough to matter. Unless he had family there, or was on the lam for some crime, why would anyone want to cross the river? Mao Zedong's China was as poor as Kim Il Sung's North Korea and nearly as repressive. A North Korean who was crazy enough to dream about going to South Korea would first have to figure out how to get out of China. That would take a miracle, and miracles were in short supply.

Then two things happened: China's economy was liberalized in the 1980s under Deng Xiaoping's reforms, leading it to quickly outpace the economy of North Korea, and the Chinese became far richer than their Korean neighbors. In North Korea, the failure of collectivist agricultural policies, bad weather, and the collapse of the Soviet Union (North Korea's patron state) combined to create a famine. Hungry North Koreans, especially those who lived in the northern reaches of the country, were faced with a choice: Stay home and starve to death, or go to China and live.

In 1991, South Korean journalist Koo Bum-hoe traveled to the border area in China and wrote a series of articles about what he learned. Reporting from Tumen City, a few miles from the North Korean border, Koo described severe food shortages that were driving families across the Tumen River into China in search of something to eat. His articles were among the first to report the coming famine and the outpouring of North Koreans to China. The trickle of refugees that he described would soon become a flood. [7]

The articles also provided rare glimpses of ordinary life in North Korea, where many were starving. He wrote about North Koreans who ate "red noodles," an imitation noodle made by grinding up the bark of a pine or acacia tree and mixing it with a small amount of corn powder. Red noodles tasted like sawdust and lacked nutrition, but they were filling.

Koo Bum-hoe also reported the North Korean government's campaign to encourage citizens to eat less for spurious "health" reasons. A person who ate sparingly was less susceptible to stomach cancer and other diseases, the hungry people were informed. Not long after Koo's articles appeared, Pyongyang introduced the campaign's macabre slogan, "Let's eat two meals a day."

While staying in Tumen City, Koo Bum-hoe picked up rumors about a North Korean family of four who had fled across the river and were arrested by the Chinese police. It was a grotesque story, and at first he didn't believe it. He finally tracked down the arresting officer, who told him what had happened. The officer, a Chinese citizen of Korean heritage, said he took pity on the family and tried to help them. Seeing that they were famished, he ordered that a Korean-style dinner of rice and an array of side dishes be served to them in jail. The officer then took the father aside and told him he would not turn the family over to the North Korean security agency if the North Korean promised to take his wife and children back to their country the next day on his own accord. The officer knew that North Korea treated repatriated refugees severely, and he wanted to spare the family from punishment.

The officer then said good night and went home. When he arrived at work the next morning and opened the door to the North Koreans' cell, he found four corpses. The mother and children had been strangled; the father had hanged himself. Koo Bom-hoe ended his article with the following observation: "It seemed as if the family had concluded that instead of going back to North Korea where they could be punished or even put to death for betraying their country that it would be better to die with full stomachs."

The North Korean famine hit the provinces bordering China first and hit them hardest. Before the famine, every North Korean had depended for his daily sustenance on food rations provided by the government-run public-distribution system. The rations were especially vital in the three northeast provinces, which had few other potential sources of food. The coast, along the Sea of Japan, is highly urbanized and industrialized, and the interiors are mountainous and rocky. Unlike the rice-growing provinces farther south, there is little arable land in the northeastern part of the country and agriculture is not a significant industry. In 1992, the government cut the official food rations by 10 percent, and the distribution system began to break down altogether. By 1994, the government appears to have decided that the citizens of the northeast region were expendable. It stopped sending food shipments altogether, preferring to channel limited food supplies to citizens of higher political status. Large numbers of starving North Koreans began crossing the river to China.

As the famine took hold, the search for food was the major factor pushing North Koreans to China. The starvation stories are legion. One survey of North Korea refugees in China asked whether they had family members who had starved to death. Of the respondents, 23 percent of men and 37 percent of women said yes.[8] A commonplace observation of North Koreans who reached China was that Chinese dogs ate better than North Korean humans. The hungry refugees marveled at watching dogs devour scraps that were more nutritious than anything they had seen for years. They also marveled at seeing dogs. In North Korea, most of the dogs had been eaten.

By the early 2000s, hunger was only one of the motives for flight.[9] Refugees cited other reasons for leaving, such as fear of persecution due to family background or frustration over lack of opportunities. By this time, North Koreans who lived close to the border had heard stories about life in China and had inklings of China's increasing prosperity and growing freedoms. Some crossed the river to find jobs. The pay wasn't lucrative by Chinese standards, but it was a fortune by North Korean ones. Men could earn ninety dollars a month in the construction industry, and women made fifty dollars a month as waitresses. The average monthly salary in North Korea was only two or three dollars, so these Chinese jobs were highly attractive.[10] Others went to China to join relatives who had already left, a pattern that accelerated in succeeding years.

It is difficult to come up with a reliable number for the North Koreans who are hiding in China. Beijing does not release information on the refugees, nor does it permit the Office of the United Nations High Commissioner for Refugees to operate there. The estimates come from international aid organizations and Christian relief groups that work quietly in the border areas. During the famine years of the mid-to-late 1990s and into the mid-2000s, there was a consensus that the refugees numbered in the hundreds of thousands. Many observers put the number as high as half a million. A leaked Chinese border police document, dated January 10, 2005, seemed to confirm these estimates. The document put the number of illegal North Korean immigrants at four hundred thousand, adding that "large numbers continue to cross the border."[11]

By the late 2000s, some observers in northeast China estimated that the numbers of North Koreans hiding in China had dropped to the tens of thousands. Large numbers of North Koreans had been arrested and repatriated. In addition, many North Koreans went home on their own initiative, unable to find work in China and unwilling to cope with life on the run. Other observers rejected such low estimates. They pointed out that North Koreans who were integrated into Chinese society—women sold as brides, for example—were so far off the radar screen that they were not easily counted. The short answer to the question of how many North Korean refugees are hiding in China: No one knows.[12]

For a North Korean who wants to escape, the first hurdle is getting to the border. Free movement around North Korea is extremely difficult. A traveler needs official permits to leave his city or county of residence, or he needs to be prepared to pay off officials along the way to let him pass. Soldiers and police officers man checkpoints on main roads at the entries and exits to most towns.[13]

The restrictions on internal travel violate Pyongyang's obligations under international law. The Universal Declaration of Human Rights stipulates, "Everyone has the right to freedom of movement and residence within the borders of each state." It further states, "Everyone has the right to leave any country, including his own, and to return to his country."[14] Such rights are also guaranteed by the International Covenant on Civil and Political Rights, which specifies that everyone "shall have the right to liberty of movement" within his own state and "shall be free to leave any country, including his own."[15]

North Korea pays lip service to its international legal obligations regarding freedom of movement within the country. But that is all it is—lip service. In 1998, under pressure at the United Nations, North Korea added a provision to its national constitution that formally guaranteed the right of movement. "Citizens shall have the freedom of residence and travel," Article 75 states.[16] But those are only words on paper. No such freedoms exist in practice. North Korea continues to enforce a system of strict control over where citizens may live and where they may travel. Pyongyang has rationalized the controls as necessary for making sure that every citizen benefits from the nationwide system of food rationing. But the real purpose for restricting citizens' movement has always been to prevent potential assemblies, protest rallies, and external contacts. If citizens can travel freely, they might obtain information from people in other regions that might in turn lead to organized dissent.

The government-mandated travel procedures call for a would-be traveler to submit an application to the accounting section of his official workplace two weeks in advance of his proposed travel date. Approval depends on a review of the applicant's ideology and his work record. If he makes it through this first level of scrutiny, the applicant next takes his request to the permit section of the local police office, which determines whether he is a security risk. Upon arrival at his authorized destination, the traveler is required to report to the head of the local neighborhood political unit to be registered. Anyone who provides accommodation to an unregistered traveler is subject to a fine or, according to the law, two months in a labor camp. Bed checks by security agencies are not uncommon, especially in the border areas.[17]

That is the official system. While it is ostensibly still in place, a parallel black-market system has mostly supplanted it. Refugees report that clerks at factories and offices sell domestic travel permits off the books. More and more people are also willing to risk traveling without permits. If caught, they count on being able to bribe officials to avoid penalties.

Train travel remains next to impossible without the proper papers, because travelers are required to present permits before purchasing tickets and on-board security checks are frequent. But the market has stepped into the breach here as well, and travelers increasingly rely on an unofficial system of private transportation known as servi-cars, which transport travelers for a fee. These unauthorized services are operated by work units and government agencies that are trying to make extra income with their government-issued cars, trucks, or buses. Even the military has gotten into the illegal transportation business, with official vehicles diverted for the use of paying passengers. A video smuggled out of the country showed private citizens handing over money to a uniformed soldier before hopping aboard an army truck.[18]

Travel to China requires a special category of permits, available to North Koreans who do business or have family in that country. Applicants must pass ideological muster and be able to pay for the permits. Overseas travel is subject to even more restrictions. Passports are a rare commodity. They are issued only to those whose loyalty to the regime is beyond question, and they must be relinquished immediately upon the traveler's return home. Even then, diplomats and other officials who are allowed to travel overseas are not fully trusted; it is assumed that their exposure to foreign thinking corrupts them. To discourage defections, diplomats posted abroad can be forbidden to take all their children with them. Sometimes the regime requires diplomats to leave at least one child at home as an unofficial hostage. If the official decides to defect, he understands that the price will be the life of a son or daughter.

No North Korean makes the decision lightly to flee to China. The law stipulates a term in a labor reeducation camp for the crime of illegally crossing the border. Those who cross the border with the intention of defecting to South Korea or seeking asylum in a third country receive harsher sentences: a minimum of five years in a political prison camp. So, too, do those who meet with Christians, Americans, or South Koreans while in China. Returnees can be subject to indefinite terms in prison, confiscation of property, or even execution. Minors over the age of fourteen are tried as adults.

The level of enforcement varies, but everyone knows the risks. In the months leading up to the Summer Olympic Games in Beijing in 2008, Pyongyang initiated one of its periodic crackdowns on border crossings. This was done at the request of the Chinese government, Western diplomats said at the time. Beijing did not want a flood of refugees from North Korea to divert world attention from the happy face it was putting on the international Games.

To make sure its citizens got that message, on February 20, 2008, six months before the opening ceremony of the Games, the regime executed fifteen people who had been arrested while trying to cross the border into China. The executions—thirteen women and two men—were by firing squad and took place on a bridge in the town of Joowon in Onsung County, North Hamgyung Province. Several of the people who were executed were found guilty of planning to go to China to get help from relatives. Others were convicted of selling their services as guides to North Koreans who wanted to go to China.

Good Friends is a Buddhist organization based in Seoul with sources in North Korea who witnessed the executions. It quoted a North Korean official on the spot as saying, "We wanted people to have the right frame of mind on this issue." The official expressed outrage that his countrymen would go to China. "This is why we carried out the executions," he said. Good Friends also quoted citizens who were ordered to watch the executions. They were matter-of-fact about it. The executions were "a matter of bad luck for those who got killed," said one witness. "They were made into examples."[19]

February 16 is the birthday of the late Kim Jong Il, who is respectfully known in North Korea by the title of Great General. Kim Jong Il, who died at the end of 2011, ruled North Korea as dictator after the death in 1994 of his father Kim Il Sung. Along with April 15, which is Kim Il Sung's birthday, February 16 is the most important holiday in the North Korean calendar.[20] During Kim Jong Il's lifetime, his birthday was marked with a military parade in Pyongyang and displays of the robotic mass dancing for which North Korea is famous. In flush times, Kim Jong Il and Kim Il Sung celebrated their birthdays by dispensing extra rations of food and soap to ordinary citizens, along with candy for the children. The elite were treated to such luxuries as long underwear from Japan, watches from Switzerland, wine from France, and, for the super-elite, Mercedes-Benzes from Germany.

On February 15, 2005, on the eve of the Great General's Birthday, the boy Joseph Kim marked the occasion in another way: He walked across the Tumen River into China. Or, rather, he ran, hoping that the border guards were too engrossed in the holiday festivities to pay close attention to their duties. It was a bitter day, with snow covering the frozen river in many spots, and he was dressed only in sweatpants, a light jacket, and a pair of sneakers. No hat. No gloves. No boots. He slipped and slid on the ice.

Joseph had made his decision the night before, when, as was often the case, he went to bed hungry. He was crashing at a friend's place because he did not have a home of his own and it was too cold to sleep outdoors. When he woke up the next morning, he almost changed his mind. He wanted to tell someone he was leaving, to say good-bye to at least one person he knew, but there was no one he trusted with such a secret. Everyone in his family had died or disappeared, and the information was too dangerous to share with a friend, no matter how close. Instead, he took a walk around town, looking at the familiar sights and bidding silent farewells to the buildings he had known all his life. He recalled his father's refusal to go to China and wondered for the thousandth time whether he was making the right decision.

Finally, in the midafternoon, hunger overcame sentimentality, and he headed toward the river on the outskirts of town. He joined a group of pedestrians who were strolling along a paved road that ran parallel to the river. When the pedestrians were looking the other way, he veered off the path, scrambled down the bank to the Tumen River, and started running. He remembers little about the actual crossing, just that his heart was pounding.

In crossing the river, the boy committed two offenses for which he could have paid with his life. It was a crime to leave North Korea without permission. It was also a crime to enter China without official papers and at other than one of the fifteen authorized border-crossing points. If he had been spotted on the ice, he could have been shot by North Korean border guards.

If Joseph had been captured on the North Korean side of the frontier he would have been arrested, interrogated, and hauled off to a detention center. If the Chinese had grabbed him on their side of the border, it would have taken a little longer, but the result would have been the same. He would have been repatriated and then imprisoned. If his jailers decided that he had fled to China for the purpose of going to South Korea—a treasonous offense—he might have faced the ultimate penalty and been hanged. The boy knew all this. It was a measure of his desperation that he was nevertheless prepared to run.

LOOK FOR A BUILDING WITH A CROSS ON IT

When Joseph reached the other side of the Tumen River, he scrambled up the bank and lay very still for a few minutes, his face pressed against the frozen ground. He waited to hear boots come crashing toward him and feel hands grab him under the shoulders, wrench him to his feet, and haul him off to a police station. But nothing happened. No boots, no hands, no police. Everything was quiet. Once his heart finally stopped pounding, he lifted his head, looked around, and scrutinized the Chinese village he had observed from the North Korean side of the river. He decided to go there to beg for food.

Eventually he pulled himself to his feet and set off toward the nearest house. He knocked on the door, forced himself to smile, and made his pitch to the woman who answered. She shook her head and shut the door. He continued to the next house and then the next, each time receiving the same reply: We can't help you. After being turned away from a dozen houses, Joseph finally found a welcome. A man opened his door wide, invited him inside, and gave him a meal. Joseph noticed that despite his generosity, the man did not appear to be any richer than the villagers who had turned him away. The man spoke Korean, and in the course of conversation he told Joseph that he was a Christian.

As Joseph was departing, the Good Samaritan advised him to walk along the bank of the Tumen River until he came to a bigger town, where, the Christian said, he would be more likely to find help. Joseph set off for the town, but night was falling and he stepped off the path and into the woods, looking for a dry place to lie down and rest. He slept for a few hours stretched out on the ground near a fire he lit with matches he had happened to bring with him. He reached the town the next afternoon and poked around until he discovered an abandoned house. The house became his home for the next three weeks. He hid there during the day, slept on the floor of a closet at night, and ventured outside in the morning and evening to beg for food. On one of his begging missions, he met an old woman who spoke Korean. If you need help, she said, go to a church. Church people help North Koreans.

"What's a church?" Joseph asked.

"Look for a building with a cross on it," the woman told him.

So Joseph set out to find a building with a cross on it. Having never seen a church, he didn't realize that crosses were usually attached to the roofs of a church, visible against the sky, not painted on a wall or door. When he eventually found a church, with the help of another Korean-speaking person he met on the street, the pastor gave him food and enough money to pay for a bus ticket to Tumen City, a two-and-a-half-hour ride away. Go to Tumen City, the pastor advised him. He gave Joseph directions to a church not far from the bus station. Someone there will help you find a place to hide, the pastor promised.

Joseph did as he was told. He went to Tumen City and found his way to the second church. From there, the Chinese Christian network took over. The pastor arranged for him to live with an elderly Chinese woman who spoke Korean. Joseph helped her with housework in exchange for a place to stay. It was too dangerous for him to leave the house—his Chinese hosts feared he would be spotted and arrested—so he stayed indoors all day. He would slip outside behind the house at dusk and kick around a soccer ball for a little while.

A few months later the church introduced him to a South Korean missionary, who in turn linked him up with the American aid organization that helped him and two other boys seek political asylum in the American Consulate in the city of Shenyang. He lived in the consulate for four months, until China issued him an exit permit. When his departure date arrived, an American consul accompanied Joseph and the other two boys to the airport in Shenyang for their flight to Tokyo and on to Los Angeles. The friends said good-bye at LAX airport and went their separate ways. One of the boys went to Seattle; the other was heading for Utah. Joseph boarded a plane to Chicago, where he caught a flight south to his new home. The date of his arrival in America was February 15, 2007, precisely two years since he had crossed the river.

Joseph's experience parallels that of many North Koreans who cross the river. The first survival tip a North Korean learns when he reaches China is: Find a Christian.

Churches in northeastern China are meeting grounds for refugees and rescuers. The North Korean who finds his way to one is likely to be safer than one who doesn't. Church people routinely dare to defy the law against helping North Korean refugees. Christian organizations, funded by private sources in South Korea or America, are among the few humanitarian groups that both want to help the North Korean refugees and work hard to do so. The sooner a refugee hooks up with the Christian network, the greater his chances of avoiding arrest and repatriation and of finding a way to disappear in Chinese society. If he wants to go to South Korea, church people can help him navigate his way to the underground railroad and obtain passage out of China.

Like Joseph, many North Koreans go to China without a plan. They are driven by hunger, fear of persecution, or a general sense that the path to a better, freer life lies across the border. At best, they may have vague notions of finding work or looking up a distant relative. Few are prepared for the rigors of life on the run in China. They make easy targets for the first person, honest or not, who offers help. Like Oliver Twist in Charles Dickens's novel about an orphan adrift in early nineteenth-century London, a North Korean can fall into the hands of the criminal Fagin as easily as he can come under the protection of the saintly Mr. Brownlow. What happens to him is largely a matter of luck.

Bride brokers and other unscrupulous people who prey on refugees make their living by seeking out new arrivals on the pretense of helping them. Bride brokers engage villagers who live near the river to report sightings of attractive young North Korean women. If Joseph had been a fourteen-year-old girl rather than a fourteen-year-old boy, chances are that one of the villagers who turned him away would instead have invited him in and offered to phone a "friend" who could "help." In short order, the "friend" would arrive in the village, take charge of the girl, and pay the villager who had tipped him off. The next stop would be the home of the girl's new "husband." As one rescuer put it, speaking of a young woman who had been sold in such a manner, it was as if the purchaser had struck a bargain for a fattened pig.

A church is unlikely to turn away a needy North Korean who knocks on its door. But its ability to provide assistance is limited by its own, usually meager, resources and by Chinese law, which forbids helping North Koreans. More often than not—unless they have received a crackdown order from Beijing—local authorities turn a blind eye to churches that give handouts to North Koreans and send them on their way. But involvement with the underground railroad is strictly taboo, a far more serious violation than providing a meal to a starving refugee. Chinese Christians have gone to jail for buying train tickets for refugees, driving them to the station, or otherwise helping them get out of China.

The Northeast is China's Rust Belt. People there are rich by North Korean standards, but not by Chinese ones. As Joseph discovered at the first church he visited, many churches cannot afford to help refugees with more than a meal, a little money, and information.

Information is the most valuable commodity. Church people help refugees obtain jobs on the black market, direct them to safe places to stay, and provide advice on how to avoid arrest. Most useful of all, they provide introductions to a network of helping hands, including Chinese-Koreans who operate shelters funded by overseas donors. Trusted refugees receive introductions to South Koreans or Americans who can help them escape from China on the new underground railroad.

Few North Koreans who reach China have ever met a Christian or know anything about Christianity other than that it is banned in their country. Refugees old enough to recall the 1930s or '40s sometimes remember going to church in their childhood or hearing about churches or people who were Christians. Hwang Gi-suk, who was born in North Korea in 1935 and now lives in South Korea, had vague recollections from his childhood of tunes that he later realized were hymns. When he was living in a shelter run by an American missionary in China, he was surprised to find he could sometimes sing along without looking at the hymnal during worship services.[1]

Younger refugees may remember hearing their parents or grandparents mention Christianity or church. Eom Myong-hui, born in

1960, had never met a Christian or seen a church before she went to China. She recalls that her mother described attending church in the 1940s. "She told me about people praying, bowing down, and gazing at an empty space, meaning the altar, I later realized. So I had heard there was a religion called Christianity, but it wasn't relevant to me."[2]

Christianity has a rich history in Korea. Protestant missionaries first arrived in the 1880s and began winning converts. Christianity flourished in early twentieth-century Korea, when the country was under the rule of Imperial Japan. It became associated with modernity, progress, and resistance to Japanese colonialism. As in China, many intellectuals and modernizers in Korea came from prominent Christian families. By the early 1940s, Pyongyang was home to so many Christians that it had earned the nickname "Jerusalem of the East."

Even Kim Il Sung had Christian connections. His father attended a Protestant missionary school, his parents were church-goers, and they took their son to worship services. The Christian message apparently didn't stick. As Bradley K. Martin has noted, "Who . . . would have imagined that the man whose rule wiped out nearly every trace of religion in North Korea—except worship of himself—had been until his late teens not only a churchgoer, but, moreover, a church organist?"[3] When Kim Il Sung came to power, he labeled Christians and other religious believers as counterrevolutionaries and targeted them for repression. Many Christians fled south. Believers who remained in North Korea were killed, jailed, or forcibly relocated to remote areas in the north of the country.

When Kim Il Sung consolidated his power after the end of the Korean War, he banned religion. By 1960, the number of houses of worship operating in North Korea—Christian, Buddhist, or other— was a grand total of zero. That held true until 1988, when, under pressure from international religious groups, the regime opened a Protestant show church in Pyongyang and permitted a few carefully selected people to attend worship services. Four churches operate in Pyongyang today—two Protestant, one Catholic, one Russian Orthodox—and serve as showcases for foreign visitors. There are no Catholic clergy in North Korea, so Mass cannot be celebrated. State-sponsored religious federations oversee the official Christian churches and the few operating Buddhist temples. The federations also interact with foreign visitors.

The overwhelming majority of North Korean refugees have little or no exposure to religion before they arrive in China, according to a survey conducted by the United States Commission on International Religious Freedom. Most have never encountered any religious activity, seen a place of worship, read religious literature, or met a religious leader. Before reaching China, their knowledge of religion is limited largely to the antireligious propaganda they learned at school and from the state-controlled media.[4]

A few North Koreans surveyed by the commission spoke of Christians who were punished for their beliefs in North Korea. Two of the interviewees provided grisly eyewitness testimony of executions of Christians who had engaged in unauthorized religious activities. In one episode, a father and daughter were shot after authorities learned that the daughter owned a Bible. In another, five secret Christians were bound, laid on a highway, and run over by a steamroller. According to the witnesses, the five condemned Christians were given an opportunity to live if they renounced their religion. They refused.[5]

And yet many North Koreans who escape to China, although they've been warned against Christians all their lives, end up turning to Christians for help. This is particularly striking given that some of the Christians are South Koreans or Americans, two other groups of people the North Korean regime has demonized. That so many North Koreans in China entrust their lives to Christians is a measure of the refugees' desperation. But it also reflects the remarkable success of the Protestant missionaries who have flocked to the Sino-Korea border area since the mid-1990s. Many of the missionaries are South Korean or Korean-American. They operate underground, without the approval of the Chinese government and at risk of arrest, imprisonment, and expulsion from the country.

Seoul and Beijing normalized diplomatic relations in 1992, opening the door for South Koreans to visit China more easily. Businessmen flooded in, and so did missionaries. The missionaries saw an opportunity to contact fellow Koreans who had been unreachable since the division of the peninsula. China bars proselytizers, so the missionaries entered the country using a range of guises that allowed them to obtain visas: teacher, student, tourist, businessman. As one American recounted, missionaries had to be creative to find ways to stay in China. This is still the case. The missionaries in China today are Protestant, representing a range of denominations and a variety of churches and humanitarian groups from South Korea and the United States. Some of the missionaries are ordained ministers; others are lay workers. Many of the humanitarian workers, even those with nonsectarian organizations, are inspired by their Christian faith to help North Koreans in China.

By the late 1990s, the severity of the North Korean famine was well known, the number of refugees in China was rapidly increasing, and the missionaries were beginning to organize. They established shelters to feed and house fugitives, and they developed systems to help them escape. They built ties to local Christians, who, as the first line of contact to refugees, would direct needy people onward to the missionaries.

One of the founders of the effort to aid North Koreans in China is Tim Peters, a lay Christian worker from Michigan. Peters is probably the best known rescuer in the business. He has testified before the United States Congress. His photograph has appeared on the cover of *Time* magazine's Asia edition. He travels the world raising awareness of the plight of the North Koreans in China, asking for money and recruiting helpers.[6]

From his perch in Seoul, Peters has become the voice of the North Koreans who are hiding in China and the unofficial spokesman of the new underground railroad. He decided early on that his Caucasian face could be a liability in this line of work, especially in northeast China, where, unlike in many other parts of China, Westerners are relative rarities. While he works closely with Korean-Americans and South Koreans who are on the ground in China, his base of operations is in Seoul, where he can speak freely.

Every Tuesday evening at seven o'clock, Peters leads the Catacombs meeting, where people who work with North Korean refugees in China gather to exchange notes. The Catacombs meeting takes place in an art gallery in central Seoul that is owned by a Korean couple who have moved to the United States. The gallery is closed to the public for the evening, and chairs are arranged in a circle in the center of the small main room under a portrait of Jesus. The meeting attracts a mix of Christian activists, visitors from the Sino-Korean border who are in Seoul on R & R, and locals who work with resettlement agencies that aid North Koreans.

Before he became involved in helping North Koreans, Peters's mission work took him to Japan, South America, and the South Pacific. In the mid-1970s, he took a fateful trip to the then authoritarian country of South Korea. He worked on human rights issues there and was eventually deported for handing out antigovernment pamphlets. He returned to Seoul for a while in the 1980s and then again, for the third time, in 1996. By then, South Korea was democratic and prosperous, and Peters asked himself why God had called him there. What need was there for him to fill? "One night it just dawned on me," he told an interviewer. "I wasn't here this time for South Korea. I was here for the North, to try to do the Lord's work and help people there. It couldn't have been any clearer."[7]

In 1996, Peters founded Helping Hands Korea, an organization dedicated to providing aid to North Koreans who flee to China. By the late 1990s, Helping Hands Korea had set up shelters for refugees and, as Peters euphemistically put it in testimony before the United States Congress, the organization was "coordinating logistical support for their escape to third countries."[8] In other words, the new underground railroad had opened for business.

Working with colleagues from South Korea, Japan, the United States, Southeast Asia, and, especially, China, Peters helped set up a network of Christians who facilitated North Koreans' escape from China. Their explicit model was the underground railroad that led African-American slaves out of the South to freedom in the nineteenth century. Like the original underground railroad in America, the new underground railroad in China was organized to operate in what Peters calls "separate, secure nodes," so as to protect the identities of both the workers and the refugees. During an operation to transport refugees, for example, the locations of the safe houses remain secret. Rather than have the guide pick up the refugees at the safe house, which would necessitate revealing the address, the house manager will escort the refugees to a public place, where their guide will meet them.

One of the hardest aspects of his work is deciding whom to help, Peters says. Resources severely limit the number of North Koreans Peters's network can transport on the new underground railroad, and there are more prospective passengers than there are spaces. He admits to sleepless nights over some of the decisions he has had to make. There is no set of established criteria for winning a ticket on the new underground railroad, but some general guidelines have emerged over the years.

"The South Koreans or Korean-Americans on the ground in the border areas are the first ones to send up a flag as to who is needy," Peters said. "They conduct interviews of refugees to find out more about their background, and they try to filter out those who may not be telling the truth. They try to find out who needs help and who needs it desperately."

Peters's first priority is to help those who would suffer most if they were to be arrested and repatriated. That category includes women who are obviously pregnant. North Korea forces repatriated women to have abortions, even in the final months of pregnancy, and it kills newborns it believes have Chinese fathers. Also on the priority list are North Koreans with medical problems that make it unlikely they could survive the rigors of detention if arrested and sent back. So, too, are North Koreans who are at risk of being identified as Christian or as having had contact with Christians; North Korea metes out especially harsh treatment to Christians.

For Peters, the toughest calls involve refugees who claim to be North Korean officials, especially if they are peddling information that they offer to trade for passage on the new underground railroad. "These are really dirty guys," Peters said. If they are telling the truth, then they were complicit in the crimes they wish to confess. Only people who participated in such abuses would have evidence that they took place, and their victims are almost certainly dead. "Most of these guys you can't trust with last year's Christmas tree," he said. "But then again, some of them might have information that would have a bombshell effect on the whole human rights situation. They might have highly incriminating evidence about what goes on inside North Korea. That's the kind of dilemma that keeps me up at night."

In 2010, Peters considered a request for help from a man who said he was a state security agent and had explosive evidence of human rights abuses in the prison system. The agent and his family had fled to China, and he wanted to negotiate a deal whereby Peters's network would help them get to South Korea. By the time a request for help reaches Peters, it is usually well authenticated, and in this case he believed the man had been a security agent, as he claimed.

He agonized over the decision. If the state security agent "really had something that would cause the international community to pay attention, to say, 'Oh, my God, it's true—we've got documented proof from someone inside the system,' that would be a huge force multiplier," Peters explained. The news would make headlines around the world, and it could have an enormous impact on his work by calling international attention to the human rights abuses in North Korea. On the other hand, the state security agent was surely responsible for the deaths of many innocent people. In the end, Peters decided to help. He negotiated a deal, agreeing to bring out the man along with one of his children.

At the time Peters related this story, the operation to extract the state security agent and his child was still in progress and the duo had not yet reached South Korea. The South Korean intelligence agency would debrief the man upon his arrival and evaluate his information. Peters still wasn't sure he had made the right decision. "We helped those two," he said "but what two didn't we help?" He may never know whether the man's information will help save North Korean lives in the future. He does know that by his decision to help the North Korean security agent and his child, he was unable to provide passage out of China for two other North Koreans who did not have blood on their hands.

South Korea's Ministry of Unification keeps track of the number of North Koreans who arrive in the South each year. The numbers showcase the growing success of the underground railroad in helping North Koreans escape from China. In 1998, seventy-one North Koreans reached safely. In 1999, as the underground railroad was gearing up, that number more than doubled, to 148 arrivals. By 2002, only three years later, the number of arrivals exceeded the thousand mark, to 1,140. By late 2000s, close to three thousand North Koreans were reaching the South every year.[9]

The new underground railroad has many conductors. It is impossible to know how many North Koreans who escape are assisted by Christians, how many are aided by other humanitarian workers, and how many pay brokers to help them get out. Sometimes conductors who do it for money work hand in hand with those who don't. Christians may hire brokers to help with part of the journey or aid them in gathering information. Some church people or humanitarian workers won't knowingly employ brokers, believing, as one Christian drily put it, that in a crisis, the broker won't be thinking in terms of the North Koreans' welfare. Others say brokers are essential and that they couldn't do their work without them.

The charitable groups that help North Koreans in China operate on a very small scale. They often are one-man operations—typically a sole missionary who is supported by his congregation back home in South Korea or the U.S. and who has lined up local Christians to work with him. During the years he lived in China before his arrest, Phillip Buck, a pastor from Seattle, guided more than one hundred North Koreans out of China. Tim Peters said in 2010 that he had helped rescue thirty-seven North Koreans in the previous year. Liberty in North Korea, a nonsectarian group based in California, set a goal in 2010 of rescuing one hundred North Koreans over the next couple of years. The numbers are small, but they add up.

For some workers in the Christian underground, the work has moved away from helping people escape to caring for them in place. Crossing Borders, an Illinois-based, Christian nonprofit, shifted its resources from the new underground railroad to providing long-term shelters in China. As Mike Kim, one of the organization's founders, put it in his book, *Escaping North Korea*, Crossing Borders is committed to "helping them live safe and happy lives" in China.[10] Mike Kim spent four years secretly guiding North Koreans out of China while working as a martial arts instructor there.

Tim Peters and his network have begun to devote more of their resources to caring for the children of Chinese men and the North Koreans brides they purchased. He estimates that there are scores of thousands of such half-and-half children, many of whom lack the official Chinese identity cards without which they cannot go to school or receive medical care.

Peters is not a fan of bringing half-and-half children out of China on the new underground railroad. "You might help a few," he said, "but then what?" He thinks group homes, run by foster parents who are Christian, are a better option and a way to help a greater number of children. Down the road, as the children get older, he would like to establish vocational schools to teach them farming, mechanical trades, hair dressing, and other productive skills.

Meanwhile, fifteen years after he helped launch the new underground railroad, Peters's work in China continues. In early 2012, he warned that this was an especially difficult period for Christians helping North Koreans in the border area. Since the middle of 2011, his colleagues on the ground had been reporting that China and North Korea were ramping up efforts to prevent border crossings. North Korea was building underground bunkers for border guards, making it easier for them to spot people crossing the river. China was said to be erecting a ten-foot-high barrier fence along the Yalu River at a popular crossing point near the Chinese city of Dandong. Peters's colleagues in the border area also reported the presence of an unusually large number of North Korean government agents posing as refugees. "The North Korean agents are there with the cooperation of the Chinese government," he said. "Why? They are trying to hinder the flow of refugees and break up the aid networks."

Peters had an additional worry: finding more Christian workers to go to China to help North Koreans. The number of missionaries in the field has been decimated by imprisonments, expulsions, and harassment by Chinese authorities. He was finding it hard to recruit workers willing to risk working in China.

On a speaking tour of Korean-American churches in the United States, he told his audiences, "I want *you*, not just your money." It was a pitch that deliberately called upon the congregants' Korean heritage. Peters reckoned it would be embarrassing for Korean-Americans to hear such a plea from someone who was not ethnically Korean. He hoped to shock his audiences into action.

Peters emphasized the same message in his speeches in South Korea, the nation that is second only to the United States in the number of Christian missionaries it sends overseas. South Korean missionaries are active worldwide—in South America, Africa, and the Indian Subcontinent. They go to places that are at least as dangerous as China, if not more so. In Afghanistan in 2007, the Taliban captured twenty-three South Korean missionaries and held them hostage. Two were murdered.

In Seoul, Peters made his pitch to an assembly of divinity students at Chongshin University. Chongshin's famous divinity school was founded in Pyongyang in 1901 and relocated south during the Korean War. Today, its graduates disperse to the four corners of the world to preach the Gospel. One would think that the school's roots in the North would give it a special interest in reaching out to North Koreans. That was not what Peters found.

Peters described his interaction with the students at Chongshin. "Who's going to India?" he asked the assembled seminarians. Lots of hands shot up. India is a popular spot for missionary work, and the South Korean students clearly were enthusiastic about the prospect of working there.

"Then I asked, 'Who's helping North Koreans?' " At this point in his story, Peters paused and looked around him. It was if he still had the prospective missionaries in his sight and was waiting to count the raised hands.

Finally, he answered his own question. "Nothing."

DEFECTORS

Until the mid-1990s, when food shortages began to push women and children across the border to China, most of the North Koreans who fled were men, and virtually all were privileged citizens with access to escape routes closed to ordinary people. Most were classic Cold War defectors, men in influential jobs who peddled information or military equipment in return for resettlement and protection in South Korea or the West. They were diplomats posted abroad, students studying at foreign universities, and renegade pilots who flew their Russian-made MiG-15s across the DMZ.

There is a one-word explanation for the gender imbalance among the early defectors: sexism. For all its talk of socialist equality, modern-day North Korea is a patriarchal society with a limited number of women in positions of authority. When the famine struck in the 1990s, women's secondary status worked to their benefit; they found it easier than their husbands or fathers or brothers did to slip away from their state-assigned jobs and sneak across the border. Young women had—and continue to have—an additional, albeit grim, advantage: They are marketable in China as brides or sex workers. Then, as now, men have a harder time finding jobs on the black market in China. Chinese families are less likely to take in men than women, which makes male refugees more vulnerable to arrest and repatriation. When famine struck in the 1990s, the flow of North Koreans to China became heavily female. Today, more than three-quarters of the refugees who reach South Korea from China are female.[1]

The early defectors almost always left North Korea for political reasons. In some instances, travel abroad had revealed new worlds, opening the defector's eyes to the realities of the North Korean regime and offering possibilities that were unimaginable at home. Others were self-declared patriots who believed their defections would prevent war and hasten the coming of a unified Korea under South Korea's freer political system. Still others were fleeing for their lives after committing some supposed transgression against the state that, had they stayed, would have condemned them to the gulag.

Few ordinary citizens escaped North Korea during the pre-famine period. The borders were sealed, and news of the outside world was scarce. Unless he had relatives in China with whom to stay, a North Korean had nowhere to go. Moreover, China was poor; it did not yet offer the comparative advantages that economic prosperity afforded it by the 1990s. In any event, North Korea's societal controls were such that a man who failed to show up at his state-assigned job for more than a few days was presumed to have deserted his duties, thereby putting his family at risk for punishment. The underground railroad did not take off until the late 1990s, when the number of refugees in China swelled near the half-million mark and Christian activists started helping them escape.

In the pre-famine days, the rare North Korean who found his way to China was on his own. Evans Revere, a former American diplomat in Beijing, recalled his astonishment at encountering two North Koreans who turned up at the door of the United States Embassy in 1982, asking for help to reach South Korea. "I may have been the first American diplomat in China to have had to deal with North Korean refugees," he said.[2]

Revere was the duty officer one evening when the Marine guard at the embassy entrance phoned to say there were two guys sitting in front of his post. They were dirty and disheveled and had plopped themselves down on the floor of the vestibule. "I can't understand their Chinese," the Marine told Revere. "Can you come down and talk to them?"

Revere went to the front entrance. After his questions in Mandarin also failed to elicit a response, something about the two men prompted him to try Korean, which he also spoke. The men responded with big smiles and a torrent of words. "I had a hard time at first placing their accent," Revere said. "But then it dawned on me. I couldn't quite believe it, but they were from North Korea."

"They said they had swum across the Yalu," Revere remembered. "Then they hitchhiked to Beijing, stole into the U.S. Embassy grounds, climbed over the back wall, and presented themselves at the front door. They said they had worked at odd jobs and stolen food along the way." It was a miracle that they had made it as far as Beijing without being arrested.

"I asked them, 'If you had some more money, can you get to Guangzhou?'" (a major city in the south of China near Hong Kong). "They said yes. So we fed them, gave them some money, and took them to the train station." The North Koreans hid on the floor in the back seat of a van so the Chinese sentries wouldn't spot them as they left the embassy compound. If the North Koreans had been soldiers or officials with important information to impart, Revere said, the United States might have been able to figure out a way to extract them from China. But they were just farmers and not worth diplomatic intervention, and they didn't know enough to ask for political asylum. The Republic of Korea had no embassy in China at the time, so the Americans did not have the option of handing them over to the South Koreans. The last Revere saw of the two North Koreans was when they hopped out of the van at the train station and waved good-bye before vanishing into the crowd.

Most of the early defectors ended up in South Korea, but a handful of North Koreans managed to disappear in the West, where they quietly established new lives. Defectors were not always good guys. The fact that they had permission to travel abroad indicated some significant degree of complicity in North Korea's brutal regime. Only trusted loyalists were allowed out of the country. At the same time, the defectors were also the only North Koreans who had any exposure to what life was like in freer societies.

Colonel Kim Jong-ryul—aka Kim Il Sung's personal shopper—is a case in point. The colonel defected during an official trip to Vienna in 1994. Kim Il Sung had just died, and Kim Jong-ryul was convinced that it wouldn't be long before a revolution broke out, North Korea erupted in chaos, and he would be purged. He faked his death, arranging for it to look like a hit by the Slovak mafia. His aim was to deceive the North Korean authorities and, he hoped, protect his family from retaliation. He then went into hiding in Austria for sixteen years. His story was not made public until 2010 when two Austrian journalists published a book in German about his defection. The title was *Im Dienst des Diktators*, or, in English, *In the Dictator's Service*.

As a kind of high-tech personal shopper for Kim Il Sung, Colonel Kim had traveled regularly around Europe for nearly twenty years, armed with a diplomatic passport and suitcases filled with cash. He bought armaments, fancy cars, carpets, furniture, and other luxury items. The luxury goods were for the North Korean leader's personal use or for him to dole out as gifts to his supporters. Colonel Kim purchased two encrypted telephones so Kim Il Sung and Kim Jong Il could talk to each other without anyone listening in.

Colonel Kim bought from Austrian, Swiss, German, French, and Czechoslovakian firms, which were only too willing to break international trade embargoes on North Korea in return for a 30 percent additional fee. He told the Austrian journalists that he did business with European customs agents and other officials, who would turn a blind eye to the illicit trade. The colonel even purchased a fleet of tanks, which he smuggled to North Korea disguised as hunting equipment. At a press conference in Vienna launching the publication of *In the Dictator's Service*, he explained why he had defected: "I wanted freedom. I needed freedom."[3] Perhaps. Or maybe he wanted to save his skin.

The highest-ranking defector to the United States was North Korea's ambassador to Egypt, Chang Sung-gil. Chang Sung-gil walked into the American Embassy in Cairo on a sweltering August Friday in 1997 and asked for protection. The ambassador's defection was the first by a senior North Korean diplomat. In 1991 and 1996, two mid-level diplomats in Congo and Zambia had defected to South Korea.

Cairo was a significant diplomatic outpost for Pyongyang, and Chang Sung-gil was a good catch. News reports of the day identified him as a fountain of information about North Korea's sales of Scud missiles to Iran, Syria, and other Middle Eastern countries, although the State Department did not confirm these sales. To the extent that Chang Sung-gil had facilitated the arms trafficking when he was North Korea's man in Cairo, he had blood on his hands; at the same time, his information was valuable. There was an added bonus to Chang Sung-gil's defection: his wife. The South Korean press identified her as a well-known actress who was acquainted with Kim Jong Il, an avid movie buff; in her debriefings, she presumably added to the intelligence community's store of knowledge about the personal habits of the secretive dictator.

Chang Sung-gil's defection was actually a three-fer. In Paris, at almost exactly the same hour on that August Friday in 1997, the ambassador's brother, Chang Sung-ho, also defected to the United

States. The brother was North Korea's economic and trade representative in the French capital, a position that would have given him detailed knowledge of North Korea's trade—legal and illegal—in Europe. He brought his wife and two children with him.[4]

North Korean students also defected. The most notorious student defections were those, in 1962, of four young men who were studying in the then Communist country of Bulgaria. The four students received asylum from the Bulgarian government in a diplomatic brouhaha that resulted in the expulsion of the North Korean ambassador from Sofia and the suspension of ties between the two countries. The diplomatic breach lasted seven years.

The North Korean students happened to be in the right place at the right time. They were among thirty-eight North Koreans studying in Bulgaria at a moment of deteriorating relations between Pyongyang and Moscow. As ties between North Korea and the Soviet Union worsened due to, among other things, Nikita Khrushchev's rejection of Stalinism, Pyongyang recalled its students from every Communist country in Europe except Stalinist Albania.

On August 9, 1962, four students in the Bulgarian capital of Sofia decided to seize the moment and exploit the rift between their country and Bulgaria. Declaring themselves as loyal Leninists, they requested asylum. In a handwritten petition delivered to the Minister of Foreign Affairs, they stated that no "threats or hardships" could "turn us aside from the right Leninist path." The letter ended, "We cherish our lives, but we cherish more our just cause."

Two and a half weeks later, North Korean agents kidnapped the four students in the center of Sofia and took them by force to the North Korean Embassy. This was an outlaw action, and the Bulgarian government declared it a "rude intervention in the affairs of the country." The incident soon devolved into farce. Two of the students managed to escape from the North Korean Embassy by tying sheets together and climbing out an upper-story window. The other two were rescued by Bulgarian police at the Sofia airport as North Korean officials tried to manhandle them onto a flight to Pyongyang.[5]

In 2010, during a visit to Seoul, two of the former students, now both in their seventies, told reporters that their protestations of support for Leninism had been false. They were not true Leninists, they said; they were only trying to win the assistance of Bulgaria's Communist government, which at the time was closely aligned with Moscow. The real reason the North Korean government had kidnapped them in an effort to force their return, they said, was that they had issued a statement calling the Korean War a "North Korean war of aggression" in contravention of the official North Korean line that the United States started the war. Their statement also included the conviction that "it is better to read the Bible than the Collected Works of Kim Il Sung."[6] Half a century after the fact, it is impossible to know whether the defectors were telling the truth or rewriting history for the benefit of their hosts in Seoul.

Once the famine arrived in the mid-1990s and escape routes opened across the Tumen and Yalu Rivers and then across China, a high percentage of the fugitives came from the northeast region of North Korea, near the Chinese border. But word of the exodus reached some people in the privileged enclave of Pyongyang. Members of the powerful elite class made the decision to flee, too.

One such man was Kim Cheol-woong, first pianist of the Pyongyang Philharmonic Orchestra until 2001, when he escaped to China. Kim Cheol-woong reached South Korea in 2003 after two years on the run in China and two repatriations to the North. "My motivation to escape was not hunger," he said later, "but to be able to play freely the music of my choice."[7]

Kim Cheol-woong was born in Pyongyang in 1974 to a politically connected family. His father worked for the Workers' Party, and his mother was a professor. At the age of eight, he was selected for a special program for young artists at the Pyongyang Music and Dance University, where he underwent fourteen years of intensive training. "For music students," Kim Cheol-woong explained, "the core requirements are of course subjects related to music, but the main stress is always laid on the theory and philosophy of Kim Il Sung and Kim Jong Il."

Among the required subjects Kim Cheol-woong studied were the Revolutionary History of Great Leader Kim Il Sung and the Revolutionary History of Dear Leader Kim Jong Il. In music, as in every art form, the purpose is to serve the state and extol the country's dictators—or so Kim Cheol-woong and his fellow students learned. The performing arts are a means to political ends.

Kim Cheol-woong recalled an episode that influenced him profoundly during his student years and taught him a lesson about the role of the artist in North Korea. The incident concerned a celebrated young pianist who had just won a minor international competition. Kim Jong Il ordered the pianist to enter the International Tchaikovsky Competition, held every four years in Moscow. It is the world's most competitive piano competition, and Kim Cheol-woong said the young pianist knew he needed more years of practice before he would be ready for it. So he decided not to enter. It was a "rationally considered choice as a pianist," Kim Cheol-woong said, but as a political matter, it had disastrous consequences for the unlucky young man. For his disobedience, the pianist was sent to the gulag on the orders of Kim Jong Il.

Many North Korean musicians studied in Russia at the time, and in 1995, Kim Cheol-woong, then twenty-one years old, was dispatched to the Tchaikovsky Conservatory of Music in Moscow. In Russia, his life was tightly restricted. He lived at the North Korean Embassy, and he was under surveillance by North Korean security guards. Even so, a new world opened before him. For the first time, he could study twentieth-century music, and he fell in love with the free harmonics of jazz. There was only one problem: Jazz was banned in North Korea.

In North Korea, jazz is "seen as 'vicious' music that confuses people's minds," Kim Cheol-woong explained. American jazz pianist Dave Brubeck made a similar observation in 1958 on a visit to Warsaw. "No dictatorship can tolerate jazz," he said at the time of that Cold War visit. "It is the first sign of a return to freedom."[8]

The North Korean regime also bans individual composers whose biographies it deems dangerous. Among them is Sergei Rachmaninoff, who wrote some of the twentieth century's greatest piano music. Rachmaninoff is verboten because he fled his native Russia after the 1917 Revolution and settled in the United States. In the eyes of the North Korean regime, a musician who betrayed his country—especially one who betrayed it in favor of the United States—is not a model anyone should emulate.

In Russia, Kim Cheol-woong discovered the lush, romantic music of the French composer and pianist Richard Clayderman. He remembers the first time he heard a recording by Clayderman. He was sitting in a café in Moscow across the street from the conservatory when the song "Autumn Leaves" came over the stereo system. He was entranced: "I had never heard music like that before, and it gave me goose bumps all over my body."

"What is it?" he asked the owner of the cafe.

The Russian scoffed at him. "You're studying at the music conservatory and you don't know? What kind of student are you?"

Kim Cheol-woong bought Clayderman's recordings in Moscow and continued to listen to them in secret when he returned home to Pyongyang in 1999. Then, one day in mid-2001, he was practicing Clayderman's "Autumn Leaves," which he wanted to play as a surprise for his girlfriend. A colleague heard him playing the illegal music and reported him to the Ministry of State Security, which oversees the country's secret police and reports directly to the supreme leader, then Kim Jong Il. Kim Cheol-woong was forced to apologize and write ten pages of self-criticism. The experience was a personal epiphany: "The fact that a pianist, just because of playing his music, was forced to apologize, caused a great sense of aversion in me, and I decided to seek the freedom of being able to play freely."

Kim Cheol-woong had heard rumors about North Koreans who had managed to get to South Korea by crossing the river to China, where they sought the help of Christian missionaries running an underground railroad. He decided to flee. In October 2001, he took a train to a town in the northeast part of the country, where he found a guide who, for $2,000, led him across the Tumen River in the middle of the night.

The guide directed him to a small village where other North Koreans were hiding. Kim Cheol-woong knocked on a random door. He told the farmer who answered that he was a classical pianist who had trained in Moscow at one of the world's preeminent conservatories. He might as well have announced that he was an astronaut who had flown to the moon. The farmer's response? "He said, 'What's a piano? I have no idea what you're talking about,'" Kim said. The farmer gave him a job helping with the harvest in exchange for room and board.

For seven months, Kim Cheol-woong never touched a piano. After three weeks helping the farmer bring in his harvest, he found a job as a logger. It was backbreaking work that left him exhausted at night. Even so, he never gave up looking for a piano. "Every day I would tell whomever I met that I played the piano," he said. Eventually another refugee directed him to a church that had a broken-down instrument. Thirty of the eighty keys did not function, but that did not matter to Kim Cheol-woong. "I could hear the missing notes in my head," he said. After seven months of not playing, "I finally felt like I was alive."

After about a year in China, he bought a fake South Korean passport on the black market and tried to use it to fly to Seoul. He was caught by the Chinese immigration authorities at the airport in Beijing. After three months in detention in China, he was put on a train to North Korea. Desperate to escape, he managed to jump from the moving train shortly after it reached North Korean soil. He immediately crossed the river again to China.

Two months later, Kim Cheol-woong was arrested a second time. This time he was nabbed as he was trying to cross the border into Mongolia posing as a Chinese tourist. He spent six months in jail in China before being deported. He was taken to the border and handed over to North Korean officials. He was about to be sent to a prison camp when he caught the eye of one of the officials, who happened to have worked with Kim's father in Pyongyang. That man helped him escape and get back to China.

His third attempt to leave China worked. On December 7, 2002, using a fake South Korean passport he had purchased on the black market, Kim Cheol-woong flew from Beijing to Seoul. At the airport, he walked to the immigration desk and announced to the officer on duty, "I'm from Pyongyang."

In recent years, Kim Cheol-woong has traveled the world with his music and his story. On a warm spring evening in 2008, he gave a private recital in Manhattan. The venue was the venerable Metropolitan Club, a white-marble palazzo designed by the renowned architect Stanford White and opened in 1894. The club overlooks Central Park from its prime location on Fifth Avenue at East Sixtieth Street. On the evening that Kim Cheol-woong took his seat at the grand piano in the ground-floor salon, the red-velvet curtains were closed to the evening light and the room was softly lit by triple-armed sconces lining the gold-and-white walls.

After the recital, which included a ballad by Richard Clayderman, Kim Cheol-woong took questions from the audience. Someone inquired about his life in South Korea. Freedom isn't easy, he replied. "One of the hardest things I have experienced since leaving North Korea is having to choose what to play."

The highest-ranking North Korean official to defect was Hwang Jang-yop, who made world headlines in 1997 when he requested political asylum at the South Korean Embassy in Beijing. Hwang's defection is one of the few times that Beijing has stood up publicly to its North Korean ally. It is the only time that the Chinese have publicly defied Pyongyang in support of a defector who wanted to flee to South Korea, although China has allowed other defectors to leave China quietly. It is unclear why Chinese authorities decided to disregard Kim Jong Il's wish that they return the defector. Hwang Jang-yop had friends in high places in Beijing, and perhaps they interceded on his behalf. Or perhaps China viewed Hwang's release to South Korea as a way of solidifying its newly established diplomatic ties with that country. It's also possible that international public opinion played a role.

At the time of his defection, Hwang Jang-yop was one of the most powerful men in Pyongyang. He was a man "with no intellectual rival," according to two scholars who have studied his background and influence.[9] He was the consummate insider, an intimate of the late Great Leader Kim Il Sung, who died in 1994, and a mentor to his son, Dear Leader Kim Jong Il, whom he had known for nearly forty years.

Hwang Jang-yop held three high-level government appointments. He was secretary of the ruling Korean Workers' Party, chairman of the Supreme People's Assembly, and president of Kim Il Sung University, which is the Harvard, Princeton, and Yale of North Korea. His most notable accomplishment, though, was authorship of the regime's guiding *juche* philosophy of self-reliance. In 1972, *juche* replaced Marxism-Leninism as the official state ideology. *Juche* thought infuses every aspect of North Korean life. Even dates are given in *juche* years. *Juche* Year 1 is 1912, the year of Kim Il Sung's birth.

Hwang Jang-yop's official responsibilities took him abroad frequently and gave him access to South Koreans perceived as friendly to the North—including the businessman who played a key role in his defection. Hwang Jang-yop plotted his defection for months. On January 30, 1997, he departed Pyongyang for an international seminar in Tokyo on *juche* ideology. After Tokyo, his itinerary called for him to visit the Japanese cities of Kyoto and Nagano before going on to Beijing. His plan was to defect in Japan or China, or if that proved impossible, in India or Thailand in April, when he was to attend a meeting of nonaligned nations in New Delhi. Accompanying him was a close aide, Kim Duk-hong, who planned to defect with him.

In Japan, Hwang Jang-yop found it impossible to break away from his minders. Japanese-Koreans who sympathized with Pyongyang "protected" him round the clock. Later, Japanese Prime Minister Ryutaro Hashimoto observed that during Hwang Jang-yop's stay in Japan, "North Korean guards were tightly huddled all around Hwang as if they knew he intended to defect."[10]

So Hwang Jang-yop kept to his itinerary and went on to China as scheduled. He arrived in Beijing on February 11; he was to spend the night there before boarding a train for Pyongyang the following afternoon. The next morning, he and Kim Duk-hong left the North Korean Embassy compound, ostensibly to do some shopping at the Great Wall Hotel. Upon arriving at the hotel, the two men sent their embassy handlers on made-up errands and met up by prearrangement in one of the hotel shops with their South Korean–businessman contact. The businessman phoned the South Korean Embassy and asked for a car to pick them up at the hotel.

The embassy refused, arguing that if Hwang Jang-yop and his aide arrived at the facility in an embassy car, it would look as if they'd been kidnapped. Instead, embassy officials told the trio to take a taxi.

So Hwang Jang-yop, Kim Duk-hong, and the South Korean businessman hailed a cab and drove to the embassy's consular section. It all happened quickly. Hwang Jang-yop and Kim Duk-hong left for their shopping expedition at 10 a.m. By 11:30 a.m., the South Korean ambassador had informed the Chinese Foreign Minister of their defection.

Immediately upon his arrival at the South Korea consular section, Hwang Jang-yop sat down at a desk and handwrote a statement that the embassy distributed later. Introspective and personal, the statement was the only human touch in what was quickly turning into high political drama.

His statement began: "Starting with my family, all the people [in North Korea] will judge that I have gone mad when they learn that I have decided to go to the South, abandoning everything. I actually feel—on not a few occasions—that I have gone mad myself."

As he wrote, Hwang Jang-yop was perhaps thinking about the relatives he had left behind in Pyongyang. They included his wife, a son, and three daughters. He went on to say that he did not expect to live much longer. He was a few days short of his seventy-fourth birthday. His statement concluded: "I hope that my family will consider me dead as of today. If possible, I only wish to help promote reconciliation between the South and the North until the last possible moment." In this and later public comments, Hwang Jang-yop emphasized that he defected for patriotic reasons. He said that his duty to his country transcended political considerations and his responsibility to his family.

In the weeks, months, and years that followed his defection, Hwang Jang-yop adhered to a constant message: Don't underestimate Kim Jong Il. As he put it in a press conference in Seoul at the time of his arrival in South Korea: "I have come to the Republic of Korea in order to warn about the danger of an armed invasion of the South by the North and to contribute to the peaceful unification of our country." He spoke repeatedly of the "warlike intention" of

North Korea's ruler and said, "I could not help but agonize in pain at the thought of the tragedy that might befall all Koreans if war were started again." He presented himself as a patriot loyal to the Korean people on both sides of the DMZ. At first he even denied that he was defecting. The word, with its connotation of betrayal, seemed to repel him. Rather, he said he wanted to move from one part of Korea to another.

Factors other than patriotism might have played a role in Hwang Jang-yop's decision to defect. He was angry at what he saw as the regime's misappropriation of *juche* ideology to create personality cults around Kim Il Sung and Kim Jong Il. It's also possible he feared that his personal political future was in jeopardy. A few months before his defection, he had been forced to write a self-criticism about three ideological mistakes he supposedly had made: He had publicly renounced war with the South whereas Pyongyang's policy was to prepare for war; he had stated that *juche* ideology was an offshoot of Marxism-Leninism, not the sole, glorious creation of the late Kim Il Sung; and he had praised Deng Xiaoping's market reforms in China, which Kim Jong Il had rejected for North Korea. Given this experience, he may have seen what he believed to be the handwriting on the wall: He was about to be purged.

Hwang Jang-yop's defection posed a diplomatic challenge for Beijing, which by 1997 was jockeying to maintain good ties with both Koreas. Despite Pyongyang's urgings, China decided not to apply the two countries' 1986 extradition agreement. Hwang Jang-yop had entered China legally on a diplomatic passport, and Beijing found it convenient to argue that the extradition agreement applied only to North Koreans who had entered the country illegally. Beijing took care not to set a precedent that other North Koreans could cite if they wanted to transit China to South Korea.

This was a high-profile case, and Beijing knew it would face international condemnation if it sent Hwang Jang-yop back to North Korea against his will, as Kim Jong Il initially demanded. It was no secret what would happen to Hwang Jang-yop if he were repatriated. But just in case anyone had lingering doubts, North Korea provided a well-timed reminder: Three days after Hwang Jang-yop requested political asylum in Beijing, an earlier defector was murdered in Seoul by unknown assailants believed to be North Korean agents. South Korea's prime minister described the murder as retaliation for Hwang Jang-yop's defection.

Pyongyang had initially responded to the defection by accusing South Korean spies of kidnapping Hwang Jang-yop. When the regime realized that China would not buckle to its wishes and repatriate Hwang, Pyongyang dropped these accusations and instead declared, "A coward may leave." This opened the door for China to work with South Korea in devising a plan for the defectors' transfer to Seoul. The two countries crafted a plan intended to lessen North Korea's public humiliation. Rather than sending Hwang Jang-yop directly to Seoul, they would first transfer him and his aide to a third country. So arrangements were made for Hwang and Kim Duk-hong to visit the Philippines for a month, after which they would travel on to Seoul.[11]

More significant, and an early hint of how it would treat the coming wave of North Korean refugees in China, Beijing decided not to recognize Hwang Jang-yop as a "refugee" as defined in the Geneva Convention on the Status of Refugees, which Beijing had signed but not yet ratified. It was careful to avoid setting a precedent that could pave the way for other North Koreans seeking refugee status. It chose to "expel" Hwang Jang-yop rather than classify him as a refugee or grant him political asylum. On March 18, 1997, five weeks after they defected, Hwang Jang-yop and Kim Duk-hong boarded a Chinese military plane and flew to the Philippines, where they stayed one month. On April 20, they arrived in South Korea.

Contrary to the dire prediction he made in his defection note, Hwang Jang-yop did not die soon after his arrival in South Korea. Rather, his fate was to be a Korean Cassandra, delivering his warnings about Kim Jong Il to successive South Korean governments that mostly chose to ignore him. In December 1997, eight months after Hwang Jang-yop reached Seoul, Kim Dae-jung was elected president of the country on a platform of outreach to North Korea, and Hwang Jang-yop was effectively silenced. The defector's warnings about the Kim regime in the North were an embarrassment to adherents of Kim Dae-jung's Sunshine Policy.

In Seoul, Hwang Jang-yop survived numerous assassination attempts, including one by North Korean agents several weeks before his death. The defector died of a heart attack in his bathtub at home in Seoul in October 2010 at the age of eighty-seven. He was given a hero's burial in a national cemetery in a ceremony attended by many dignitaries, including the Unification Minister, a former president, and members of Parliament. One attendee called him a "great teacher." His coffin was covered with the flag of the Republic of Korea. The government of President Lee Myung-bak presented him posthumously with a medal.

Hwang Jang-yop's death reignited the debate over his motives for calling attention to North Korea's human rights abuses. Some believed him to be sincere. They cited the many attempts made on his life as a measure of his bravery. And as proof that he was dedicated to regime change and democracy, they pointed to his fiery radio broadcasts to North Korea on the refugee-run Free North Korea Radio. Others countered that he was merely seeking publicity.

Still others suggested that the old defector was driven by guilt over what happened after he left Pyongyang. Information does not readily make its way out of North Korea, but when it's useful to regime purposes, the authorities make sure that certain news is delivered. And so, not long after Hwang Jong-yop's arrival in Seoul in 1997, word filtered back about the fate of the family and colleagues he had left behind. More than three thousand of his family members, friends, and associates were arrested, including distant relatives who had no idea they were even related to the defector.[12] Hwang's wife was said to have committed suicide. So, too, the reports said, did one of his daughters. She was said to have jumped off a bridge to her death while being transported to a prison camp. Two other daughters, his son, and his grandchildren were lost in the gulag.

This is the reality of life in North Korea—and the truth that Hwang Jang-yop told again and again after his defection.

PART II

IN HIDING

There we were informed by a friendly colored man of the danger we were in and of the bad character of the place towards colored people, especially those who were escaping to freedom; and he advised us to hide as quickly as we could.

—WESLEY HARRIS, SLAVE
THE UNDERGROUND RAILROAD RECORD
NOVEMBER 2, 1853

BRIDES FOR SALE

How much does a North Korean bride cost?

Steven Kim, an American businessman from Long Island, New York, may be the world's leading expert on the market for North Korean brides. He acquired this expertise accidentally. He likes to say it was God's plan.[1]

In the late 1990s and early 2000s, Kim lived in China, where he oversaw the manufacture of chairs that he sold to Wal-Mart, Home Depot, and other retail clients in the United States. He was based in an industrial area near the southern boomtown of Guangzhou. On Sundays he would get up early, pack his passport, and drive across the border to Hong Kong to attend a church in Kowloon that had a Korean-language worship service. The round-trip took most of the day, but the inconvenience was worth it. As a Christian living in China, he had few opportunities for worship. The former British colony of Hong Kong, although formally part of China since 1997, was an enclave of freedom. Under the terms of its return to Beijing, Hong Kong guarantees freedom of religion.

Then one day a more convenient alternative presented itself. Kim happened to hear about a secret church not far from his apartment. The church catered to the South Korean businessmen who worked in the Shenzhen industrial zone. It wasn't registered with the Chinese government, as required by law, so it operated underground, billing itself as a cultural association. There was no sign on the door and no cross on the roof. The hundred or so congregants learned about the church by word of mouth.

Kim was soon a regular attendee. One Sunday he noticed two shabbily dressed men seated in a corner of the room. After worship, he went up to them, said hello, and learned to his astonishment that they were from North Korea. They had escaped across the Tumen River to northeast China and then traveled two thousand miles south to Guangdong Province. It took them two months. They hoped to find a way to slip across the border into Hong Kong.

"They came to church asking for help," he said. "But the church would only feed them, give them a few dollars, and let them go."

Kim was outraged. "I asked the pastor, 'Why do you let them go?' "

"Because we're afraid," the pastor replied. "If we're caught helping North Koreans, the church will be shut down."

Kim took the two men home.

That was the start of his rescue work. Kim began to assist North Korean refugees clandestinely. He provided safe houses in southern China; he gave them food, clothing, and money; and, eventually, he organized secret passage across China to third countries. He tried unsuccessfully to find them jobs in the furniture factories with which he did business, but the Chinese factory managers were afraid to help. They knew that hiring a North Korean was a serious crime.

It wasn't long before Kim gained a reputation along the new underground railroad as someone refugees could count on for assistance; some started coming south to seek him out. Pastors of churches in northeast China would call him and ask him to take in refugees. Many of the people he helped were women fleeing from the Chinese men who had purchased them as brides.

By his count, Kim helped more than one hundred North Koreans get out of China before he was arrested in 2003. It was a warm afternoon in late September, and he was leading a prayer meeting in his apartment. He and nine North Koreans—three men and six women—were seated in a circle on the floor. There was a knock on the door, then police burst in. Convicted of the crime of helping illegal migrants, Kim spent four years in a Chinese prison. He was released in 2007. He now runs an American nonprofit dedicated to rescuing trafficked women by spiriting them out of China on the new underground railroad.

In China, Kim named his rescue mission Schindler's List, a reference to the 1993 movie about Oskar Schindler, the Czech businessman who saved more than one thousand Polish Jews from the gas chambers at Auschwitz during World War II. Kim sees himself and other Korean-Americans who help North Koreans as modern-day Schindlers, committed to saving North Koreans from the depredations of two authoritarian governments, North Korea and China. When he worked in China, many of Kim's furniture clients in New York were Jewish, and he would ask them quietly for money to support his work helping North Koreans escape from China. "They understood what I was doing," he said simply. Later he changed the name of his organization to 318 Partners, after Article 318 of the Chinese criminal code, the law under which he was convicted.[2]

Today, Kim works out of his home on a quiet street in suburban Long Island about an hour's train ride from Pennsylvania Station in Manhattan. It is a luxurious contrast to his prison accommodations in China, where he slept on the cement floor of the cell he shared with a dozen felons.

His office is set up in a corner of the family room, where a computer sits on a small desk. But the nerve center of his operation is his cellphone, which rings repeatedly on the morning we meet. Calls come in from contacts in South Korea, China, and Southeast Asia regarding a rescue operation that is in the works. It is not until lunchtime, when most of Asia is asleep, that his phone finally goes quiet.

North Korean women are "commodities for purchase," Kim explains. The process of recruitment, transfer, and delivery of the brides has become systematized. He describes a network of human traffickers who operate as "suppliers," "wholesale providers," and "retail sellers."

The supply chain typically begins in the young woman's hometown in North Korea and ends when she is delivered to her new husband in China. The most popular marketplaces for North Korean women are in the three Chinese provinces that border North Korea—Liaoning, Jilin, and Heilongjiang—but North Korean brides are sold throughout China. The buyers are Chinese men, both ethnically Korean and majority Han. Many are farmers. Some have physical or mental disabilities that make them unsuitable as husbands in the eyes of Chinese women. In almost every case, the men are buying the one thing they want most in life: a wife.

Why would a Chinese man go to the trouble and expense of buying a North Korean bride? The answer has to do, above all, with China's long-standing population policies.

For more than three decades, China has pursued one of the world's strictest family planning policies. Most couples are allowed to have only one child. The one-child policy became part of China's constitution in 1978 and went into effect in 1979. Since then, the government has enforced it through fines, imprisonment, forced abortion, sterilization, and even, human rights groups charge, infanticide. The fertility rate has dropped to fewer than two children per woman today compared with close to six children per woman in the early 1970s.[3]

The one-child policy has had its intended effect of slowing the rate of expansion of China's population. But there has been an unwelcome side effect: an unnaturally high male-to-female ratio. A scarcity of young women is a fact of life in China today. In 2009, according to research published in the *British Medical Journal*, the number of males younger than twenty exceeded the number of females by more than thirty-two million.[4]

Left to herself, Mother Nature will bring more boys than girls into the world. The sex ratio at birth is roughly consistent worldwide: It's between 103 and 107 boys for every 100 girls. But boys tend to be less healthy than girls and have a higher mortality rate during infanthood. By the time the newborns reach their reproductive years, the sex ratio is about even.

This pattern does not hold true in China, where sex ratios are grossly lopsided. In 2005, the birth ratio was 120 boys for every 100 girls, according to the *British Medical Journal*. In some rural provinces, more than 140 male births were reported for every 100 female births.[5] "Gendercide" is how the *Economist* magazine characterized the problem in a 2010 cover article.[6] The word appeared in bold letters over a photograph of a pair of pink-bowed baby shoes. The shoes were empty.

The obvious result of the gender imbalance is a surplus of bachelors. The Chinese have a euphemism for permanently unmarried men: *guanggun.* They are "bare branches" on the family tree. The unmarried men are often desperate—for companionship, for sex, for household help. In rural areas, the bride problem is exacerbated by young Chinese women's preference for urban life and modern-minded husbands. Young women are fleeing the farm in droves, attracted by well-paying factory jobs and more comfortable urban lifestyles. In the three provinces bordering North Korea, the ratio of young men to young women is a staggering 14-to-1, according to an estimate from the Committee for Human Rights in North Korea.[7]

One former North Korean bride, now living in the United States, has a matter-of-fact explanation for the appeal of North Korean brides. North Korean women have a reputation of being clean and submissive, she told me. In a society that is modernizing as quickly as China is, such traditional wifely virtues are prized, especially in rural areas, where contemporary notions about women's roles have not penetrated. Brokers take "orders" from Chinese bachelors or their families for North Korean brides.

Women may hold up half the sky, in Mao Zedong's famous phrase, but they are still treated as second-class citizens in much of modern China. Today's gender imbalance gives the lie to Mao's dictum. Chinese families' traditional preference for boys lives on. Many couples still favor sons, both to carry on the family name and support them in their old age. In rural areas, sons are prized for the value of their labor. The birth of a son heralds the arrival of an extra farmhand as soon as the boy is old enough to hold a hoe.

Not so long ago in China, an unwanted baby girl might be drowned in a bucket at birth or left unattended to die. Such atrocities might still be occurring. But abortion is the preferred method of getting rid of unwanted baby girls. "Sex-selection abortion accounts for almost all the excess males," the *British Medical Journal* concludes. Because of the one-child policy, abortion is both widely available in China and widely accepted as a means of contraception.

Many couples take pains to make sure their one permitted child is male or, if they are allowed to have two children, that at least one is a boy. That is increasingly easy to do, thanks to ultrasound technology that allows a couple to determine the baby's sex early in the pregnancy. The first ultrasound machines were introduced in China in the early 1980s. They reached county hospitals by the end of that decade and rural hospitals by the mid-1990s. Since then, ultrasonography has become very cheap and is easily available even to the rural poor. The popular test costs about $12, well within the means of most couples. China has laws forbidding the use of ultrasounds to determine the sex of the unborn children, but they are ignored.[8]

China's sex imbalance has reached epic proportions. Steven Mosher, of the Population Research Institute, calls it a tale of "marital musical chairs" in which tens of millions of young men will be left standing. He paints a bleak picture of social disruption. "Rates of prostitution and homosexuality will increase as these unwilling bachelors seek alternative outlets for their urge to mate," he cautions. "Rates of recruitment for both the People's Liberation Army and for criminal gangs will increase as these 'excess' men seek alternative families. Crime, which is mostly committed by unattached males, will skyrocket."[9]

Mosher is not the only observer who is worried about the growing disparity between the sexes and how it could reshape Chinese society. Even the Chinese government has initiated programs to teach citizens about the value of girls. For now, however, one of the responses to the shortage of young women comes by way of North Korea, through the buying and selling of female flesh.

In what Steve Kim calls Stage One of the supply chain, the supplier, or recruiter, lures a woman away from her home with promises of a lucrative trip to China. Recruiters are either North Korean nationals or Korean-Chinese, and usually male. They typically hang out around urban train stations in the border regions and chat up attractive young women who pass by. Their marks are often rural women who have come to the city to sell an agricultural product they grew on an illegal private plot or scavenged from the forest.

Sometimes the recruiter targets a pretty young woman, follows her home, and tries to enlist her parents in his persuasion game. The recruiters travel from village to village, keeping an eye out for potential brides.

Kim explains what happens next. "When they see a widow with a beautiful daughter they say: 'Why do you leave your daughter like that? If you send her to China, then she can get money and have an education. Why don't you send her?' They keep talking and gain trust, and then—'OK,' the mother says, 'I trust you. Take her.'

"Then he takes the girl into China and sells her. This is one of the tricks." Kim shudders. "Horrible."

The recruiter's pitch is usually a variation on one of three themes: Come to China, and I'll introduce you to someone who will give you a good job. Or, I'll take you to a Chinese market where you can sell your goods for more money than you can get in North Korea. Or, I'll help you find your relatives in China.

He makes a tempting promise: You can come home after a few months with more money than you could make in a year here. For a young woman with no job prospects and whose family may be destitute, or nearly so, it can be an irresistible offer.

There is also a gullibility factor at work. In the northern reaches of North Korea, near the border with China, stories abound of girls who have gone to China and never returned. But even if they have heard such stories, many women are young enough, inexperienced enough, or desperate enough to believe that "it won't happen to me."

One former bride I interviewed—she called herself Naomi—described how she was befriended by a traveling salesman from China who offered to guide her to the address where relatives of her father lived. She left home in the middle of the night.

"I didn't want my parents to know I was leaving," Naomi told me. She knew she was taking a risk and didn't want them to dissuade her. "I thought I would go for a few days and come back."[10]

It wasn't until she reached China that she realized that the wares her salesman-friend were selling were human, and female. She was delivered to a Chinese farmer, exchanged for the North Korean wife he had purchased a month earlier but who had turned out to be ill. The unwritten contract under which the first woman had been purchased apparently contained a damaged-goods clause.

If trickery doesn't work, recruiters have been known to resort to kidnapping. Hannah, another former bride, described how she had been abducted and taken to China. She was a teacher in Pyongyang, and during the school vacation she accompanied the mother of one of her pupils to the border region. Hannah hoped to make a little extra money by helping her friend carry back the fashionable Chinese-made clothing she was planning to purchase from a Chinese salesman and resell in the capital.

On the evening they concluded the deal, the Chinese salesman invited the two women to dinner. The food was drugged, and the next thing they knew, both women woke up in a dark room, hands and feet bound, heads groggy from the narcotic.

As Hannah struggled to come to, she heard her friend cry out, "Teacher, I think we've been sold."[11] They were in China, destined for forced marriages. They never saw each other again.

"I never knew such things happened," Hannah told me.

Sometimes the pseudo-marriages are voluntary—at least in the sense that the woman has the theoretical option of turning down a man's offer. It is not unusual for a North Korean woman to agree to live with a Chinese man as his wife. But it is wrong to consider it a true choice. It is "a means of survival or livelihood," says Lee Keum-soon, a senior researcher with the Korean Institute for National Unification in Seoul. Lee has interviewed hundreds of North Korean women who have settled in the South. In many cases, she says, a voluntary marriage is indistinguishable from a forced marriage.[12]

Marriage is almost always a better option for a North Korean woman than prostitution or online sex work. A woman who cannot speak Chinese would not be able to work in public places such as a restaurant or a store because the risk of arrest would be too high. The North Korean woman "would quickly realize that there was no alternative but to establish a 'live-in' relationship with a Chinese man to avoid a police roundup," Lee observes. "She would have to choose to 'live-in' as a relatively safe means of staying in China."[13]

The supplier's job ends when he delivers the women to the Chinese side of the Tumen or Yalu River. His fee, Steve Kim says, runs between $80 and $300 per woman, depending upon the quality of the "product" and the difficulty of the crossing. Out of that sum, the supplier is expected to cover any bribes he must pay to North Korean border guards for information about safe crossing points or for an agreement that they'll look the other way at a prearranged time. North Korean officials themselves sometimes get into the business of trafficking women, Kim says. He cites the case of a twenty-two-year-old woman he helped who identified her recruiter as a retired military officer.

Stage Two of the supply chain begins on the Chinese side of the border, where "wholesaler providers" are waiting to receive the women. The wholesaler's job is to escort the women from the border region, past Chinese ID checks, to a safer place farther inland. That is typically somewhere in the Yanbian area of Jilin Province, one of the three provinces that border North Korea. Yanbian's full name is Yanbian Korean Autonomous Prefecture, and it is home to a large number of ethnic Koreans. It's a good place for North Koreans to hide in plain sight, or in the case of the North Korean brides, be hidden.

From there, some of the women are sold directly to Korean-Chinese men who live in the region. From the woman's point of view, this is usually the better option. Life with a Korean-Chinese man, in a community where the Korean language is spoken, is preferable to life with a Han Chinese man who speaks only Mandarin and whose culture and food will be unfamiliar to the woman.

Other brides move on to Stage Three of the supply chain and are resold to "retailers" for between $500 and $800 each. The retailers then sell the women directly to their clients, usually Han Chinese who live in other parts of the country, Steve Kim says. The price ranges between $1,200 and $1,500 per woman, depending upon her age and appearance.

There are variations on the pattern Steve Kim describes, but the basic outline, as also described by aid workers, remains the same: recruitment, transfer, and delivery.

In some cases a North Korean woman will cross the river on her own before linking up with a broker. Traffickers prey on women in the border regions using the same sorts of pitches they use to recruit women in North Korea. According to the State Department's Trafficking in Persons Report, trafficking networks of Korean-Chinese and North Korean men operate in northeast China and along the Chinese–North Korean border, "where they seek out North Korean women and girls."[14]

By the time a woman arrives in China, she is more vulnerable than she was at home. Listen to the voices of a few such "brides," as compiled by the Committee for Human Rights in North Korea. Sometimes the woman is talked into living with a Chinese man for her own "safety." Sometimes she is threatened with exposure if she doesn't comply. Sometimes she is told nothing; she is simply sold.

Case 11: "Only when we arrived in a village in Heilongjiang did I hear that I was going to get married. I didn't have a choice because I didn't even know where I was."[15]

Case 13: "We met with one ethnic Korean man by chance, and he said we should get married to a Chinese citizen to be safe. While I was not sure whether I should follow him or not, he took me to Mishan in Heilongjiang and sold me to a Han Chinese man."[16]

Case 14: "I crossed the Tumen River with three other people, and we all went to the house of ethnic Koreans nearby. This household had an orchard. They let us work there for a while, giving us food and shelter. One day, three men, including one dressed in a soldier's uniform, came in a taxi and took me to Longjing, where I was sold to an ethnic Korean man."[17]

At some point along the supply chain, the North Korean woman wakes up and realizes what is happening to her. She then has two choices: Go through with the marriage, or try to escape. This is not really a choice. The woman is on her own in a strange country. She knows no one. She doesn't speak the language. As she quickly finds out, in escaping to China from North Korea, she has exchanged one form of bondage for another. Most accept the inevitable and agree to be sold. They reason, not illogically, that life with a Chinese husband, even an abusive one, is preferable to arrest, repatriation, and imprisonment in North Korea.

The rule of law—to the extent that it prevails in China and to the extent that a North Korean with no exposure to such a concept is capable of understanding it—doesn't apply to North Korean refugees. If a woman has relatives in China, they often urge her, not without reason, to strike a bargain with a Chinese man who will feed and house her in exchange for her labor and sexual favors. If she contacts the police or other Chinese officials, she can expect worse treatment. If the police abide by the law, they will arrest her and send her back to North Korea. If they are corrupt, they will sell her to another bride broker.

Bang Mi-sun's story is typical. Bang Mi-sun crossed the Tumen River, motivated, she later said, by one thought: "I might find refuge in China."[18] Her husband had died of starvation in North Korea. Her elder daughter had disappeared, and her two younger children needed her help. She hoped to find work in China.

Instead, on the other side of the river, she found the police waiting for her. The Chinese police "were getting ready to apprehend me and send me back to North Korea," she said, unless she agreed to be sold. Speaking at a press conference in Washington, D.C., she described what happened next: "My first buyer sold me to another buyer, and then that buyer sold me in turn to another buyer, each buyer for additional profit. "

"I was being sold like a beast," she said. "I remember these Chinese brokers would call us, those who were being sold, 'pigs.' Well, I was the best pig they had. I was sold at top price." Her first husband told her he paid 7,000 yuan for her—the equivalent of about $850. "He told me he would kill me if I did not listen to him."

A few days after Bang Mi-sun started living with her new husband, she won a reprieve of sorts: Brokers abducted her and sold her to another man. "I found out that there are brokers who would take the people who had been sold and take them away and sell them again to a third party," she said. "I never knew that this buying and selling of people existed. . . . I was sold again and again."

After her last marriage, Bang Mi-sun was arrested by Chinese police and deported to North Korea. She was beaten and sent to a labor reeducation camp. She eventually escaped again to China and made her way to South Korea. At the Washington press conference, she stood on a chair, lifted up her skirt, and displayed the deep furrows in her thighs, scars of where she'd been tortured.

She asked, "Why do North Korean women have to be treated like pigs and sold like pigs and suffer these things?"

North Korean brides are "thrice victimized," says Ambassador Mark Lagon, former director of the U.S. State Department's human-trafficking office. "They have fled starvation and human rights abuses in North Korea," he notes. "They are subject to abuse as undocumented migrants in China. And if they are sent back to North Korea, they face severe punishment, even execution in some cases."[19]

According to the Office to Monitor and Combat Trafficking in Persons, which Lagon headed, more than eight hundred thousand people are trafficked worldwide across borders every year. The vast majority—80 percent—are women and girls. That is roughly the same percentage of North Korean refugees in China who are female, according to human rights groups.

Lagon describes the plight of North Korean women in China as different from that of trafficked women elsewhere in the world, or even in China, where Southeast Asian women also are sold as brides.

North Korean women in China experience the "usual vulnerabilities of undocumented migrants, who are subject to manipulation by employers, debt bondage, and so forth, worldwide," he says. But China's treatment of North Korean women is worse. "There's a particular cocktail here of an insensitive and arguably cruel immigration policy in China that make them even more vulnerable."

Lagon is referring to China's policy of treating trafficked North Korean women as criminals or deportable aliens, not as victims. Chinese law recognizes North Korean refugees only as illegal immigrants. There is no screening process to determine whether a woman is a victim of sex trafficking, that is, whether she has been forced into prostitution or marriage with a Chinese national. She has zero recourse under Chinese law.

Every North Korean bride I have interviewed used the words "marriage" and "husband" when describing her personal situation. That was true even if she had another husband and family back home in North Korea. But in the eyes of Chinese law, the living arrangement of a North Korean woman with a Chinese man has no legal status. The marriage cannot be registered with the Chinese government because the woman has no official identity papers. If a man tries to register his marriage, he runs the risk that his wife will be exposed as an illegal migrant and subject to arrest and repatriation. At the very least, the husband will open himself up to bribery from officials who want money in exchange for ignoring his wife's illegal status.

Like most of the Christians who are in the business of rescuing North Korean refugees, Steve Kim and 318 Partners rely on information from women who have escaped to seek out more people to help. Just as the widespread use of cellphones and the Internet has streamlined the export industry in China in the past decade, so, too, have high-tech communications media streamlined the escape industry. A ticket on the new underground railroad often begins with a cell-phone call.

After brides escape, "they tell us there are ten, fifteen more women like them in their village," Kim says. "And then they call them."

He lifts his hand to an ear, pretending to be a rescued North Korean woman making a phone call to a friend in China. "'Yeah, I'm here. It's so-o-o good. Why don't you come?'" The bride who has escaped then gives her friends in China Kim's phone number or the number of a colleague in Seoul.

"If they want, they contact us," he says. "That's how it happens."

The next step is a phone interview with Kim. Does the woman fully understand the risks of escape? Is she willing to take the chance that she could be arrested and repatriated? If she has children with her Chinese husband, is she prepared to leave them behind?

Some women decide not to leave. "Many women have adjusted to their new lives even though they were trafficked," he says. They have enough to eat. Their living conditions are far better than anything they experienced in North Korea. Their neighbors help shield them from arrest when security officials come snooping.

"The husband is happy and they're not complaining," Kim says. "They're taking it as destiny. They tell me, 'Don't bother our family.' They are living peacefully."

If a woman wants help, and Kim agrees to do so, he goes to work quickly. He figures out how much the rescue will cost and begins to organize his network on the new underground railroad. If the woman is still living with her Chinese husband, the first step will be to arrange for her to get to a secure location from which she can begin her journey.

Then he sends out a plea for money to his email list of supporters. Typical is an appeal from a January 2010 newsletter: "We have received another call for help from three trafficked North Korean women in China," the newsletter states. "They are all from the same hometown in North Korea. According to the older woman named Choi, they have escaped from the captors [and are] hiding in a northern city of Jilin province. We ask your support in prayers and financially."[20]

The basement price of one of 318 Partners' rescues is $1,300. Most cost much more—$3,000 or above. Money is so tight that Kim sometimes asks the rescued women to pledge to pay back $1,000 of the costs once they get to Seoul and receive financial help from the South Korean government.

There is a crude justice in such financial accountings: $1,000 is also the approximate price of a North Korean bride.

HALF-AND-HALF CHILDREN

Before we reach the secret house orphanage in the Korea-town section of a city in northeast China, my hosts instruct me: "Don't ask the children about their mothers. It's too sad for them."[1]

The boys and girls we are en route to visit are the children of North Korean brides and their Chinese husbands. They represent the most vulnerable subgroup of the North Korean humanitarian crisis in China—abandoned children. Caring for these children is a growing focus of Christian missionaries in China, and small, secret house orphanages have sprung up across the Northeast. They usually are set up and paid for by American or South Korean Christians and staffed by local Chinese Christians. The orphanage I am about to visit is run by Crossing Borders, a small Christian nonprofit based in Illinois and dedicated to serving North Koreans in China. Crossing Borders operates several orphanages there.

The children aren't strictly orphans, but given that both parents are absent, they are effectively so. Their mothers have been arrested and repatriated to North Korea, or they've left of their own accord on the new underground railroad. The fathers either don't want the children or don't have the means to care for them. Aid workers estimate that there are tens of thousands of half-Chinese, half–North Korean children in that part of China.[2] Like other demographic issues involving North Korean refugees, there are no reliable statistics, only informal estimates. No one really knows how many half-and-half children exist overall or what percentage of these kids are abandoned.

Half-and-half children pose a special set of ethical and legal problems for those who want to care for them—especially for activists who are contemplating whether to help them get out of China on the new underground railroad. Does anyone have the moral right to remove a child from his country of birth without the consent of at least one of his parents and in contravention of Chinese law? What is best for the child?

Even if a half-and-half child were to make it safely out of China to a neighboring country, his chance of reaching South Korea or another country is slim. There is a high risk that the host government of the country where he took refuge would return him to China. This has happened. Half-and-half children usually lack documentation of any sort. They seldom have birth certificates or proof of citizenship. Seoul is willing to accept half-and-half children when they are accompanied by their North Korean mothers, but it is understandably reluctant to take unaccompanied children whom China might claim as citizens. Neither the South Korean government nor the Christian rescuers want to be accused of kidnapping Chinese children.

The bottom line is that many aid workers reckon they can help more children more effectively by taking care of them in China. In most cases, the aid workers opt to care for the children in place rather than take them out of the country. In the words of an American missionary whose organization shelters half-and-half children in China, "We hope they'll grow up to be productive citizens."

The five children I am about to visit are typical of the half-and-half children. In every case, the child's mother disappeared. Either she was arrested and repatriated to North Korea or she left home voluntarily in search of the underground railroad and a new life in South Korea or another country. But the reason for her absence matters less to the child she has left behind than the absence itself. "The children miss their mothers very much," I am told. Many bear emotional scars.

When Chinese police arrest a North Korean woman who is living with a Chinese man, they leave her children behind. Refugees tell stories of half-Chinese children being ripped from their mothers' arms by Chinese policemen. It's possible that Beijing's policy is motivated in part by a recognition of the Chinese father's parental rights. But another reason for leaving the children in place is practical: Beijing knows that North Korea will reject these children if China tries to repatriate them with their mothers. Because the children are half-Chinese, the North Koreans deem them to be of "impure" blood and unworthy of entering their country. Both North Korea and China are in violation of the international Convention on the Rights of the Child, which prohibits separating children from their mothers.

Chinese racism against North Koreans, as bad as it is, is overshadowed by the virulence of North Korean racism against Chinese. In the view of many North Koreans, theirs is the "cleanest race," possessing a unique moral purity. The worst invective is reserved for Americans—official propaganda describes Yankees as animals with "snouts," "paws," or "muzzles"—but North Korea's Chinese allies are also denigrated.[3]

This attitude is exemplified by an anecdote told by a South Korean professor who conversed with a North Korean scholar at a conference in Beijing. In his presentation at the conference, Mo

Jongryn, the South Korean professor, made passing reference to the growing number of South Koreans who are marrying foreigners. Later, the North Korean scholar approached Professor Mo. He was aghast. "You are diluting the purity of our race," he wailed.[4]

Nowhere is North Korea's attitude about racial purity more apparent than in its treatment of pregnant women repatriated from China. For the perceived crime of carrying "Chinese seed," their North Korean jailers force the repatriated women to undergo abortions, even in the final weeks of pregnancy. There are numerous eyewitness reports of pregnant women being beaten or required to work at hard labor until they abort spontaneously. One such technique is called the Pump. The pregnant woman is forced to stand up and squat down repeatedly until she aborts or collapses of exhaustion. In cases where the repatriated woman gives birth, her newborn is taken away from her. The infant is drowned, smothered, left outside in the elements, or clubbed to death.[5]

The South Korean government debriefs every refugee who arrives in Seoul and reports its findings in an annual publication. Many of the refugees have spent time in North Korean prisons, and the section on pregnant women is a parade of horrors. The matter-of-fact, staccato language of the government report only heightens the atrocity:

- "Gave birth to a baby . . . but they put vinyl cover [over the baby's face] and left it to die, accusing the baby of [being] Chinese."[6]
- "Gave birth to a baby on way to hard labor. Baby died."[7]
- "Hospital aborted baby at seven-month pregnancy because she had lived with a Chinese man."[8]
- "The agents forced her to run one hundred laps around a track because she had a Chinese seed in her. She collapsed after sixty laps and the baby was aborted."[9]

The five children I visit at the tiny orphanage in China all come from a remote rural village in Heilongjiang Province in the extreme northeast of China. Their mothers fled to China in the late 1990s and were sold as brides. Heilongjiang, which translates as Black Dragon River, is the Chinese name for the Amur River. The province borders the Russian Far East on the north and the Chinese autonomous region of Inner Mongolia on the west. It is the northernmost part of China, subject to sub-Arctic weather in winter and harsh living conditions for much of the year. China's economic miracle hasn't reached most parts of Heilongjiang yet, and the children's home village is very poor. Indoor plumbing was new to at least one of the children when he arrived at the orphanage. Another child, accustomed to being hungry, was amazed to find rice served at every meal. He had to learn how not to overeat.

These motherless children are fatherless as well, or the fathers are as good as dead to the children. The kids are in the orphanage in the first place because their fathers either cannot afford to take care of them or they do not want to. Centuries-old racial prejudices remain strong, and if the father is Han Chinese, he can be ashamed of having a half-Korean child. Once a man's North Korean wife is gone, some husbands want nothing further to do with their children. Whatever the reason, in the case of the five little ones at the orphanage I visit, the men handed their sons and daughters into the care of the village church. The church in turn delivered them to the American couple who are my guides.

Mary and Jim—they asked me to use pseudonyms—are a retired couple from the Midwest. They never told me their last name, and I never asked. We were introduced through an associate of theirs in New York City. Our first meeting took place in Seoul, where we rendezvoused at a prearranged time at the information desk of a popular mega-bookstore on the city's main avenue. It was a get-acquainted meeting, and I must have passed inspection, for they later agreed to meet again in China and take me to one of their foster homes. Crossing Borders, with which Mary and Jim work, had turned down my first request, made directly to the group's board of directors a few months earlier.

Back home, Mary was an accountant and a homemaker and Jim worked in a trading company. Their children are grown. Like most of the Americans working with North Koreans in China, they are of Korean heritage and speak fluent Korean. Despite that ethnic background, neither would be mistaken for Chinese or even South Korean. Their jeans, backpacks, and sneakers are giveaways, as is Jim's long hair, which sweeps across his forehead in a Ringo Starr–like bob. Both look American through and through. I easily spot them coming through the crowd when we meet near a congested train station in a city in northeast China.

Mary is effervescent and outgoing and acts as the couple's unofficial spokesperson. "After our younger child graduated from college, we decided we wanted to do mission work together," she tells me. "It was the right moment for us. We were thinking of going to Africa, but then this opportunity came up. We realized that this is the way God is leading us."

The couple is in China on work visas, and Jim's official job is with a company owned by a relative in South Korea. But their real work is with Crossing Borders. They manage a string of foster homes located in two cities in the northeast and divide their time traveling among them. The foster homes care for orphaned North Korean children as well as children whose mothers are North Korean. The couple also runs a shelter for young North Korean women who are in danger of being sold as brides.

This kind of second career is not for everyone. The work is far from home, poorly paid, and dangerous. If they are caught, there is a good chance they will go to jail; they would certainly be deported and barred from returning to China. "We thought about it carefully," Mary says, while Jim nods his assent. "We thought that after a life of work, we wanted to spend the rest of our lives helping someone. The U.S. is wonderful, and we had a good life, but there's not a lot of time left for us, and we want to use it well."

The Chinese foster parents who staff the orphanages are hazarding much more than Mary and Jim are. They face a constant risk of exposure by a nosy neighbor, a suspicious friend, or even a child in their care who reveals information to someone he shouldn't trust. If the foster parents are arrested and sent to prison, putting the pieces of their lives back together won't be easy. They will always be under suspicion. The foster parents also are putting their own biological families at risk. All the foster parents are married couples. If they're parents as well, they'll be separated from their child if they are arrested and jailed.

In the mid-2000s, aid workers in China began sounding the alarm about the special difficulties surrounding half-Chinese, half-North Korean children. This was about the time that the first wave of such children was reaching school age, their mothers having arrived in China during the famine years. The children are in legal limbo. As far as the Chinese government is concerned, they're invisible because they aren't listed on the family's official household registration card known as a *hukou*. Without a *hukou*, children can't attend school or obtain medical care.

Under Chinese law, a child born in China is entitled to citizenship if one parent is a Chinese citizen. But there is a catch. To obtain the right of citizenship for their child, parents must register their newborn, a process that requires them, among other things, to identify themselves, their address, and their citizenship. The *hukou* is a passport-like document, containing personal information about every member of a household. The data recorded in the *hukou* include gender, date and place of birth, ethnicity, current address, previous address, citizen ID number, height, blood type, education level, occupation, and work address. The *hukou* is an essential document, required for virtually every interaction with the state. Students are required to present copies of their *hukou* to enroll in school. Adults must show their *hukou* when they change jobs or move to a new residence. A *hukou* is required to obtain medical treatment.

The father of a Chinese–North Korean child is thus compelled to make a wrenching choice: Does he register the baby, an act that will expose the nationality and location of the child's mother? If he does so, his wife will be vulnerable to arrest and deportation, and he and his family will be susceptible to shakedowns by authorities. Or does he forego the registration, making it difficult, if not impossible, for the child to receive health care and an education? It is a kind of Sophie's Choice: the life of the mother or the well-being of the child.

Fathers who care about their half–North Korean children sometimes take desperate measures to make sure they receive an education. Officials at an elementary school sometimes can be bribed to admit a child without a *hukou*. But the enrollment is unofficial, and the school will not keep formal records of the child's work; when it comes time for junior high school, it again will be as if the child did not exist. Parents also have been known to borrow or buy the *hukou* of a full-Chinese child. There is even a market in counterfeit *hukou*. But all these options are expensive, risky, and unreliable. They also require proactive steps on the part of a responsible father.

If they can afford it, Chinese fathers sometimes apply for *hukou* for their children after their North Korean wives have left or been arrested. There is a fine for late registration, and the authorities sometimes demand to see a police document verifying that the North Korean mother is gone, a piece of paper that requires yet more bribes.

Mary and Jim have managed to obtain *hukou* for all the children under their care, thanks to funding from Crossing Borders. Real IDs are preferable, because the children will use them for the rest of their lives, and Mary and Jim are willing to pay a premium for government-issued registration cards. If a child has a Chinese father who is identifiable and willing to put his half–North Korean child on his family's *hukou*, their organization will ante up the funds for the late registration fee and attendant bribes. If the father is absent or unwilling to add his half–North Korean child to the family *hukou*, Mary and Jim will purchase fake IDs on the black market. There are a few fully Korean children in their orphanages, and obtaining fake IDs for them costs the most—up to $8,500 per child.

Mary and Jim are extremely careful about security, and with good reason. The legal status of their foster homes is at best ambiguous. Under Chinese law, foreigners are not permitted to perform these kinds of social services, and, in any case, proselytizing is forbidden. Teaching Christianity to the children is against the law.

The explanation given to neighbors of their house orphanages or to inquiring officials is that the foster parents are operating a *jun tag* business. That is, they are taking care of the children of ethnic Korean-Chinese who have temporarily moved to South Korea. There are more than four hundred thousand Korean-Chinese working in South Korea, so this is a plausible scenario. Korean-language newspapers run ads for *jun tag*, which are often run by retired teachers. The foster father of the orphanage I visited used a variation on the *jun tag* story, telling neighbors that he was caring for the children of relatives who had gone to South Korea to work. He instructed the children to call him and his wife "Uncle" and "Auntie." The families worship at home on Sundays, preferring not to call attention to themselves by attending a local church. The children are warned not to talk about Jesus outside their home.

The network of foster homes that Mary and Jim supervise operates on a monthly budget of about $10,000. This covers rent, a small salary for the foster parents, food, school supplies, and clothes for the thirty children under their care. There is little left over for extras. The children go without dental care or birthday presents. At Christmas, Jim dresses up as Santa Claus and gives each child one gift.

Mary and Jim learned the hard way about the need for tight security. Early in their stay in China, one of the foster parents threatened to expose them. He said he would turn them over to the police and reveal the location of their apartment and all the house orphanages if they did not pay him a bribe. Mary and Jim immediately called home for advice, and the board of Crossing Borders dispatched one of its directors to China, where he negotiated hush money with the foster parent. Since that episode, Mary and Jim keep their home address secret. They each carry two cellphones—one for talking to foster parents, the other for talking to each other. Sensitive matters are saved for face-to-face conversations. They also took the precaution of opening two foster homes in a second city so that they have bolt-holes for the children in case of another such emergency. The couple says the trust issue is the hardest part of their job. "We want to trust everyone, but we can't," Mary says. "That kind of stress is the worst."

Their focus on security extends to our meeting. When I connect with Mary and Jim at the train station in China, it's just after six o'clock in the evening and still light. Mary suggests that we kill forty-five minutes at a nearby McDonald's while we wait for dusk. We are going to take a cab to the foster home, and she wants us to arrive after dark so we'll avoid prying eyes. Every Chinese neighborhood has an official busybody, a government watchdog who reports to the local authorities. The last thing the foster parents need is for a neighbor to spot me walking into the apartment and start asking questions about what a *gweilo*, a foreigner, is doing there.

A little before seven, Mary glances out the window at the darkening sky and says, "Let's go." She hails a cab, negotiates a price with the driver, and we pile in. It is fully dark by the time we reach

Korea-town; there are no streetlights, and it's hard to make out the faces of the people on the sidewalk. Jim called the foster father a few minutes before our arrival, and he is waiting for us as we get out of the car. We don't linger. Introductions will come later. He and Jim lead us quickly through a maze of alleyways between blocks of identical high-rise apartment buildings. Eventually we enter a doorway, someone flips on a light, and we start to climb the stairs. The stairway and landings are clean and tidy. We know we are in Korea-town by the huge brown earthenware pots outside the doors. They hold kimchi, or pickled cabbage, a staple of every Korean meal and the culinary accomplishment by which every Korean housewife is judged.

When we reach the fourth floor, the foster father sprints ahead, opens the door to his apartment, and pandemonium erupts. Five children race to the vestibule and shout "hello!" in English, the "l's" sounding more like "r's." One child helps us remove our shoes and shoves slippers onto our feet; two others grab the bags from our grip; and the other two run to the kitchen to fetch boxes of cookies, which they thrust into our hands the moment we step up from the vestibule into the living room. I am ushered to a white plastic chair that one of the children has put out for me. Mary, Jim, and the foster father sit nearby.

After greeting each child by name, Mary takes charge. She has the children sit cross-legged on the floor in front of me. One by one, each child rises, bows formally, and introduces himself. The children are suddenly tongue-tied, too shy to answer questions with more than a word or two. Later Mary describes each child's background for me, and I am able to piece together their stories based on her information along with what the children told me.

The children have been living in the house orphanage for a year now, and they look well fed, energetic, and healthy. Mary says they were malnourished when they first arrived. To my American eyes, they look like they are only nine or ten years old even though their real ages are twelve and thirteen. The emotional deficits are harder to notice or remedy.

"Kuon" lost his mother when he was six. The police raided his home on a cold night in December after the family had gone to bed. They handcuffed her and took her away while Kuon remained asleep. When he awoke, she was gone. After his mother left, Kuan stayed home alone all day while his father went to work. He eventually went to school for a while, but his father was too poor to buy even a notebook for his son, so the boy dropped out. Kuon is luckier than many of the half-and-half children: His father is a good man, I am told, and loved his North Korean wife. He called Mary and Jim angels from heaven for welcoming his son into their orphanage.

The other two boys were less fortunate in their families. "Sung Hoon" has no memory of his mother, who was arrested and sent back to North Korea when he was only seven months old. His father was too poor to take care of him, so the boy went first to an uncle's house and then to a state orphanage before finding his way to Mary and Jim's foster home. "Hak Chul's" father died of cancer when he was ten, and his North Korean mother left home shortly after that. The boy went to live with an uncle, but the uncle abused him and was only too happy to turn him over to Mary and Jim. Hak Chul's chubby face is round and cute, but it belies his unhappiness. He cries frequently and won't join in games with the rest of the children.

The two girls are polar-opposite personalities. "Eun Hee" has a ballerina's body. She is tall, slender, and perfectly proportioned. Mary says she likes clapping games, but on the evening we meet, it is hard to imagine her loosening up enough to take part in any such lively activity. She sits with her hands folded in her lap, and her eyes never leave my face. She is silent and serious and doesn't smile. Her mother, who was arrested when Eun Hee was six, was abusive, and Eun Hee has a nightmarish memory of being nearly strangled to death by her. Her father is disabled and cannot work. Her grandfather took care of her before handing her over her to Mary and

Jim. When I ask her what she wants to do when she grows up, she thinks a moment and then gives a surprising reply: She wants to be a scientist.

"Kim Sun" also comes from an abusive home, but she somehow seems the child most capable of rising above it. Of all the children they care for, she is the one in whom Mary and Jim place the most hope. She is quick-witted and intelligent. She is already second in her class at a Korean-language elementary school even though she is a native Chinese speaker and doesn't understand Korean very well yet. When Mary and Jim and I speak English together, I hear her softly repeating some of our words. "Thank you" comes out "sank you" and "sixty-seven" is "sixty-seben."

Like many of the half-and-half children, Kim Sun comes from a violent home. She was abused by both her father and her uncle, who took her mother as his "wife" after her father died, when Kim Sun was five. She retains vivid memories of her mother, who left home when Kim Sun was ten, abandoning the girl to her violent uncle. Shortly after that, the uncle agreed to send her to Mary and Jim's orphanage. Although most of the other children in the foster homes make occasional holiday visits back to their home villages, Kim Sun has nowhere to go and spends her holidays in the foster home or with Mary and Jim.

Mary and Jim think Kim Sun is smart enough to go to university one day, and they are committed to seeing her and the other half-and-half children through to adulthood. If, that is, they can afford it. The children are only in fourth or fifth grade now, but the Americans are already worried about paying for junior high school and high school, should the children qualify. Schooling is ostensibly free in China, but parents are obligated to pay for books, supplies, and uniforms. These costs add up as children reach higher grades. If a child needs special attention, teachers expect "extra" payments. In addition, the half-and-half children often need after-school tutoring to help them keep up. Many have not attended school full time before moving to their foster homes and are a grade or more behind. Others have emotional problems that interfere with studying. Foster parents usually don't have time to provide the necessary tutoring, or they are poorly educated themselves and can't keep up with the curriculum after the early grades.

For the meantime, Crossing Borders can pay the bills, though just barely. One day, after the children are older, Mary and Jim may decide to send them out of China on the new underground railroad, they told me. They and other Christian aid organizations that work in China are also exploring ways to get half-and-half children out of China legally and have them adopted in the West. For this to happen, the children's legal guardians would need to be identified and agree to give up their rights.

It's getting late, way past the children's bedtime. We have been talking a long time, and the children are getting sleepy. But before Jim and the foster father walk me out to the street to find a taxi, Mary wants to tell me one more story about the half-and-half children. "Usually they don't talk about their mothers," she said. It's too painful. But sometimes the subject comes up naturally in conversation, as it did with one little girl Mary supports in a foster home in another city. Mary was reading the children a bedtime story, when the child told her that Cinderella was her favorite fairy tale. The girl saw herself in the story of the impoverished, motherless child rejected by her stepfamily. The girl liked the story, Mary said, not because Cinderella married a prince or became rich. She liked it because Cinderella was happy even though she didn't have a mother.

SIBERIA'S LAST GULAG

The trunk line of the new underground railroad runs through China, but a branch line originates in Russia.

This leg of the underground railroad serves a sad subset of North Korean fugitives: men who escape from logging camps in Siberia and the Russian Far East, where their government has sent them to work in conditions that amount to slave labor. There are an estimated thirty thousand to forty thousand North Koreans working in Russia. Many are loggers, but others work in construction, mines, and other industries.[1]

During their stay in Russia, an unknown number of the North Koreans take the opportunity to escape. Human rights activists put the number of runaway loggers as high as ten thousand, although that might be inflated.[2] Since the mid-1990s, roughly one hundred ex-loggers have arrived in Seoul from Russia with the help of Christian activists. Others have found their way across the Russian border to China, where they managed to get work on the black market or obtained passage on the new underground railroad, eventually reaching South Korea.

The North Korean lumberjacks and other contract workers are in Russia as part of a business deal negotiated by the Kim family regime more than forty years ago. Pyongyang has a long-standing commercial arrangement with Moscow to provide low-cost labor for Russian logging operations in the birch and pine forests of the far eastern reaches of the country. [3]

This is the desolate area, in Siberia and the Russian Far East, that used to be home to the forced-labor camps of the Soviet gulag. The North Koreans who toil there today have in some locations taken the place of the political prisoners banished to the camps by the old Soviet dictators. The logging sites are so remote, the work so arduous, and the living conditions so onerous that it is difficult to find Russians who will agree to do the jobs. Pyongyang is only too happy to step in—for the right amount of foreign exchange, of course—and sell the services of its citizens.

It has done so since 1967, when North Korea and the Soviet Union concluded an agreement to supply workers for the Russian timber industry. Under the original deal, struck by North Korea's founding President Kim Il Sung and then Secretary General of the Soviet Union Leonid Brezhnev, North Korea provided the workers and managed the logging sites. The Soviet Union furnished the forests, fuel, and equipment. Pyongyang sent in the lumberjacks, usually for three-year terms of work and always under the close watch of the North Korean security agents who accompanied them.[4] The lumber was sold abroad, and the profit was divided between the two nations. Japan was an early client; China is said to buy the lumber today.

Then came the collapse of the Soviet Union in 1991. The logging camps in the former gulag were an embarrassment, a symbol of the totalitarianism that the Russian people had rejected. When the Soviet–North Korean agreement on the camps expired at the end of 1993, Russian human rights groups pushed for the inclusion of human rights protections for the North Korean loggers in the new accord that was then under negotiation. The human rights commissioner of the Russian Parliament, himself a former prisoner of the gulag, declared that a secret protocol in the original Soviet–North Korean agreement would be henceforth illegal. That protocol had authorized North Korean security agents to operate on Russian soil and stipulated that Soviet police would arrest any North Korean logging-camp runaway and turn him over to North Korean agents. A revised agreement was signed in 1995 that included protections for the North Korean workers. Those protections have been largely ignored and are disregarded even today. The treatment of the loggers has shown little improvement, and human rights advocates say Russian law-enforcement officials continue to cooperate with the North Korean security agents to track down and repatriate runaway lumberjacks.

The loggers' work is a modern-day form of slave labor. Much of a worker's salary goes to the North Korean government. The North Koreans are forced to undertake backbreaking work over long hours under austere conditions. The lack proper training, safety equipment, and even clothing warm enough to protect them from the freezing Siberian winters, where temperatures can reach twenty degrees below zero. In the hours when they are not working, the workers are confined in prison-like facilities policed by North Korean guards. They are required to attend the same kind of government propaganda sessions they are forced to take part in at home. The camps have their own prisons, where workers who commit ideological crimes are punished with low rations and violent treatment.

Media reports about the logging camps began to surface in the early 1990s. Russian journalists, exercising their post-Soviet freedom to report on hitherto forbidden subjects, were the first to cover the story. Western media soon picked it up. One of the early reports ran on the front page of the *Wall Street Journal* in 1994. Moscow bureau chief Claudia Rosett described her clandestine visit to several logging camps in the municipality of Chegdomyn, two hundred miles northwest of the Siberian city of Khabarovsk. She painted a vivid and disturbing picture of what she saw there. Recent news reports suggest that little has changed in the nearly two decades since she wrote her articles.

Rosett described a camp that "could be almost anywhere in North Korea." A giant portrait of Kim Il Sung looked out across the wooden barracks. A sign in huge red Korean letters exhorted the loggers: "Democratic People's Republic of Korea, to Victory!" Loudspeakers played anthems glorifying the North Korean state.[5]

It was winter and bitterly cold when Rosett visited. She recounted how, despite the weather, the North Korean gatekeeper at one camp was shod in sneakers with no laces or socks. It was an image, she later wrote, that haunted her for years. In her words, it was that of a man "peering out from that transplanted bit of North Korea into a world where asking for even a taste of his rightful human portion of liberty could bring him torture and death."[6]

At another camp she observed loggers toiling in torn pants and felt shoes. The North Koreans were bone-thin, fed on rations of cabbage and rice supplied by Pyongyang. Hungry loggers sometimes slipped away from the camp to beg door-to-door from the Russians in a nearby settlement, the same way that North Koreans who cross the Tumen or Yalu River into China knock on the doors of houses in the first villages they encounter. She quoted a local housewife: "One Korean came here, and you could see he was just starving. I gave him bread and salt pork."[7]

Stalin once shipped political undesirables to work, and often die, in camps like these. For North Koreans, however, being sent to a logging camp is not a punishment; it is a privilege. For North Koreans lucky enough to be selected to work in Russia, the logger's life is a dream job, the opportunity of a lifetime. The reality of life in North Korea is reflected in the fact that workers compete vigorously for the opportunity to be sent to Siberia. The logging jobs are allocated by factories. Workers who want to become loggers pay bribes to the officials who make the selections.

"Mr. Chang," a pseudonym for an ex-lumberjack now living in Seoul, explained how the selection process worked when he competed for a logging job in the mid-1990s. He believes it operates the same way today.

First, a worker must belong to what is known as the "loyal" class of citizens with "pure" family histories. That means that he must have no ancestral ties to South Koreans, capitalists, or Christians.[8]

Second, Pyongyang requires that the applicant be married and have at least one child. In the cruel reckoning of the regime, wives and children act as hostages, ensuring the return of the logger. Mr. Chang, who was employed at a car factory in a city not far from the capital, explained that he met the basic requirements because he came from a good family—he has relatives who work for the government in Pyongyang—and he has a wife and daughter.

Third, an applicant needs to pay off the decision makers. To get the logging job, Mr. Chang paid a bribe of $300 to a Workers' Party official at his factory. He considered himself lucky for having struck a good bargain. Some of his colleagues had to pay bribes of as much as $1,000. Others went into debt to get the jobs, pledging to bring home gifts of hard-to-get items such as TVs or refrigerators. "You can't imagine how tough the competition was to be selected as a worker," Mr. Chang said. "For example, if there are three openings in a factory of fifteen hundred workers, everyone will be competing for these three openings."

Mr. Chang had high hopes for his logging job. The money was far better than it was at home, even with the big cut of his salary that went to the government. He also anticipated that he would have the opportunity to buy goods not readily available in North Korea. Mr. Chang didn't know how much his government actually received for his labor, but of the salary that he knew about, he remitted 70 percent to his hometown government. He received 30 percent in the form of vouchers for use in Russian stores.

Mr. Chang left for Russia in 1995 with high expectations. They were soon dashed. He received his promised salary the first month, but payment was erratic in subsequent months. By the end of the first year, payment stopped altogether. He decided to run away. Railroad tracks ran through the forest near his camp, and he managed to hop on a freight train headed to Khabarovsk. There he found an off-the-books job working on a construction site, but it wasn't long before he was arrested for being in Russia illegally. Hoping to avoid being sent back to the logging camp, he told the police he was a Chinese citizen of Korean heritage and had come to Khabarovsk looking for work. He was desperate to avoid being turned over to North Korean security agents. In his calculation, being confined in a Russian jail for the crime of illegal entry into Russia was far preferable to being sent back to the logging camp and then incarcerated for the crime of running away. Authorities eventually found out his true nationality, and he was turned over to the North Korean secret police. Instead of returning him to the logging camp, the agents put him and other escaped loggers on a train to North Korea.

Human rights organizations reported at the time on the treatment of runaway loggers in the custody of North Korean security police in Russia. They were kept in iron chains and sometimes had casts forcibly put on both legs in order to keep them from escaping again.[9] Mr. Chang was fortunate—no fetters, no casts. When the train slowed down, he and two friends jumped off, suffering only minor cuts and bruises. It was evening, and they ran into the woods. As they watched the lights of the retreating train in the fading light, they decided to walk along the track until they reached a town, where they would seek work. Mr. Chang spent the next three years wandering from place to place in Siberia, staying one step ahead of the Russian police and North Korean agents. He begged, did odd jobs, and occasionally resorted to theft. Eventually a Christian activist helped him get to China. After four years on the run in China, another Christian helped him reach South Korea.

Mr. Chang doesn't remember the name of the Christian who helped him in Russia, but it might have been Phillip Buck, an American pastor of Korean heritage.[10] Pastor Buck was one of the early developers of the new underground railroad in China. He began his mission work in 1992 in Russia, though, with runaway North Korean loggers. He developed techniques there that he later used to greater success in China.

"I wanted to be close to North Korea," he explained years later about his decision to move to the Russian Far East as a missionary. While he lived in Russia, he would often pay a visit to Khasan, a tiny border settlement south of the Far East city of Vladivostok on the Tumen River. The pastor would stand on the bank of the river, gaze at his native country, and pray.

In Russia in the early 1990s, Pastor Buck was shocked at the lack of concern the South Korean government showed for the North Korean loggers. Despite its rhetoric about welcoming North Koreans to the South and despite its constitutional obligation to do so, the South Korean government had little interest in helping North Koreans reach safety, he said. Most of the loggers he helped in Russia were turned away by the South Korean Embassy or Consulate if they went there to ask for asylum.

In her 1994 *Wall Street Journal* article, Claudia Rosett reported that ninety loggers had requested asylum at South Korean consular facilities in Moscow and Vladivostok, only to be denied. She called the presidential Blue House in Seoul and received an explanation that was amazing both for its content and its candor. "The government isn't accepting them, in order to avoid getting on the nerves of North Korea," a spokesman for President Kim Young-sam told her. Pyongyang had warned Seoul that it would consider any loggers who were granted asylum by South Korea as having been kidnapped. It threatened "decisive countermeasures," the presidential spokesman said.[11]

Pastor Buck operated safe houses in Khabarovsk and Vladivostok, where he also ran a church. Escaped loggers would learn about the pastor and his work through the local Korean grapevine and show up on his doorstep. He would provide a place to stay and give them food; if they decided to seek asylum in South Korea, he would offer to help them get out of Russia. North Korea had security agents in the region, and the kind of work Pastor Buck was doing was dangerous. In 1993, a South Korean missionary couple was murdered; the wife was strangled and the husband was bludgeoned to death. The Russian police did little to investigate the killings, which Pastor Buck believes were carried out by the North Korean security police. He led a demonstration in front of a police station in Khabarovsk, demanding a more thorough probe, to no avail.

The pastor advised North Korean loggers against approaching the South Korean Consulate in Vladivostok. It was too risky, he told them. It was a good bet that the consulate was under surveillance by the North Korean security service, and a logger on the run risked being kidnapped before he could reach the consulate's front door and then shipped back to North Korea.

Even South Korean diplomats weren't safe from North Korean agents in Russia. In 1996, a South Korean consul by the name of Choi Duk-keun was murdered in Vladivostok. The circumstantial evidence strongly suggested that it was a North Korean hit job. Choi Duk-keun was responsible for monitoring North Korean activities in the region. He was walking up the stairs to his seventh-floor apartment when he was hit on the head and stabbed twice in the stomach. He was carrying his passport and more than a thousand dollars in cash when he was attacked, but the assailant stole nothing. The National Institute of Scientific Investigation in Seoul performed an autopsy on the dead consul's body and determined that he had been killed by a poisoned needle.[12]

Pastor Buck counseled the loggers in his care to travel to Moscow and apply for asylum at the South Korean Embassy. He bought them tickets on the Trans-Siberian Railway and gave them money for expenses on the long journey. It takes nearly a week to travel the 5,300 miles from Khabarovsk to Moscow—across the vast Siberian taiga and over the Ural Mountains. Before the loggers left, he would pull out a city map of Moscow and trace the route from Yaroslavsky Rail Terminal, the terminus of the Trans-Siberian, to the South Korean Embassy, and he would coach them on what to say when they got there. Two or three loggers would travel together, bunking in the cheap "hard-class" compartments. Of the hundreds of loggers the pastor helped in some form in Russia, only a handful reached South Korea.

One-quarter of a million North Korean men have worked in Russia since the late 1960s, according to scholar Andrei Lankov.[13] The exposure of 250,000 North Koreans to Russia's more open society is bound to have had some effect on their thinking about their own country; perhaps the comparative liberty also affected the people to whom they recounted their experiences once they returned home. Even during the Communist era, Russia was a more liberal and prosperous society than North Korea. Half a continent away from Moscow, Siberia was the Wild East, the Soviet equivalent of the American Wild West, where residents got away with conduct forbidden elsewhere in the country.

A visitor to Siberia during that time period would have seen capitalism in action on a small scale—an apple seller on a city street or a merchant on a train platform hawking bread and hard-boiled eggs. Such sights would have been marvels to the North Korean workers changing trains in Khasan or Khabarovsk before heading into the forests. So, too, would have been the bright lights of the Soviet towns through which they traveled en route to their camps. The well-fed, warmly clothed Russians, though poor by first-world standards, would have seemed rich beyond measure to North Korean eyes.

By the 1990s, the Russian Far East was inundated with South Korean products and South Korean businessmen. There was so much business activity that Seoul opened a consulate in Vladivostok in 1992. North Korean loggers might have seen South Korean goods on display in Russian stores. North Koreans, although they hear from an early age that South Korea is an oppressive and poor country, suddenly became acquainted with the products of a modern industrialized country and realized that their image of the South was inaccurate.[14] Pastor Buck, an American, recalls that the Russian Far East "wasn't a very nice place to live, but it was far better than in North Korea."

Also in the 1990s, loggers sometimes got hold of radios that allowed them to listen to KBS, South Korea's state-owned radio station. KBS broadcast special programming to Korean speakers in North Korea, and its signals reached Russia, too. Korean-language radio programs also aired on Russian radio stations. In his book *Under the Loving Care of the Fatherly Leader*, Bradley K. Martin quotes an ex-logger who talked about the impact that listening to KBS had on him. "They had people criticizing the government on various issues," the ex-logger exclaimed. "So I experienced some ideological change. My friend and I kidded each other, 'Let's go to South Korea.' Ultimately it was that ideological change coupled with fear of execution that prodded me to defect."[15]

Twenty years later, North Korean loggers in Russia continue to work under conditions that have remained remarkably similar over the decades. The loggers "reportedly have only two days of rest per year and face punishments if they fail to meet production targets," the U.S. State Department noted in its 2011 report on human trafficking.[16]

In 2009, a reporter for the British Broadcasting Company traveled to a logging camp, where he observed facilities nearly identical to those described by Claudia Rosett in the mid-1990s. The camp the BBC reporter saw was home to fifteen hundred loggers, some of whom lived in mobile homes decorated with portraits of Kim Il Sung and Kim Jong Il. The reporter saw a giant monument inscribed with the words, "Our Greatest Leader Kim Il Sung Lives With Us Forever." The Russian director of a small local timber firm that had a contract with the logging camp told the BBC reporter that the North Koreans work year-round, with two days off per year. One logger said he earned the equivalent of $200 a month, but that he hadn't been paid in three months.

Under the administration of President Lee Myung-bak, who took office in 2008, South Korea says it no longer turns away lumberjacks who reach one of its consular facilities in Russia. On a sub-zero day in March 2010, two runaway loggers approached the South Korean Consulate in Vladivostok. The consulate is a turreted, red-brick building that looks as if it had been a merchant's mansion back in czarist times. The North Koreans climbed over the wall, ran past the guards, and entered the consulate, where they requested political asylum. Several weeks later, they arrived in Seoul.[17]

Also in March 2010 and also in Vladivostok, another North Korean logger made his bid for freedom. He was not so fortunate. The man, known only as "Kim," was waiting in a car outside a hotel, where he was to meet with officials from an international aid group who promised to help him reach the South Korean Consulate. As he was sitting in the automobile, another car pulled up to the hotel. Several men in civilian clothes got out and told the driver of Kim's car that his passenger was a criminal. They proceeded to put handcuffs on Kim, forced him into their car, and drove off.

Kim left behind a note, penned the previous day and given to a South Korean Christian at a safe house in Vladivostok. The note read: "I want to go to South Korea. Why? To find freedom. Freedom of religion, freedom of life."[18]

He was not seen again.

OLD SOLDIERS

When "Mr. Jung" joined us at our table in the cocktail lounge of a hotel lobby in Seoul, the man who had arranged the meeting, our mutual friend, did not recognize him. It was as if a stranger had suddenly filled the empty chair across from us.

"I just had my eyes done," Mr. Jung announced with a broad smile, clearly delighted that he had fooled his old colleague. His eye job was the latest in a series of face-changing operations he had undergone. He explained: "I've had plastic surgery to change my appearance so I can go back to China."[1]

Our friend complimented Mr. Jung on his new look and then, remembering his manners, performed the introductions. "No names, please," said Mr. Jung, shaking my hand. I agreed to keep his real name confidential, and his new name—"Mr. Jung"—is born. Given the line of work he is in, it can be safely assumed that "Mr.

Jung" is only the latest in a long line of aliases he has used in his years on the job.

Mr. Jung is a rescuer. His area of professional expertise is bringing home South Korean prisoners of war who have been held against their will in North Korea since the Korean War ended in 1953. He was part of a clandestine network of South Korean civilians who operated in the Sino-Korean border area during the 1990s and into the early 2000s. Their mission: Find the POWs in North Korea, facilitate their escape to China, and return them to South Korea. His rescue operations were authorized and funded by senior officials in the administration of President Kim Young-sam.

In 2010, the South Korean government estimated that there were at least five hundred South Korean POWs from the Korean War still alive and being detained illegally in North Korea.[2] Pyongyang said what it has been saying since 1953: It holds no South Korean POWs against their will.

This is a lie. The evidence—collected from, among other sources, the handful of POWs who have escaped to the South in recent years—overwhelmingly supports the South Korean government's assertion that some of its soldiers are still alive and being forcibly detained by North Korea. Time is running out. The men who fought in the Korean War are now elderly. A soldier who was twenty years old when the war began in 1950 would be older than eighty today.

These old soldiers have been held illegally by North Korea since the conclusion of the Korean War. Their detention is a violation of the Geneva Convention's requirements on the prompt return of POWs after hostilities end. It also violates the 1953 Armistice Agreement to the Korean War, which required the immediate repatriation of POWs. The terms are set out in Article III of the Armistice Agreement, which reads in part: "Within sixty (60) days after this agreement becomes effective, each side shall, without offering any hindrance, directly repatriate and hand over in groups all those prisoners of war in its custody who insist on repatriation to the side to which they belonged at the time of capture."[3]

Tens of thousands of South Korean soldiers went missing at the end of the Korean War. At the time of the armistice, the United Nations Command could not account for the whereabouts of nearly eighty-two thousand South Korean servicemen. Only one-tenth of this number—8,343—were repatriated during the three POW exchanges that the United Nations Command and North Korea conducted shortly after the cease-fire.[4]

Over the years, successive South Korean governments have devoted Herculean efforts to tracking down the status of each missing soldier. South Korea has checked names of the missing against the original war-time military rosters. It has taken testimony from military defectors and others who escaped from North Korea. As the years passed, 22,562 South Korean soldiers whose names appeared on the original list of the missing were identified as having been killed in action. The change in status to "killed" from "missing" was important to the soldiers' families. It gave them emotional closure, allowed them to perform funeral rites, and permitted them to benefit from government grants available to relatives of deceased soldiers. Korean names can be very similar, and some names on the original lists of the missing were found to be duplicates. By 2011, the South Korean government had reduced the official number of soldiers deemed to be missing in action to 19,409. Where are they? The Ministry of Unification answered the question in a bland statement: "It is reasonable to assume that a significant number of South Korean POWs have not been repatriated but are being held by the North Korean side."

It might have been out of some perverse sense of competition with the South that Pyongyang made the decision not to return thousands of South Korean POWs after the war. The Geneva Convention of 1949 mandated the immediate return of POWs after hostilities ended, but the United States insisted that the POWs who had been captured by U.N. forces have a choice: They could decide whether to stay in South Korea or return to North Korea. After months of negotiation, North Korea reluctantly agreed to the American demand. To Pyongyang's embarrassment, some forty-nine thousand North Korean POWs held in the South chose not to return. They were released into South Korean society.

Then, as now, Pyongyang maintained that the South Korean POWs who stayed in North Korea after the war did so by choice. The record, as compiled by American and South Korean experts, proves otherwise. A few South Korean POWs may have decided to stay, but the overwhelming majority had no choice. In many cases, they did not even know that the war had ended.

Exhibit A is a classified study the United States Department of Defense compiled in 1993.[5] According to the Pentagon report, which is now declassified, thousands of South Korean POWs died in the Soviet gulag along with many American POWs. The Pentagon researchers found that after the end of the war, American and South Korean POWs were transferred from North Korea to prison camps in the Soviet Union. The transfers took place under a secret program approved by Stalin.

The Pentagon study was conducted with the cooperation of the new Russian government, which facilitated interviews with former Soviet military officers and others who had firsthand knowledge of what happened to the South Korean POWs. The report cited many eyewitness accounts. These accounts were so broad, so numerous, and so convincing, the report's authors argued, that it was impossible to dismiss them.

Among the interviewees was a former Soviet general officer, Khan San-kho,[6] who provided information on South Korean POWs. Lieutenant-General Khan, a Soviet citizen who was ethnically Korean, had been seconded to the North Korean People's Army during the Korean War. General Khan told the American investigators that he had assisted in the transfer of thousands of South Korean POWs to prison camps in the Soviet Union after the war.[7]

The South Korean POWs were distributed among three to four hundred Soviet prison camps, the general said. Most of the POWs were sent to camps in Siberia or the Soviet Far East, but some were shipped off to Central Asia. The South Korean POWs were put to work in mines or built roads and airfields. Most did not survive long, he said.

Another source of information for the Pentagon researchers was Zygmunt Nagorski, a Polish-born American journalist. Nagorski reported the transport of thousands of South Korean POWs to Soviet prison camps in a 1953 article for *Esquire* magazine.[8] His sources were two agents of the Soviet Interior Ministry and an employee of the Trans-Siberian Railroad. Like General Khan, Nagorski said that the mortality rate among the POWs was high.

Other South Korean POWs were detained in North Korea. There is a larger body of evidence about what happened to them, thanks to North Korean defectors who have provided information about their fate. Information has also come from the small number of former POWs and their North Korean family members who have escaped to South Korea since the mid-1990s. According to these sources, the South Korean POWs detained in North Korea were interned in prison camps until the late 1950s or even into the 1960s. The POWs did not know the war had ended or that there had been an exchange of POWs between North and South. No one ever asked them whether they wanted to go home.

Many South Korean POWs died in the North Korean prison camps. Those who survived were eventually released, but the conditions of their new lives were hardly better than the conditions they'd known in prison. Most were assigned to one of the groups sent to labor in coal or copper mines in desolate areas of the northeastern provinces, the region sometimes called Korea's Siberia. It was undesirable work, difficult and dangerous. The mines were so remote that escape was impossible even if the former POWs had the physical stamina and local knowledge to try.

The former POWs were given citizen ID cards, and one could say that, in some ways, they blended in with ordinary North Korean society. Many were forced into marriages with war widows or war orphans—women tainted by family associations with South Koreans and who were otherwise unmarriageable. Lee Yeon-soon, the daughter of a former POW, said her father had been assigned a wife and was married in a mass wedding. The authorities simply matched up names and told people they were husband and wife,[9] said Lee, who is now living in Seoul. As former POWs, the South Koreans remained under close surveillance by the government.

The establishment of diplomatic ties between Seoul and Beijing in 1992 made it easier for South Koreans to travel to China. It opened up the Chinese side of the Sino-North Korean border to South Korean visitors, including those seeking intelligence on North Korea. By the mid-1990s, the flow of refugees from North Korea to China was accelerating. The refugees were a deep well of information about North Korea's closed society, including South Korea's missing POWs.

A small group of senior officials in the government of South Korean President Kim Young-sam saw an opportunity to rescue POWs and decided to act. They authorized and funded a secret network dedicated to gathering information about the POWs captive in North Korea; the goal was to bring them home. The network was composed of about twenty South Korean civilians, including Mr. Jung, and fifty Chinese associates. At least one member of Kim Young-sam's cabinet was aware of the program. It's unclear whether the president himself knew of its existence.

Mr. Jung and the other South Koreans on the rescue team posed as Chinese-Korean traders. They moved back and forth across the border, looking for goods to buy in North Korea and resell in China.

The business deals were real, but they were a smokescreen for the most important commodity the agents were seeking: information on the whereabouts of the POWs. They also gathered information in northeast China, where they sought out North Koreans who had come across the border as well as Chinese citizens who had visited North Korea. They carefully pumped them for information about POWs.

If the South Korean agents heard a rumor about a POW who was said to be living in a certain part of the country, they would concoct a reason to go there on business. When the right moment presented itself, they would approach the POW and, if he was receptive, offer to help him escape to China and then South Korea. They would develop an extraction plan. They might ask the POW to figure out on his own how to get to a designated meeting place in China—then they would supply him with enough cash to do so. POWs sometimes refused to leave without their North Korean families. If so, Mr. Jung and his team would also help relatives reach South Korea, but their first priority was always the POW himself.

China was the base of operation for Mr. Jung and his colleagues. He wore many guises there. Sometimes he would pose as a Chinese border guard. With his Chinese-language skills and a uniform he had purchased on the black market, he was able to help more than one POW or family member get out of a tight situation. In at least one instance, he hired a counterfeiter to print a fake South Korean passport for a POW, whom he then put on a plane to Seoul. He and his network also developed their own branch of the underground railroad to ferry POWs across China to safety in Southeast Asian countries. From there, the POWs would go on to South Korea.

The South Korean officials who authorized the POW rescue program entrusted oversight of the operations to an intermediary, the man who introduced me to Mr. Jung in the Seoul hotel. This intermediary was a young, energetic South Korean who traveled the world on business. He had no official position, but he was well connected with the South Korean defense and intelligence establishment, and he had done favors for the government in the past. He would go to China on "business" to meet with Mr. Jung, or Mr. Jung would fly out of China and consult with the intermediary in another Asian city.

In Seoul, the intermediary interacted with a handful of government officials. The South Korean government would provide pertinent information, offer operational guidance, and supply funding. If the extraction team in China identified the location in North Korea of a possible POW and wanted to approach him, the intermediary would take that information to his government contacts. The officials would try to verify the man's identity, using military and other records. This identity-checking was important. No one wanted to aid in the escape of an imposter or, worst of all, a North Korean sleeper agent.

If the information checked out and the man was confirmed to be a former South Korean soldier, the officials would put the intermediary or another trusted source in touch with the POW's family in South Korea. The family might be asked to supply a family photograph, which would be passed along to Mr. Jung and his associates in China. A member of the extraction team would then take the photo into North Korea and show it to the POW as a way of gaining his confidence. North Korean society is built on deceit and suspicion, and the South Korean agent would need to prove his bona fides; producing a family photo would help demonstrate that an agent really was who he said he was, not an operative of the North Korean regime seeking to entrap the POW.

The intermediary also would coordinate with his government contacts in Seoul to plan the final stage of the rescue. The South Korean government might arrange for the coast guard or a vessel from another government agency to be in the vicinity when the ship on which a POW was traveling was scheduled to enter South Korean waters. If the rescue team had guided the POW out of China to a neighboring Southeast Asian country, the South Korean government might authorize its ambassador to work with that country's government on obtaining an exit permit for the POW.

The government officials left most of the operational details to the intermediary and the China-based extraction team. The South Korean government could not be caught running illegal people-smuggling operations on Chinese or other foreign soil. It needed plausible deniability in case a member of the rescue team was arrested. Mr. Jung and his colleagues understood that they would be on their own if they were arrested.

The rescue team scored its first success in 1994, when Second Lieutenant Cho Chang-ho became the first South Korean prisoner of war to return home in forty years. The South Korean government never took public responsibility for Cho Chang-ho's escape, but it was widely assumed that it had played a hand in his rescue. In 1994, the new underground railroad was not yet up and running. It was highly implausible that Cho Chang-ho could have organized his escape on his own, without help from the South Korean government, especially in the mere sixteen days Cho spent in China.

Cho Chang-ho's homecoming captured the heart of the South Korean people. He became known as the fallen soldier who returned. It also highlighted the plight of the POWs who by now, after four decades of captivity in the North, were mostly forgotten in South Korea.

When the Korean War broke out on June 25, 1950, Cho Chang-ho was a freshman at what is now known as Yonsei University. Yonsei is one of South Korea's most prestigious institutions of higher education, and the young Cho Chang-ho had a promising future ahead of him. But the war intervened, and he interrupted his studies to join the army, where he served as a second lieutenant in an artillery battalion. In September 1951, Chinese troops fighting alongside North Korean forces captured Cho. He spent twelve years and six months in prison camps before finally being released in the early 1960s. He was sent to work in a North Korean coal mine.

When the armistice was signed in 1953, Cho Chang-ho's name did not appear on the list of prisoners held by the North Koreans. In 1977, South Korea's Ministry of National Defense changed his official status from "missing in action" to "killed in action." His name was enshrined with the names of other war dead at the National Cemetery. In the minds of his government and family, he had passed away.

In 1994, he returned from the dead.

On October 3, 1994, Lieutenant Cho, now sixty-four years old, escaped from North Korea to China by paddling across the Yalu River on a wooden raft. Sixteen days later, Mr. Jung and his team arranged for Lieutenant Cho to board a Chinese fishing boat that smuggled black-market goods from South Korea to China. Back in Seoul, the officials who were being kept apprised of Cho's escape thought that the fishing-boat plan to extract him from China was too risky, so they refused to pay for it. Mr. Jung and the intermediary decided to go through with their plan anyway. They approached the Cho family, who agreed to pay for the boat.

The fishing boat carrying Lieutenant Cho sailed into South Korean waters in the predawn hours of Sunday, October 23, 1994. Mr. Jung had alerted the intermediary that Lieutenant Cho was en route, and the intermediary in turn informed his government contacts, who, despite their earlier skepticism about the fishing-boat plan, agreed to cooperate. The officials arranged for a patrol vessel belonging to the South Korean fisheries service to be in the area, seemingly by chance. When the Chinese fishing boat, by prearrangement, flashed a distress signal, the South Korean patrol boat responded quickly. Lieutenant Cho Chang-ho climbed aboard. The rescue took place in the Yellow Sea off South Korea's western coast.

In the days that followed, the news of Cho Chang-ho's miraculous homecoming was on the lips of every South Korean. Television networks broadcast interviews with the pajama-clad former soldier from his hospital bed in Seoul. He was filmed with his older sister and younger brother, who were sitting by his bedside alternately weeping and smiling. He was asked about his new family in North Korea, where he had one daughter and two sons. He was interviewed about what he wanted to do when he got out of the hospital. Visit his childhood church, he said.

But the scene that became an icon was the shot of him with Defense Minister Lee Byung-tae, who visited him at the hospital. From his hospital bed, the former POW saluted the defense chief and announced, "Second Lieutenant Cho Chang-ho of the artillery unit, military service number 212966, reports his safe return." In describing that scene, the South Korean daily *Dong-A Ilbo* later wrote that "the nation shed tears."[10] President Kim Young-sam also paid the POW a visit.

Upon his release from the hospital, the second lieutenant was promoted to first lieutenant before being honorably discharged from the army in a ceremony at the Korea Military Academy. A parade was held in his honor. He had lunch with the president at the Blue House. In the years that followed, Cho Chang-ho went on to build a new life. He completed his degree at Yonsei University and married a South Korean woman. He became an advocate for South Korean POWs still captive in North Korea. He urged the South Korean government to speak out more aggressively against human rights abuses by the North Korean regime.

In 2006, Cho Chang-ho visited Washington, D.C., where he testified in the House of Representatives about his forty-three years in captivity. "Even as I speak," he told the American legislators, "there are many, many South Korean prisoners of war still in North Korea awaiting a helping hand from the outside world."[11] He died in Seoul a few months after his return from Washington. His remains were buried in South Korea's National Cemetery where, years before, his name had been enshrined among those of the war dead.

President Kim Young-sam left office in January 1998. He was succeeded by Kim Dae-jung, who pursued a policy of détente toward North Korea. That approach became known as the Sunshine Policy, and it culminated with Kim Dae-jung's historic summit with North Korean dictator Kim Jong Il in Pyongyang in 2000.

The POW rescue team did not fare well during the Kim Dae-jung years. The man who had served as the intermediary between the rescue team in China and the South Korean government still had well-placed contacts who were willing to help quietly, mostly in the form of providing information. But coming up with the money to fund the extraction operations was tough, and the intermediary turned to private sources such as POW families for financial help. Mr. Jung has nothing good to say about those years. "In the Kim Dae-jung era, right before the summit in Pyongyang," he said, "I had several POWs lined up to go to South Korea, but the government canceled." The South Korean government presumably didn't want to risk disrupting the summit. The arrival of former POWs in Seoul would have reminded the South Korean public of the true nature of the dictatorial regime in North Korea.

The unwillingness of the Kim Dae-jung administration to risk confrontation with Beijing or Pyongyang over South Korea's POWs is apparent in the story of another old soldier, Chang Mu-hwan. In 1998, four years after Cho Chang-ho's escape and shortly after Kim Dae-jung took office, a popular *60 Minutes*–style show on South Korean TV caused a national uproar when it broadcast the story of an elderly POW who had escaped to China from North Korea.[12] The POW was stuck in China, risking arrest and repatriation to North Korea, and unable to get home to South Korea. The South Korean Embassy refused to help.

The TV program recorded the efforts of Chang Mu-hwan, then seventy-two years old, as he sought help from the embassy in Beijing. The camera closed in on Chang's trembling right hand as he placed a phone call to the embassy. When a woman answered, the old man identified himself as a POW and asked for assistance. A transcript of his conversation with the embassy reads as follows:

Chang: I'm a South Korean POW. My name is Chang Mu-hwan.
Embassy: So?
Chang: I'm Chang Mu-hwan, and I would really appreciate it if you could help me out a little...
Embassy: Listen, why exactly are you calling?
Chang: Isn't this the South Korean Embassy?
Embassy: Yes, that's correct.
Chang: All right, then. I'm in [the name of location is redacted] now, and I was just thinking that the embassy could probably help me out. That's why I'm calling.
Embassy: Of course we can't.
Chang: But I am from North Korea. I...
Embassy: Oh, no, we can't. (She hangs up.)
Chang: But I'm a South Korean prisoner of war...[13]

Chang Mu-hwan eventually made it to South Korea with the help of private aid workers. He had spent forty-five years in captivity in North Korea.

In 2002, Mr. Jung was arrested in China and charged with espionage. There was no trial, and the length of his sentence was unspecified. For the first two years of his imprisonment, the Chinese questioned him periodically, he said. After eight years in prison, including three in solitary confinement, he was released in 2010 and deported to South Korea.

Since the return of Second Lieutenant Cho Chang-ho in 1994, a total of seventy-nine South Korean POWs have made their way home, according to a tally the South Korean government released in

2010.[14] South Korea has also welcomed nearly two hundred family members of POWs. Other POWs have not been so lucky. Several escaped to China but were arrested and repatriated to North Korea, which claimed them as citizens.

The Kim family regime in Pyongyang remains acutely sensitive to the POW issue. It continues to assert that every former South Korean soldier who lives in North Korea is there by choice. To reinforce this point, it occasionally puts a POW before a television camera and uses him for propaganda purposes. The POW dutifully talks about how wonderful his life is in North Korea and how content he is to live in the people's paradise.

Pyongyang pulled this stunt in 2010 at one of the rare family reunions organized by the Red Cross organizations of both countries for relatives who had been separated during the Korean War. At the reunion, four former POWs were reunited with family members from South Korea. The participation of the four POWs came as a surprise in South Korea. Before Pyongyang put the four men's names on the reunion list, neither their families in South Korea nor the South Korean government had any idea that these soldiers had survived the war. The event threw doubt on the accuracy of South Korea's lists of the dead and missing. How many other POWs whom no one knows about are still alive and living in North Korea?

Ask a South Korean today about the POWs detained in North Korea, and a typical response is to speculate that these old soldiers may not want to come home. They have lived in North Korea for more than half a century, the speculation goes; they have new families and are happy where they are. The surprise inclusion of the four POWs in the North-South reunion in 2010 fueled this line of thinking; all the POWs said publicly that they were in North Korea by choice. But of course, Pyongyang never puts the question to the POWs themselves—or if it does, the question is framed in such a way that the POW knows that he puts his life at risk, or that of his family, if he gives a wrong answer.

When President Lee Myung-bak took office in 2008, he pledged to work for the return of the POWs. The government won't talk publicly about its work to get the POWs back, but some information has emerged. One aspect of that work appears to be exerting pressure on Beijing to release POWs who have crossed the river to China. On a visit to Beijing in the summer of 2011, Lee's defense minister reportedly pressed China to give exit permits to five POWs who had sought sanctuary in South Korean consular facilities in Beijing and Shenyang.[15] The fate of these five POWs is unknown.

Meanwhile, South Korea has made no progress with North Korea on the POW issue. Relations between South and North worsened in 2010 when the North Korean military attacked South Korea and killed South Korean citizens: In March of that year, forty-six sailors died when a North Korean submarine torpedoed the South Korean naval ship *Cheonan*, on which they were serving. In November, North Korea shelled the South Korean–held Yeonpyeong Island. Four South Koreans were killed, including two civilians.

In 2011, the Lee administration suggested that South Korea might try to purchase the freedom of the POWs still captive in the North. Unification Minister Yu Woo-ik cited the West German *Freikauf* program as a model. *Freikauf,* meaning "buy freedom" in German, was the secret Cold War program through which West Germany paid ransoms to East Germany in order to bring out some 33,755 dissidents and political prisoners held there. A Korean *Freikauf* program is unlikely to work, however, not least because Pyongyang refuses even to acknowledge that any South Korean POWs are being held against their will.

At the time of his inauguration, President Lee said he wanted to mark 2010, the sixtieth anniversary of the outbreak of the Korean War, as the occasion to launch a joint effort with Pyongyang for the recovery of the remains of South Korea soldiers who died on the other side of the border. This has not happened. It probably was not a realistic goal in the first place, as the American experience shows.

In 2005, the United States abandoned its program to recover the remains of American soldiers in North Korea, due to concerns about nuclear tensions and the safety of the recovery teams. The United States conducted thirty excavation missions in North Korea from 1996 to 2005, finding the remains of what it believed to be 230 American soldiers. The program was marked with dishonesty and fakery on the part of Pyongyang. North Korea moved the American soldiers' remains, stole American equipment, and billed the United States at inflated rates for the cost of its assistance. It is a measure of the importance the United States attaches to recovering the remains of its fallen soldiers that it nevertheless decided in late 2011 to restart the program. But the program never got off the ground. The U.S. suspended it again in March 2012 after North Korea announced plans for a missile test that violated a United Nations ban.

Meanwhile, Mr. Jung, his plastic surgeries nearly complete, was preparing to sneak in to China to continue his work. Unlike many of the South Koreans, Americans, and Chinese providing assistance to North Koreans who are trying to escape, Mr. Jung said he is not motivated by his Christian faith. His motivation is patriotism. The American government worked hard over the years to get back the remains of its soldiers from the Korean War, he said, even if it eventually suspended the program. But South Korea is not even trying to get its living soldiers back. Bringing POWs home to South Korea should be Seoul's first priority, he argued. Because it isn't, he will do the job.

If Mr. Jung is lucky, he will succeed in repatriating a few more old soldiers. But the task is harder now than it was in the 1990s, when he was first on the job. The POWs are elderly, and many of them are too frail for the rigors of an escape. Eighty-year-old men cannot paddle themselves across the Yalu River on a wooden raft, as Second Lieutenant Cho Chang-ho did in 1994.

Successive South Korean governments have spent decades trying to negotiate their return, without success. The United Nations, under whose flag they fought, has forgotten them. Somewhere in North Korea, five hundred South Korean prisoners of war have been held for nearly sixty years. They are unlikely ever to see their homeland again.

PART
III

ON THE RUN

The unfortunate mother was detected and sold South.

—THE UNDERGROUND RAILROAD RECORD
NOVEMBER 1853

HUNTED

On December 23, 2006, Adrian Hong expected to be on a plane heading home to Los Angeles, where he would spend the Christmas holidays with his parents. Instead, he was in Beijing, holed up in a room at the Intercontinental Hotel in the city's financial center. He was pacing the floor and waiting nervously for a phone call that was several hours overdue. A few minutes after ten o'clock in the morning, there was a knock on the door. He peered through the spy hole and saw a housemaid with a stack of towels in her arms. When he opened the door, his heart sank. Arrayed behind her were five men in suits, men he could tell at a glance were plainclothes police. They were there to arrest him for the crime of helping North Korean refugees in China.[1]

Earlier that day, unbeknownst to Hong, two of his colleagues, American women in their early twenties, had been picked up by police on a highway near Beijing and arrested in connection with the same crime. The trio worked for Liberty in North Korea, a California-based nonprofit dedicated to helping North Korean refugees. The organization is known by its acronym, LiNK. Its mission is helping North Koreans escape from China on the new underground railroad. Hong co-founded LiNK in 2004 when he was an undergraduate at Yale University.

Hong and the two women stood accused of helping six North Koreans plot to reach the American Consulate in the city of Shenyang in northeast China, where they planned to ask for political asylum. Hong, LiNK's executive director, was the mastermind of the operation. The women, who had been sheltering the refugees in a safe house in another city, were helping him execute it. But on the afternoon the group intended to enter the consulate, the rescue operation went badly awry. The story of the Shenyang Six, as the refugees came to be known, speaks volumes about the hardball tactics the Chinese government employs against North Korean refugees. It also shows how Beijing tries to intimidate the United States and other governments into silence about its harsh treatment of North Koreans.

At noon on Friday, December 22, 2006, Hong, his colleagues, and the six North Koreans were in place at a KFC a few hundred yards from the entrance to the American Consulate in Shenyang. The group had arrived early that morning from the northern city of Yanji after a twenty-hour train trip. Now it was time to embark on the last and most dangerous leg of their journey. They ordered some sandwiches and sat down at a table near a window, close enough to see the Stars and Stripes waving over the main gate. Hong took out his cellphone, dialed the phone number of the consulate, and asked for a political officer. Two months earlier he had shepherded three North Korean boys to the same consulate.[2] That operation had succeeded—the boys were safely ensconced in the consulate waiting for permission from Beijing to leave for the United States—and he had every expectation that this rescue mission would, too.

"This is Adrian Hong," he told the American at the other end of the line. "I've been here before. I have more packages to deliver. Please let the consul general know I'm in town."

The reaction of the consular official was the first hint that something could go wrong. Instead of saying that he would come right out to the main gate and usher them past the Chinese guards and into the consulate, the American asked for Hong's phone number and told him that someone would call him back. A few minutes later, Hong's phone rang and the caller identified himself as a consular official. His tone was icy as he informed Hong that the consulate would not accept the group. "We suggest that you take the North Korean refugees and go to the UNHCR in Beijing." In other words, let the United Nations High Commissioner on Refugees handle this problem. The Americans didn't want anything to do with it.

Hong couldn't believe what he had just heard. Not only had an official of the United States refused to accept the North Koreans, but, by speaking openly on the telephone, he had effectively turned them over to the Chinese government. American diplomatic posts in China are subject to round-the-clock electronic surveillance, and it was a fair assumption that their phone call had been monitored. Sure enough. Within minutes, Hong saw a van pull up in front of the KFC, and six burly men jumped out. They were not wearing uniforms, but it was obvious they were security officials. A few minutes later, six more men appeared in another van.

Hong knew they were in trouble, but he forced himself to remain calm. He instructed the group to go down the street a few blocks to a café, where he would meet them later. Then he picked up his briefcase and walked in the opposite direction to an ATM machine at a nearby bank. While pretending to use the cash machine, he took out his phone and called the State Department in Washington, D.C., hoping to find someone who would countermand the decision made in Shenyang. It was after midnight in Washington, but

State's operations desk answered immediately. He was transferred to two duty officers, who quickly patched in David Sedney, the No. 2 person at the U.S. Embassy in Beijing. Sedney told Hong the same thing: We can't help you; take the refugees to the office of the United Nations High Commissioner on Refugees in Beijing. As Hong pressed the end-call button on his cellphone, he looked around him. The street was now empty of traffic. The intersection in front of the consulate had been cordoned off, and he counted more than one hundred uniformed law-enforcement officials standing by.

Hong had to come up with a plan quickly. He joined the rest of the group at the café and explained the situation. He offered to escort them back to the shelter in Yanji, but none of the North Koreans wanted to go back into hiding. They decided they had no choice but to head for the UNHCR office in Beijing, as the American official had advised. Their next stop was a hotel, where they hired a van and a chauffeur to drive them through the night to Beijing, about four hundred miles away. Worried that his photograph had been captured on the Chinese security cameras outside the consulate, Hong decided it would be best if he traveled separately. He told his colleagues he would meet them at the Intercontinental in Beijing, and, after seeing the group off in the van, he headed to the airport and caught a flight to Beijing. About four o'clock the next morning, December 23, the police stopped the van on the highway and arrested the two LiNK workers and the six North Koreans. They were taken back to Shenyang, where they were put in a jail on the outskirts of the city.

The six North Koreans included two orphan boys, ages sixteen and seventeen; a twenty-two-year-old woman; and three women in their forties. One of the older women was the mother of one of the three boys who had made it to safety in the American Consulate in October and was awaiting permission from Beijing to leave for the U.S. Another woman had relatives in Hawaii. A third had family in South Korea.

After Hong's arrest in Beijing, he was flown to Shenyang and transferred to the jail where his colleagues and the Shenyang Six were being held. A week later, on New Year's Eve, Hong and his two LiNK colleagues were deported, thanks in part to the efforts of the U.S. government, which interceded on their behalf with the Chinese authorities. Under Chinese law, they could have spent years in jail for helping the refugees.

As he was being escorted from prison, en route to the car that would take him to the airport for his flight back home to Los Angeles, Hong passed the cell that held the two boys he had tried to rescue. He pulled away from his escort, ran to the barred window on the cell's door, and yelled a few words of encouragement to the two boys inside. As he walked out of prison, a sense of failure overwhelmed him. "There is nothing like looking in the eyes of someone who thinks they are going to die," he said. "They both had that look—like there was no hope."

For refugees, there is one thing worse than life on the run in China; it is being caught and repatriated to North Korea. For rescuers, there is one thing worse than being arrested and jailed in China; it is the capture of the North Koreans under their care and the knowledge that the people they were trying to help now face detention, deportation, and possibly death.

Every North Korean hiding in China lives under the shadow of possible arrest—the knock on the door in the middle of the night, the police raid on his place of work, the arbitrary stop and ID check on a train or public street. Evading capture is the ruling factor in every decision a North Korean makes—where to live, where to work, whom to marry. How well will his employer protect him? Do her in-laws have the means to bribe local officials to overlook her illegal status? Can the missionaries who offer protection be trusted?

Every North Korean in China also knows what awaits him should he be arrested and repatriated back across the river. A prison sentence is a given. Under the North Korean penal code, "willful flight to another state" can be deemed treason and subject to the death penalty. Helping someone flee across the border also can be punished by death. [3]

In practice, the severity and duration of the punishment varies from prisoner to prisoner and jailer to jailer. The rule of thumb is that anyone who the authorities believe has had contact with South Koreans, Americans, or Christians while in China is considered guilty of a political crime and receives the worst treatment. That usually means incarceration in a political prison camp or a labor correction camp. A repatriated North Korean who fled to China looking for food or work is not punished as severely. He generally receives a lesser sentence and has a better chance of survival.

The first stop for a repatriated refugee is a detention and interrogation center on the border, where he is questioned and sentenced. According to David Hawk, who interviewed numerous refugees for his comprehensive study of North Korea's prison system, the interrogations follow a set pattern. The first questions are "'Why did you go to China, where did you go, and what did you do in each place?'" And then, more ominously: "'Did you meet any South Koreans?' 'Did you go to a Christian church?' 'Did you watch or listen to South Korean TV or radio?' and 'Were you trying to go to South Korea?'"[4]

An affirmative answer to any of this latter category of questions means an automatic sentence in a political prison camp or a labor reeducation camp. In the hope of avoiding the worst, the returnee's challenge is to stick to "no" answers even in the face of a few days of hunger or beatings. Staying out of a political prison camp or a labor reeducation camp greatly increases a prisoner's chance of survival. A returnee's sentence has nothing to do with the rule of law. There seldom is a trial or any kind of judicial proceeding before the returnee is sent to prison.

Many returnees end up in short-term detention centers. These jails, often in the prisoner's home province, also are characterized by brutal conditions: hard labor, sub-subsistence food rations, torture. But the sentences generally are shorter. Even so, many inmates die in detention or are granted sick releases to die at home. The local detention centers sometimes also house common criminals, who may be separated from the returnees for ideological reasons. The jailers want to keep the returnees from corrupting the criminal—that is, spreading the word about the freedom and prosperity in China.[5]

Seo Won-kyong's story of arrest, repatriation, and detention is typical of what happens to many North Koreans who are hiding in China. Seo was arrested after police raided the lumber factory where he was working in Heiliangjong Province and he failed to produce a Chinese ID card. After two months in a Chinese jail, he was repatriated to North Korea, where he spent a month in jail on the border before being shipped off to a detention center in his home province. "It was a horrible place," he said. It was "worse than anything I had ever experienced."[6]

Seo Won-kyong considered himself fortunate not to have been sent to a political prison. He credited this stroke of luck to two factors. When a refugee is repatriated, the Chinese police routinely hand a copy of their arrest report to the North Korean authorities. In Seo's case, the Chinese report somehow failed to mention the contacts he'd had with foreigners and Christians. That was his first lucky break.

His second break had to do with money. At the time of his arrest, Seo had with him about eighty American dollars. He knew it would be confiscated by the Chinese police, and he managed to swallow the money before being strip-searched at the Chinese jail. He later recovered it by picking it out of his feces. When he was sent back to North Korea, he used the money to bribe the officials in charge of assigning the returnees to prisons; he paid them to ensure his transfer to a local detention center. Even so, he almost died of starvation.

His food rations consisted of a single layer of boiled corn, served three times a day on an aluminum plate.

After nearly three months of this diet along with occasional beatings and incarceration in an unheated cell in winter, he was near death. The prison officials apparently decided they didn't want him to expire on their watch. Seo Won-kyung described the humiliating procedure by which the warden determined which prisoners were on the brink of death. Prisoners were ordered to drop their trousers and bend over. An official then pinched their buttocks to see how much flesh was left, making a calculation about whether an inmate was likely to live or die. Seo Won-kyung was assigned to the soon-to-die category and transferred to a jail nearer to his hometown. An official at the hometown jail recognized him and got word to members of his family. His wife was permitted to visit and bring him food. Seo's health improved slowly, and he was released in an amnesty in honor of Kim Il Sung's birthday. The date was April 15, 2005, four months after he had been forcibly returned to North Korea.

After Seo had fully recovered, he escaped again to China. This time he took one of his two teenage sons with him. His wife and second son soon followed them across the river. In China, the sons listened to Voice of America and Radio Free Asia and decided they wanted to go to the United States. A Voice of America reporter directed them to Steven Kim, whose 318 Partners organization helped the family get out of China on the new underground railroad. After spending eight months in Vientiane, Laos, the Seos finally arrived in New York City on June 3, 2009.[7]

China's repatriation policy dates back to the early 1960s, when it concluded a secret agreement governing the border area with North Korea. In 1986, the two countries signed another bilateral agreement. It mandated the return of North Koreans who crossed into

China. Beijing's official position is that it strictly adheres to this obligation and that there are no exceptions.

Despite the clarity of China's no-exceptions policies on the repatriation of refugees, enforcement is erratic—and, as many observers point out, if Beijing wanted to shut down the new underground railroad, it could do so. Instead, in recent years it has allowed more than two thousand North Koreans to escape every year. Professor Zhu Feng, a national-security expert from Peking University, put it this way: China's policy implementation is to "keep one eye open [and] the other eye closed—officially, we will repatriate, but in practice we keep the net quite loose." He calls China's repatriation policy "cold-blooded" but candidly describes Beijing's policy dilemma: "The problem is that if China refuses to repatriate, that would signal that Beijing wants to bring down the North Korean regime."[8]

Enforcement varies from jurisdiction to jurisdiction, official to official, year to year, and is generally is left to local or provincial authorities. Beijing occasionally issues a crackdown order when it has a political objective. According to aid workers in China, that was the case during the lead-up to the 2008 Beijing Olympics. By cracking down on North Korean refugees and their helpers during that period, the authorities apparently hoped to avoid international publicity about China's mistreatment of the North Koreans. They didn't want any headline-grabbing escapes to call international attention to its policies. The new underground railroad virtually ceased operations during this period as police activity ratcheted up. Beijing also tightened enforcement during the 2009 celebrations for the sixtieth anniversary of the founding of the People's Republic as well as in the months before the opening of the 2010 Shanghai Expo. It did so again after the death of Kim Jong Il in December 2011.

In contrast, enforcement was haphazard during the famine of the mid-1990s, when as many as half a million North Koreans fled to China. The influx of refugees may have overwhelmed the capacity of law-enforcement agencies to track down refugees and repatriate them. By the early 2000s, however, Beijing had developed and implemented measures to better enforce its repatriation policy. In 2001, posters began to appear along the Sino-Korean border ordering Chinese citizens to turn in refugees and warning of steep fines for helping them. The rules were posted along the Tumen River, in Chinese and Korean, and stipulated: "It is forbidden to financially help, allow to stay, harbor, or aid in the settlement of people from the neighboring country who have crossed the border illegally." The fines were stiff, ranging from the equivalent of $600 to $1,200. China also instituted a bounty system, with a hierarchy of payouts to citizens who turned in refugees or provided information on those who helped them. An informant could earn the equivalent of four dollars for reporting the location of a secret shelter. He would receive almost twice that sum that for turning in an individual refugee.[9]

In December 2002, Beijing launched the One Hundred Day Campaign to root out refugees and return them to North Korea. The One Hundred Day Campaign was a systematic and well-organized dragnet, and thousands of refugees were repatriated during that campaign. Foreigners legally living in the Northeast who were suspected of helping the refugees were warned they would be fined, deported, or jailed. Some aid workers under suspicion were required to sign oaths to the effect that they would not provide assistance to North Koreans.[10]

For the most part, though, enforcement of China's repatriation policies is left to local jurisdictions. Like the majority of social, political, and economic transactions in China, the process is inconsistent, elastic, and highly corrupt. If a refugee or his benefactor has the means to pay local officials to look the other way, he often can escape arrest and repatriation. Refugees refer to these payouts as "fines." The more precise word is "bribes." Rescuers keep track of the market price for bribes and build them into their budgets for safe houses and escapes on the new underground railroad. Justin Wheeler, an American who has led twelve North Koreans out of China in two missions, said he traveled with $3,000 in cash. "If police ask for IDs," he said, "they will let you go if you pay them $250 or $300 a head."[11]

China takes the preposterous position that the North Koreans in its country are not refugees. They are economic migrants, it argues, and hence not covered as refugees under its international legal obligations. Foreign Minister Li Zhaoxing expressed his country's callous attitude toward North Korean refugees in a succinct statement in 2004: "These refugees that you talk about do not exist. . . . [They] are not refugees but are illegal immigrants."[12]

When defending their country's policy to Americans, Chinese officials like to use the analogy of Mexicans who enter the United States illegally. They conveniently ignore the fact that Mexicans are not abused by their home country before crossing illegally into the United States or thrown into prison when they are repatriated. Unlike the Kim family regime, the government of Mexico does not deliberately deny its citizens food, nor does it operate a gulag for political dissidents. Mexicans who are sent back to Mexico from the United States are not jailed, starved, tortured, or executed.

China's policy on the North Korean refugees violates its obligations under international treaties it has signed. Its repatriation policy is a violation of the 1951 Convention Relating to the Status of Refugees and the 1967 Protocol to that Convention. China has been a party since 1982. The Refugee Convention defines as refugees those who have fled their home country because "of a well-founded fear of being persecuted" in that country "for reasons of race, religion, nationality, membership of a particular social group, or political opinion." The Convention prohibits the refugees' host country from expelling them except on grounds of national security or public order. [13]

North Koreans who enter China with a well-founded fear of persecution meet the Convention's definition of refugees, says Roberta Cohen, an expert on international refugee law. China, however, automatically sends them back. It does so without interviewing them about their reasons for escaping from North Korea. It has no screening process to determine who is a refugee, nor does it permit the office of the United Nations High Commissioner for Refugees to interview North Koreans to determine whether they endured persecution at home.[14]

Under the Refugee Convention, fear of persecution is the only factor used in determining someone's refugee status. Cohen argues that the definition applies to the North Koreans who flee to China in search of food because the North Korean government has denied them access to food for political reasons. In North Korea, food is distributed based on party loyalty. The army and members of the Workers' Party take priority over ordinary citizens. Many of the North Koreans crossing into China during periods of food shortages come from the underprivileged classes who are deliberately starved by their government, which typically routes precious food supplies to favored groups. "Their quest for economic survival could well be based on political persecution," Cohen says.[15]

The most compelling argument in support of China's obligation to grant refugee status to North Koreans in China is what happens to them when they're repatriated. There is no question that returnees face persecution and severe punishment. Under UNHCR rules, this qualifies them as *refugées sur place* and entitles them to protection. Even if their reasons for leaving their county of birth don't fit the Convention's definition of ordinary refugees, the fact that they will face persecution and punishment if they return does so. The Convention bars *"refoulement,"* the diplomatic term for returning refugees to places where their lives would be endangered.

China has gotten away with its inhumane repatriation policy for years, with only occasional criticism from human rights groups. Neither the United Nations nor individual governments have challenged China directly and publicly in an international forum. In early 2012, South Korea finally seemed to find its voice. The National Assembly passed a resolution urging China to stop sending North Koreans back home. Rep. Park Sun-young staged a hunger strike in front of the Chinese Embassy in Seoul. The South Korean government raised the issue of Beijing's repatriation policy in the United Nations Human Rights Council in Geneva, but even then it declined to mention China by name.[16]

The South Korean public, too, seemed to be waking up to the fate of its North Korean brothers and sisters hiding in China. Protestors held daily rallies in front of the Chinese Embassy, marched in the Place des Nations near the United Nations office in Geneva, and enlisted celebrity support for their cause. A grassroots organization called Save My Friend used social media to publicize China's complicity in North Korea's brutality against its own people and to launch an online signature campaign urging the United Nations to take action. North Korea's abuse of its citizens is "one of the greatest atrocities of our time," Save My Friend wrote on its website. By forcibly repatriating North Koreans, it said, China is guilty of supporting the deaths of thousands of innocent lives.[17]

Another aspect of China's mistreatment of the North Korean refugees is its willingness to turn a blind eye to North Korean security agents who operate on its soil—and in some cases commit illegal acts such as extortion and kidnapping. China's security officials aren't the only ones to keep tabs on refugees and rescuers. North Korean agents do so, too, and they do so with apparent impunity within China's borders.

Some of the North Korean agents in China pretend to be refugees and infiltrate the shelters and hideouts of real refugees. Some seek out Christians or brokers to help them find passage to South Korea on the new underground railroad. Once in Seoul, they either have a specific mission to carry out—such as the failed assassination attempt on defector Hwang Jang-yop in 2010—or they become sleeper agents, awaiting activation by Pyongyang. Other North Korean agents operate in China as spies, gathering information on refugees and the activists who help them, and earning extra cash by extorting hush money from them. North Koreans in China report cases of fellow refugees who vanish, presumably abducted by agents. Rescuers have also disappeared.

Kidnapping other countries' citizens on other countries' soil is nothing new for North Korea. Pyongyang has long been in the abduction game, starting with the Korean War, when some eighty thousand South Koreans were abducted and taken to the North. Since the war ended in 1953, the South Korean government estimates that North Korea has kidnapped nearly four thousand South Koreans. Many were fishermen who had the misfortune to sail too near North Korean waters. The list of South Korean victims also includes a South Korean movie star—a favorite of Kim Jong Il—and her director husband. The actress was lured to Hong Kong, kidnapped from the famous Repulse Bay beach, forced onto a boat, and taken to North Korea. A South Korean student at the Massachusetts Institute of Technology was kidnapped while on vacation in Vienna.[18]

Citizens of France, Italy, Jordan, Lebanon, the Netherlands, Malaysia, Singapore, Thailand, and other countries have also been kidnapped by Pyongyang. Many Japanese citizens have disappeared as well, some snatched by North Korean agents who sailed to Japan and sneaked into the country undetected. Three Japanese citizens— two tourists, one exchange student—were kidnapped in Europe. The most famous abduction was that of Megumi Yokota, a thirteen-year-old girl kidnapped while walking home from an after-school badminton practice in the western Japanese city of Niigata. In 2002, Kim Jong Il confirmed to visiting Japanese Prime Minister Junichiro Koizumi that North Korean agents had kidnapped Megumi and other Japanese citizens.[19]

In China, the best-documented disappearance is that of the Rev. Kim Dong-shik, of Chicago. Pastor Kim, a citizen of South Korea, was a legal resident of the United States and the father of an American citizen. His disappearance caused a political stir in both Seoul and Washington—though not enough to stop his subsequent torture and murder by the North Koreans.

Pastor Kim vanished from the border city of Yanji on January 16, 2000. The details of his kidnapping and death emerged several years after his disappearance when one of the members of the squad that abducted him was arrested and prosecuted in South Korea. Pastor Kim's kidnapping was ordered by a senior state-security official in Pyongyang, the kidnapper said. The senior official was in charge of North Korea's program of abducting refugees and rescuers in China whom Pyongyang considered threats to the regime.

Pastor Kim was born in South Korea in 1947. He graduated from Koshin University in Busan, South Korea's second-largest city, and was ordained as a Presbyterian minister. For many years he was employed as a minister in South Korea on behalf of the Chicago Evangelical Holiness Church, a Korean-American congregation in Illinois. In 1993, he moved to China to work as a missionary. North Korean refugees were just starting to cross the border in large numbers, and Pastor Kim decided to help them. In Yanji, he set up refugee shelters and established a school for refugee North Korean children. He was one of the early conductors on the new underground railroad. In 1999, he helped a small number of refugees escape from China.

A few months before his abduction, the pastor befriended a North Korean woman whom he believed to be a refugee. She was a North Korean agent. On January 16, 2000, the woman arranged to meet with Pastor Kim at a local restaurant under the pretext of introducing him to two other North Koreans who needed help. As they were leaving the restaurant, Pastor Kim, who was disabled, was wrenched out of his wheelchair and forced into a taxi. The taxi sped to the Tumen River border town of Sanhe, where the North Korean agents transferred him to another taxi before crossing the bridge into

North Korea. The trip would have required them to pass through Chinese immigration control.

The details of what happened next are murky, but it is known that Pastor Kim was transported to a political prison camp. He appears to have been beaten and starved to death after refusing to renounce his religion. The exact date and location of his death are not known, but according his family, his remains are believed to be in People's Army Camp 91, a garrison on the outskirts of Pyongyang.[20]

In January 2005, a month after the Seoul Central District Prosecutor's Court confirmed Pastor Kim's kidnapping, the Illinois delegation to the U.S. Congress wrote a letter to North Korea's permanent representative to the United Nations asking for information on the U.S. resident. The letter called Kim Dong-shik a hero and spoke of his "selfless efforts to assist refugees escaping in an underground network to third countries." The lawmakers compared him to Harriet Tubman, "who established an underground railroad allowing for the escape from slavery of those held in bondage before President Lincoln issued the Emancipation Proclamation." They also cited Swedish diplomat Raoul Wallenberg, who "rescued Jewish refugees trapped in Hungary" during World War II. "We revere Reverend Kim Dong-shik," the Members of Congress concluded, "as also being a hero who assisted with the escape of the powerless and forgotten."[21]

The letter from the Illinois congressional delegation ended with a declaration that until North Korea revealed what happened to Pastor Kim, they would not support its removal from the State Department's list of state sponsors of terror. Among the signatories was then Senator Barack Obama of Illinois. Three and a half years later, in October 2008, the Senator, who was now running for President, reversed his position and supported President George W. Bush's decision to take North Korea off the terror list.

The Shenyang Six were more fortunate than Pastor Kim, and their story has a rare happy ending. In July 2007, six months after they were arrested and jailed, the Chinese government quietly allowed the six North Koreans to leave the country. Beijing would not permit them to go to the United States, as they wished, so they went to Seoul. Their release was thanks to behind-the-scenes work by the American government, which helped persuade Beijing to make an exception to its repatriation policy.

Some might see the American efforts on behalf of the Shenyang Six as an act of atonement for the consulate's earlier rejection of the refugees, when they were seeking asylum. Questioned at the time about its decision to turn away the six North Koreans, the State Department would say only that there were sensitive issues involved, that its decision was made carefully, and that any publicity about the incident would have grievous repercussions. In private conversations, senior officials defended the decision, explaining that the consulate was sheltering other North Korean refugees at the time and that it feared negotiations on their behalf would break down if it gave sanctuary to the Shenyang Six.

The incident took place during the George W. Bush administration, when Christopher Hill was assistant secretary of state for Asia and Pacific affairs and the boss of the American officials in China. Not everyone in the Bush Administration was happy with how State handled the Shenyang Six. Shortly after his return to the States, Adrian Hong said that an official at the National Security Council apologized to him for what had happened in Shenyang, telling him, "Heads would roll."

Members of Congress spoke out in support of Hong's efforts to rescue the refugees. In March, a statement by Hong on the Shenyang Six was read into the Congressional Record at the request of Congressman Ed Royce, a Republican of California. Hong wrote: "It is absolutely unacceptable and shameful that a United States post will turn away legitimate asylum seekers, especially those that are targeted for capture and repatriation by local authorities." [22]

There has not been a repeat of the Shenyang Six incident. In its wake, American diplomatic posts in China have been instructed to welcome North Koreans seeking political asylum. That is, however, less likely than ever to occur. At the time of the Shenyang Six incident, the security around the American Consulate in Shenyang was considerable. Afterward, Beijing tightened security even more. To reach the entrance to the consulate today, a visitor must pass through two gates and two sets of Chinese guards. Unless he displays a passport from the United States or another country, the odds of making it into the consulate and to safety in American territory are next to nonexistent.

JESUS ON THE BORDER

"I didn't want to become a Christian," the pastor said, offering a wry smile. "It was an accident."[1]

Eom Myong-hui was describing her personal faith journey from atheist to committed Christian, from member of the Korean Workers' Party to Protestant minister. Among North Korean escapees, she is unusual, though not alone, in becoming a pastor. She is far from unusual, however, in her Christian beliefs. A large percentage of the North Koreans who reach China make the same spiritual journey.

One of the remarkable aspects of the North Korean diaspora is the high number of men and women who, once they leave their country, choose to become Christians. Protestant missionaries in the Sino-Korean border area are highly successful in winning converts to their religion, and the charitable example of the Chinese-Korean Christians who help the refugees sets a powerful example.

There is no way of knowing how many refugees become Christians. Nor is there any way of knowing how many conversions are genuine. But reports by refugees suggest that many North Koreans in China make the decision to become Christians and that they are sincere in their faith. Refugees also report a growing interest in Christianity in North Korea itself. That interest is spurred by refugees who tell their relatives about their new religion and—somewhat amazingly, given the penalties if the regime gets wind of their work—by North Koreans who return to their country to preach the Gospel.

One reason for the attraction of Christianity among North Korean refugees in China is easy to pinpoint: Christians run almost all of the aid organizations. So, too, much of the informal assistance that refugees receive comes from Christians, especially local Chinese. Christians are the only people who seem to care. In a country where helping North Koreans is against the law, there are few others to whom a refugee can turn for protection and support.

It would be a mistake to dismiss North Korean converts as mere "rice Christians," the cynical label applied to converts in pre–Mao Zedong China who were presumed to have accepted a strange Western religion solely for the purpose of receiving the benefits provided by the missionaries. Although it's impossible to judge the depth of anyone's faith, the fervor with which many North Koreans have adopted Christianity seems real. It is consistent with the enthusiasm, in post–Cold War Europe, that many citizens of former Communist countries showed toward Christianity. Even in China, which remains officially atheist even while loosening restrictions on religion, Christianity is rapidly winning converts. There are at least seventy million Christians in China today, or 5 percent of the population.[2] That is nearly the same number of people who belong to the Communist Party. A top Communist Party official felt it necessary to warn in 2011 that party members are required to be atheists. "Our party's principled

156

stance regarding forbidding members from believing in religions has not changed one iota," he said.[3]

North Koreans who become Christians in China do not jettison their faith when they reach South Korea. If anything, they often seem more committed and eager to share their new religion with fellow refugees. Christianity is widespread in the North Korean community in South Korea, where there are numerous so-called defector churches. These are often small congregations made up mostly of North Koreans.

Once a refugee arrives in South Korea, it is the government, not the church, that is his principal caregiver. The South Korean government provides an array of services, including a three-month resettlement program, vocational training, housing, and cash settlements. The government support is of course unconnected to a refugee's religion, which belies the theory that North Korean converts are merely "rice Christians."

In contrast to the government's support, the South Korean people themselves often can be unwelcoming. South Korean Christians are an exception in paying attention to refugees. Although the government provides for the refugee's basic needs, South Korean Christian organizations provide personal connections and spiritual support. South Korea is the second-most Christian nation in Asia, after the Philippines. In the 2005 national census, approximately 30 percent of the population of forty-eight million identified themselves as Christian.

Pastor Eom spent several years in China before eventually escaping to South Korea on the new underground railroad. She became a Christian in China, studied for the ministry in South Korea, and eventually emigrated to the United States. She worked for a while at a church in Virginia before moving to the Dallas area to accept a job at a Korean-American church. She lectures widely in Korean-American churches, relating her own personal story and discussing the attraction of Christianity for many North Korean refugees.

Pastor Eom was a math and biology teacher in North Korea. She was so good at her job that she won an award for being a model citizen. In the 1990s, during the famine, she went into the business of selling Korean antiques and specialty foods such as ginseng root across the border in China. Both the business itself and the trips to China were illegal, but times were hard, the trade was lucrative, and she had a husband and two young daughters to feed at home.

As she tells it, converting to Christianity began as a business decision. Her principal buyer—and the person on whom her livelihood depended at the time—was a Chinese-Korean man who would visit North Korea to pick up the wares she was peddling. After they had been doing business together for a while, he confided to her that he was a Christian. She knew it was dangerous to associate with Christians, but she was afraid of losing his business, so she listened politely. "When he started talking to me about Christianity, I didn't respond in any negative way," she said. "I just nodded my head and listened. I wanted to be on his good side. My only purpose was making money." She told no one that she had spoken to a Christian.

The buyer turned out to be an evangelist working for a South Korean church. He was a bit of a shady character, she said, and in retrospect she believes he was less interested in building a successful business than in recruiting North Koreans to Christianity even at the expense of exposing them to punishment at the hands of the North Korean regime. She later learned that he operated on a quota system, with the South Korean church paying him a bonus for every North Korean he introduced to the church's underground mission in China. She figured this out after he tricked her into visiting the mission house by promising to pay her the money he owed her only if she would come and pick it up. When she arrived at the mission house, he told her that before he would give her the money, she had to complete a "New Believers" course. She had no choice but to comply.

To her surprise, she found herself receptive to the Christian message. After three weeks of studying the Bible, her perspective shifted.

"I started sensing that maybe there is a God," she said. "There was a glimmer of light that began to shine on me."

But she still wanted to go home. After a month in the Chinese mission house, she crossed the border back into North Korea, accompanied by the buyer-evangelist. They were caught. North Korean police arrested them and took them to a detention center, where they were interrogated. Pastor Eom was in a bind. What should she say when she was asked, as she knew she would be, if she had met any Christians in China? Contact with Christians was a crime punishable by time in a political prison. "But I couldn't really say no," she said. "The person I was caught with was a known Christian, at least to the authorities. So the way I answered that question was to say, of course he talked to me about Christianity, but I didn't believe him. That's how I did it."

Interrogations in North Korea are not mere question-and-answer sessions. More persuasive measures are employed. Pastor Eom was beaten by her interrogators, who kept trying to get her to confess to being a Christian. She denied it. Finally, they gave up. Her denials, coupled with her past record as a model citizen, had an impact, and the police decided to let her go. She was released with a warning.

When she got home and told her husband what had happened, he was furious. "Christianity is no good," he told her and berated her for putting their family in jeopardy. She tried to persuade him that her business relationship with the Chinese-Korean man was too important to jeopardize, but he wouldn't listen. She showed him a palm-sized Bible her business partner had given her. Her husband grabbed the Bible out of her hand, took it to the kitchen, and burned it. A few months later, a friend tipped her off that she was about to be arrested again. She fled to China.[4]

Asked why so many North Korean refugees become Christians, Pastor Eom cited her own faith journey. "Not a lot of conversions are genuine at first," she said. Refugees are usually desperate, and some falsely claim to be Christians in order to get the aid they need.

Pretending to accept their benefactors' religion is also a way North Koreans can show respect and appreciation to the Christians who help them, she explained.

But, as in her case, the message often sticks. "There's a seed planted in their hearts," she said. "And some of the refugees eventually become true Christians. Because they have been exposed to the pastors, to missionaries, to prayer, to the Christian lifestyle, it has a profound effect on their thinking." How so? "At first they can't believe that someone would want to help others for the sole benefit of helping, just for the purpose of serving God." But seeing is believing. Once North Koreans realize that the Christians who help them aren't motivated by the hope of personal gain and run serious risks by helping them, she said, they often take a closer look at the religion. The example of Christians who put their faith into action is a powerful recruiting tool.

On one level, North Koreans are ready for the Christian message, Pastor Eom argues. The old socialist system has broken down, and Kim Il Sung, once revered as a deity, has been exposed as a fraud. "A lot of people know that they have been lied to all their lives" by the government, she said. At the same time, they are wary. She explained: "They are not ready to put their faith in another unseen force, in another unseen god, like Kim Il Sung, that they cannot see or touch. They don't want to be fooled again." It takes a while for North Koreans to understand that Christian faith is different from worship of Kim Il Sung.

Pastor Eom does not hold a high opinion of many of the foreign missionaries who work in the Sino-Korean border area. She thinks many have unrealistic expectations about the effectiveness of their evangelism. In her view, a lot of the South Korean and Korean-American missionaries are under the mistaken impression that just because they speak the same language and share the same ethnicity, they have an advantage in talking to North Koreans about the Gospel.

The most effective way to spread Christianity in North Korea, she argues, is through North Koreans who have escaped. That is already happening, as North Koreans who have left the country talk about Christianity in phone calls to their relatives at home. As North Koreans inside North Korea observe the spiritual transformation of their relatives who have become Christians, it will be the beginning of what Paster Eom calls "the opening of the hearts and minds of all North Koreans for the Gospel, for Christianity."

Like Pastor Eom, Kang Su-jin had an experience with a Christian evangelist who treated her in a devious way. When she arrived in China from North Korea, a South Korean Christian made her an offer too good to refuse: Study the Bible, become a Christian, and return to North Korea as a secret missionary. "That was the deal," Kang Su-jin said. If she said yes, the missionary promised to reward her at the end of her studies with a gift of 3,000 Chinese yuan. That was the equivalent of about $500, a small fortune in North Korea.[5]

Kang Su-jin evaluated the missionary's offer in purely practical terms. Since she was planning to return home anyway after she accumulated some cash, she thought, *Why not?* In return for studying the Bible, she would receive room and board and, above all, a safe haven that would keep her out of the line of sight of the Chinese police. She decided she would go through the motions of becoming a Christian—baptism, Bible study, and the like. But she did not plan to become a real Christian, and she certainly did not intend to proselytize when she returned home. "So only for the money, I decided I would stay and study," she explained

In the end Kang Su-jin changed her mind about returning to the North. Two unexpected things happened. First, she became a real Christian. Her change of heart about Christianity was much like that of Pastor Eom's. As she tells it, the Bible study she had undertaken for pecuniary reasons took hold. "My eyes were opened to Christianity," she said. Second, she decided to go to South Korea. She came to realize the danger of returning to North Korea, where Christians are viewed as traitors. She put it bluntly: "I became afraid to go back."

Kang Su-jin's escape story ends well. She met an American pastor in China who was a conductor on the new underground railroad. He found a home for her in a safe house. She spent a few months in the safe house, spending her time cross-stitching murals of the Last Supper and other religious scenes while she was waiting for her turn to leave. The pastor guided her across China and helped her cross the border into Laos; from there, she eventually made her way to South Korea. In South Korea, she has built a new life running a nonprofit agency that helps North Korean women who have been trafficked. She has been reunited with family members who also escaped from the North. She is still a Christian.

An unknown number of North Koreans have made the decision that Kang Su-jin rejected. They have returned to North Korea as Christian evangelists. The practice began in the late 1990s, when the number of North Koreans in China was at its height and Christian missionaries were hard at work in the borderlands.

Proselytizing in North Korea is life-threatening work. The government's harsh treatment of Christians is well known, and the North Koreans who make the decision to return to their country to spread their faith are keenly aware of the risks they are taking. They literally are risking their lives.

Mere possession of a Bible can be a capital crime in North Korea. So it was for Ri Hyon-ok, a thirty-three-year-old woman who was executed in 2009 for distributing Bibles in a city near the border. Ri Hyon-ok was also accused of spying and organizing dissidents. Her husband and three children were sent to the gulag.[6] Her execution was public. The government was sending a message: Christianity is dangerous; stay away from it.

Worship is also an offense, as it was for twenty-three Christians arrested in 2010 in a raid on their illegal house church. The worshippers had been to China, where they became Christians before returning to North Korea. Three were executed; the others were sentenced to the infamous Yodok political prison camp. [7]

There is much more clandestine Christian worship in North Korea today than there was in the late 1990s or early 2000s, according to Scott Flipse of the United States Commission on International Religious Freedom. "That's all I can tell you," he said. "I don't know the numbers, and there's no way to count them." How many Christians are there in North Korea? "You've got some people claiming there are one hundred thousand Christians in North Korea," he replied. "You've got some people claiming ten thousand. All we know is that it is happening and that it's happening at a much larger level than it was ten years ago."[8]

The late Song Jong-nam was one of the North Koreans who converted in China and returned to North Korea to spread his faith. His story was pieced together by his younger brother, Song Jong-hun, who now lives in South Korea. Song Jong-hun said his brother became a Christian in China, inspired by the example of the South Korean missionary who helped him. The missionary worked undercover as the manager of a timber mill, where he hired North Korean refugees and gave them a place to live. The elder Song returned voluntarily to North Korea in 2004 with the intention of proselytizing. In 2006, the police found Bibles at his home and arrested him, charging him with spying for South Korea and the United States. He was sentenced to execution by firing squad. Song Jong-hun, by now in South Korea, heard about his brother's sentence and launched a campaign to draw international attention to his plight. He later learned, from a man who had been incarcerated with Song Jong-nam, that his brother had died in prison.[9]

A North Korean teenager recounted a similar story to four thousand fellow Christians from 190 countries at the Lausanne Congress on World Evangelization in Cape Town, South Africa, in 2010. The girl, Son Gyeong-ju, described how her family had fled to China, where they became Christians. Her father disappeared after he went back to North Korea to teach Christianity. He "chose to return to North Korea—instead of enjoying a life of religious freedom in South Korea," she told the audience. He wanted "to share Christ's message of life and hope among the hopeless people of his homeland," she said. The girl escaped on the new underground railroad and now lives in South Korea.[10]

Steven Kim's main work, as mentioned earlier, is rescuing trafficked women through 318 Partners, the nonprofit organization he set up on Long Island, New York, after his return to the United States from jail in China. But in addition to this work on the new underground railroad, he also supports a mission to send Bibles to North Korea and plant churches there. The Bible-smuggling operation was relatively easy to organize, he said. It's not difficult to find North Korean border guards who, for a price, will look the other way when a courier crosses the river with a load of Bibles. All it takes is enough money.

Planting churches is far more difficult, and far more dangerous. 318 Partners already has opened four secret house churches in North Korea and has plans to open twenty more. The churches were founded by North Korean refugees whom 318 Partners recruited and trained in China over a two-year period. The future evangelists received vocational training in addition to their religious instruction. The aim was to help them get jobs or set up small businesses on the black market once they returned to North Korea. The vocational training was an afterthought, Steven Kim said. He and his colleagues couldn't figure out how to get financial support to the evangelists after they went back to North Korea, so they hit on the idea of giving them training that would allow them to become self-sufficient.

Open Doors, founded in 1955 by a Dutchman who smuggled Bibles behind the Iron Curtain, is a Christian ministry dedicated to helping persecuted Christians worldwide. It estimates that there are four hundred thousand secret Christians in North Korea—and that the number of Christians there is growing quickly. The organization also estimates the number of Christians imprisoned for their religious beliefs to be between fifty thousand and seventy thousand.

Some of the secret Christians in North Korea belong to what Open Doors refers to as the catacomb church. They are remnants of the church that flourished before the establishment of the Democratic People's Republic in 1948 and the ban on religion. These Christians took their worship underground. They have been worshipping in secret for more than half a century and introducing their children to their faith. Carl Moeller, who heads Open Doors USA, explained how Christians in North Korea's catacomb church have survived. "They are like the Jews in Spain in the 1400s," he said, referring to Jews who pretended to practice Christianity after the Catholic monarch ordered them to convert to Christianity or face expulsion from the country. "They became good Communists on the outside but remained believers on the inside." Open Doors estimates that fifty to sixty thousand of these Christians worship in the catacomb church in North Korea today.[11] A catacomb Christian whom Open Doors sheltered in China gave the organization a tattered copy of a New Testament he'd smuggled out of North Korea. The New Testament dated back to the early 20th century. The family of this catacomb Christian had hidden it ever since Kim Il Sung declared religion illegal.

Open Doors works with North Koreans in both China and North Korea. It operates shelters for refugees in China, it sends Bibles and other religious literature into North Korea, and it supports North Koreans who want to go back to their country as missionaries. Unlike some other missions in China, Open Doors does not recruit North Koreans to be evangelists. It believes that the decision to go knowingly into a life-threatening situation must originate with the individual. "We don't have a program to train refugees to go to North Korea, but if they want to go, we will support them," Mueller said. "People love their home country. As strange as that sounds, North Koreans love North Korea. By becoming Christians, they have found freedom. They have a message of hope. They think of their families and want to share that message."

A typical Christian church in North Korea is tiny. The congregation may consist of only one family, or even just a husband and a wife. Children are excluded from worship until they reach the age when they can keep a secret. A few families occasionally will get together to risk group worship if they can find a way to avoid attracting attention, Moeller said. On Kim Il Sung's birthday, for example, many gatherings are devoted to celebrating him, and a group of house churches might take the opportunity to worship together under the guise of partying.

Voice of the Martyrs also focuses its work on persecuted Christians. Like Open Doors, Voice of the Martyrs dates back to the Cold War, when religion was banned in the Soviet Union and Eastern Europe. It was founded in 1967 by Richard Wurmbrand, a Romanian pastor who emigrated to the United States after spending fourteen years in jail because of his religious beliefs. Voice of the Martyrs says it has smuggled ten thousand Bibles into North Korea. It also has dropped Christian literature from balloons launched in South Korea.

Voice of the Martyrs sponsors a program aimed at evangelizing North Korea's elite. It does so by using a technology considered old-fashioned in most of the rest of the world: fax machines. Like every technological device that allows users to communicate with the outside world, fax machines are tightly controlled in North Korea. Their use is strictly limited to government offices and state-sponsored businesses that trade overseas. Voice of the Martyrs spent a year collecting the fax numbers of such enterprises. It now faxes them weekly Christian messages and Scripture passages. The faxes apparently get through. After one round of faxes, Voice of the Martyrs received an anonymous return fax written in Korean. "We know who you are," the fax began. "We warn you that if you send this kind of dirty fax again something very bad will happen to you. Don't do something you will regret."

Seoul USA is another ministry that helps North Koreans. Based in Colorado Springs, Colorado, Seoul USA is a network of Christians who aim to mobilize Christians worldwide to support the underground churches in North Korea. Among its projects is the Underground University, a mission school in Seoul that trains North Korean refugees as evangelists.[12] After one year of study, the graduates are dispatched to work with North Koreans in one of four mission areas: North Korea, China, South Korea, or among North Korean students and diplomats abroad. Inside North Korea, Seoul USA's mission includes launching and operating what it calls "repression-proof mini–house churches." These are tiny congregations, often made up of members of a single family.

In recent years, two American Christian activists have entered North Korea illegally, hoping to draw international attention to the plight of Christians in that country. To their supporters, they are committed Christians seeking to share their faith. To their detractors, they are at best misguided, at worst mentally unbalanced.

The first was Robert Park, a twenty-nine-year-old man from Arizona, who walked across the frozen Tumen River on Christmas Day in 2009. He carried a Bible and a letter to the dictator at the time, Kim Jong Il, demanding that he free all political prisoners in North Korea and then resign. As he touched North Korean soil, Park shouted, "I bring God's love." An American friend of Robert Park described him as a "zealous Christian." "Robert is fiercely adamant" about the human rights situation in North Korea, the friend said, "particularly the suffering of the Christians in the gulag."

Robert Park was arrested and taken to Pyongyang. After he read a confession on North Korean TV, North Korea announced he had repented and let him go. He was freed after forty-three days in detention. Park later said his apology was fake and had been dictated to him. In an interview on South Korean TV, he gave a harrowing account of his imprisonment, which he said included beatings, torture, and sexual abuse. In early 2012, Park said he would bring a lawsuit against North Korea in a U.S. court.

On January 25, 2010, exactly one month after Robert Park crossed the Tumen and entered North Korea illegally, Aijalon Mahli Gomes, from Boston, followed his example. Gomes had known Robert Park in Seoul, where they had both lived and worked for a while. They attended the same church. Gomes was an English teacher in Seoul and a frequent protestor against North Korea's human rights violations. Like Robert Park, he was arrested immediately upon entering North Korea. Unlike his friend, he received a much more draconian sentence: eight years of hard labor and a fine of $700,000 for illegal entry. Seven months after his arrest, North Korea granted him amnesty and released him in the custody of former American President Jimmy Carter, who was visiting Pyongyang.

Not all Christian activists agree about the wisdom of sending North Koreans into North Korea to proselytize. There are conflicting views about how best to deliver the Christian message to North Koreans. The question, put simply, is this: Do you evangelize in North Korea, or do you evangelize only to those who have escaped?

Open Doors' Carl Moeller believes that carrying the Christian message into North Korea is necessary. Jesus told us to go into all the world and spread the Gospel, he said, quoting the Gospel of St. Mark. "That doesn't mean just the places where we can go with a legal visa." He added: "Jesus said, I will build my church and the gates of hell will part. That's what's going on in North Korea."

Tim Peters, the Seoul-based American missionary who has been working with North Korean refugees since 1996, takes a different view. "Yes, we need to send Bibles in, and I do that," he said. "But ever since I started my work with the refugees, I very firmly have been of the conviction that the way to help the North Koreans the most is to help them as they come out." It is "common sense," he said, "that we try to help people once they come out of the iron grip of the regime—that means the refugees."

Like Moeller, Peters turned to Scripture to back up his opinion. He quoted the Gospel of St. Matthew: *When you are persecuted in one place, flee to another.*[13] In Peters's view, sending Christians into North Korea is at cross-purposes from what the Scripture says. He emphasized that there might be exceptions—cases where "the hand of God is at work and we shouldn't stand in the way." But he is deeply troubled by the practice of sending new Christians back into North Korea to win converts to Christianity. "The Scripture says *flee* persecution," he said. "It doesn't say run into it. It doesn't say put a little baby Christian on the tracks where an oncoming locomotive is going to run over him."

The American evangelist Billy Graham visited Pyongyang in 1994 at the invitation of Kim Il Sung, who was then 81 years old and nearing the end of his life. Graham was traveling through Asia on one of the international crusades that have taken him to more than 180 countries and territories. His wife, Ruth Bell Graham, accompanied him. The trip to North Korea was something of a homecoming for Mrs. Graham, who was the daughter of Presbyterian medical missionaries in China and had gone to high school in Pyongyang in the 1930s. That was an era when Pyongyang was home to so many Christians that it was known as the Jerusalem of the East.

Kim Il Sung knew his audience. He regaled the Grahams with stories about attending church with his mother when he was a boy, and he told them about a Presbyterian minister who was an early influence on his life. In Hong Kong, where the Grahams flew from

Pyongyang, I spoke with the American evangelist. He speculated that "some of [Kim Il Sung's] early experiences may be influencing him now."[14] With age can come wisdom.

Pastor Graham also pointed to the explosion of interest in Christianity elsewhere in Asia and attributed the growing numbers of Christians there in part to the rapid changes that Asians are experiencing in their culture, economy, and politics. "There's a void," he said. Asians are turning to Christianity to fill that spiritual hole. Why should North Koreans be any different?

Numbers are uncertain, but Billy Graham is right that Christianity appears to be winning converts in much of Asia. China has at least seventy million Christians and maybe as many as one hundred million. Pastor Graham noted that Christianity is growing rapidly in Thailand, a Buddhist country, as well as in predominantly Muslim Malaysia. There is a resurgence of Christianity in Vietnam, which has about five million Catholics now, compared with a million and a half in 1975. Fundamentalist Protestantism is catching on in the Philippines, which is overwhelmingly Catholic.

"Christianity does teach freedom," Pastor Graham said. If Christianity it were to come to North Korea, that would be a good omen. "God through the Bible teaches freedom of choice in everything."

The North Korean leader died a few months after the Grahams' visit, and he gave no sign that he had rejected his atheism or that his early exposure to Christianity had had any tempering effect on his regime's brutal policies toward Christians. The only worship allowed in North Korea remained the same: that of the Kim family.

But Billy Graham's essential point about Christianity—the connection to freedom—is the reason the North Korean regime fears it. Communism collapsed in Eastern Europe in part because the Christian message of freedom took new hold in places where it long had been repressed. In China, Christianity exploded after Beijing lifted some of its restrictions on religious freedom. The government now appears to be trying to reassert control over unregistered churches as part of an overall crackdown on dissent. The examples of Eastern Europe and China would be well known to Kim Il Sung's son and successor, Kim Jong Il, who continued his father's antireligion policies. They would also be well known to current dictator Kim Jong Eun, who appears to be following in the footsteps of his father and grandfather.

Eom Myong-hui, the North Korean woman who became a pastor, says Christianity points the way to freedom. "In my view, Christianity is about the individual, about accepting responsibility," she said.

That is anathema to Pyongyang.

THE JOURNEY OUT OF CHINA

There are many routes out of China on the new underground railroad, and every escape story is unique. Each carries its own logistical challenges, risks of arrest, and personal terrors. The train out of China sometimes is just that, an actual train that carries the North Korean runaway to a location near the border of a neighboring nation. The fugitives and their conductors move across the country by other means as well: express bus, private car, airplane, boat, and, more often than not, their own foot-power. The only way to evade the border controls of an adjacent country is usually to walk across an unpatrolled section of the Chinese frontier.

Whatever mode of transport North Koreans use to exit China, the journeys share common features. Behind every successful journey is a community of workers who make it happen. No North Korean can survive long in China without assistance, and no North Korean can get out of China on his own. Similarly, no conductor on the new underground railroad, whether he is a humanitarian worker or a broker, can operate independently. He requires a network of people to support him and the North Koreans in his care. He needs locals to purchase the bus or train tickets; greeters to meet the travelers when they arrive in a new city; couriers to escort them to their overnight accommodation; linguists to translate from Korean to Chinese and vice versa; agents to procure fake travel documents; householders to provide meals and shelter. Sometimes these people are paid for their assistance and their silence. Other times the helpers work voluntarily, out of a sense of Christian charity or simple human kindness.

The story of the Reverend John Yoon suggests the perils that conductors on the new underground railroad face, even when they are well organized, well funded, and well intentioned.[1] Failure brings penalties, usually jail, for the conductor, and it brings arrest, repatriation, and possible death for the fugitives he was trying to lead to freedom.

Pastor Yoon was in high spirits. The American minister had just succeeded in leading thirty-two North Koreans out of China. They had walked undetected across the Chinese border into Laos just after dawn the previous day. At noon, a motorboat, hired in advance, met them at a dock on the Laotian side of the Mekong River. The boat whisked them over to Thailand, where they also disregarded border formalities and landed on a deserted beach. There they were met by a South Korean missionary, who served as their guide in Thailand.

The group was now safely settled in a large tourist hotel in the fourteenth-century river town of Chiang Saen in northeast Thailand, and Pastor Yoon felt that he could finally relax. The operation had been a success so far. He was confident that the final leg of their journey, to the South Korean Embassy in Bangkok, was equally well planned and would go off without a hitch. In the morning, two minibuses were scheduled to show up at the hotel and pick up the group, passing (as far as the drivers were concerned) as a group of tourists from a church in South Korea who were enjoying a vacation in rural Thailand. To reinforce the fiction that the refugees were Christian tourists, Pastor Yoon had prepared two placards to put in the front windows of the buses. The signs said, "Emmanuel," Hebrew for "God is with us" and, for Christians, another name for Jesus Christ. The plan was for the group to relax and lie low for five days in Chiang Saen and then take a train to Bangkok. By this time next week, praise God, they all would be in Bangkok. Nothing was likely to go wrong now, and he expected that the refugees would find permanent homes in South Korea within a few months.

It had been a difficult journey, complicated to orchestrate and frustrating to implement. Pastor Yoon had spent weeks collecting information, deciding on an itinerary and lining up a network of reliable, trustworthy people to assist the travelers at the various stages of their trip. In China, most of the people he relied on were Chinese and Christians. Some were of Korean heritage; others were majority Han Chinese. In Laos and Thailand, he had hired locals and lined up South Korean acquaintances to go there and act as facilitators once the group arrived.

Several weeks earlier, at the pastor's behest, missionary friends had traveled to Kunming and then across the border to Laos. They were traveling on legitimate visas and were posing as tourists. But they weren't genuine tourists. The real reason for their trip was to gather information about the Laotian border crossing. Pastor Yoon had the missionaries take photographs of the terrain on both sides of the border, the border-control posts, the nearby roads, and other landmarks. The missionaries sketched out a map of the area, noting the wooded areas where the refugees could hide, and recommending a path that would skirt the official checkpoints. Crossing the Laotian-Chinese border illegally should not prove difficult, they informed Pastor Yoon. Drug runners had been doing it for years, smuggling opium from the Golden Triangle into Kunming and from there into all parts of China.

In Laos, the missionaries had also gathered information for Pastor Yoon about the going rates for bribes. They found out that the Laotian border police expected a "gratuity" of between thirty and fifty American dollars for every undocumented person they discovered. If the police came across an illegal immigrant and weren't paid off, their policy was to take him to the official border crossing and force him to walk back into China. For a North Korean, that meant he would be arrested, sent to a detention center in northeast China, and repatriated to North Korea.

Based on this information, Pastor Yoon decided to make sure that every North Korean in his group had enough cash on hand to bribe his way out of a jam. Before they crossed the border, he gave each refugee $150 in ten-dollar bills. He told them to offer the Laotian security official a bribe of thirty dollars if they were captured. If the worst happened and some of the North Koreans were arrested, he reassured himself that they would be able to bribe their way out of jail. The pastor wouldn't begrudge any such payments. Rarely did freedom come at such a low price.

The refugees' journey through China had begun in Yanji City, a gritty city in Jilin Province in the northeast of the country, not far from the Sino-Korean border. The thirty-two men and women had been staying there, scattered among a string of apartments rented by Pastor Yoon and his wife. It was not safe for thirty-two North Koreans to travel together as a group across China, so the pastor had divided them into units of four or five travelers. He decided that they would be less likely to attract suspicion if they traveled by the express train, rather than by the local train or a bus. It was more expensive, but it was safer. The Chinese police would not be on the lookout for refugees on the pricey express train.

In Yanji City, Pastor Yoon saw each group off at the train station. It wasn't safe for him to acknowledge them directly, so he took up a position apart from them on the train platform and communicated through eye contact and small body gestures—hands clasped together in prayer, an almost imperceptible bow. He had made his formal farewells the day before each group's departure. He invited them to his home, said a prayer, and urged them to have courage. God was watching over them, he promised, and would keep them safe. Before he said his final good-byes he reminded the refugees one last time of the instructions he had given them during a pre-trip briefing: Sit in the same car of the train, he ordered, but sit separately. Don't sit together. That way, if one person were arrested, the others might be spared. Don't worry if you see a policeman come through the car. That's routine. But if the police begin to check IDs, go to the restroom and wait there until the ID checks are over. He also advised them to look occupied. Hold a Chinese magazine or newspaper, flip the pages, and pretend to be reading it even though you can't read Chinese. The last thing you want is to appear nervous and attract attention.

The trip to Beijing by express train took about twelve hours. In Beijing, Pastor Yoon arranged for a pastor with whom he had worked before to meet each group at the train station and escort them to the train they would board for the next leg of their journey. The pastor took the refugees to a hotel, provided dinner, and then escorted them back to the train station in time to catch their next train. The refugees' final destination was Kunming, two thousand miles to the southwest. Kunming is the capital of Yunnan Province and very close to the border of Laos. It was a journey of about two days—forty-eight hours for those who took the slower train, thirty-eight hours for those on the express.

Meanwhile, Pastor Yoon traveled separately to Kunming by plane. He met each group upon their arrival at the train station and took them to the different hotels where he had booked rooms. Once everyone had arrived in Kunming, they convened at the bus station, where they boarded an overnight bus to the town of Jinghong, very close to the Laotian border. After breakfasting together at a restaurant near the bus station, the group boarded a local bus, which took them to the wooded outskirts of Jinghong. Here they split up again into small units of four or five people. At intervals of an hour, with Pastor Yoon or an associate leading the way, they walked over a mountain until they reached the Laotian frontier. Once in Laos, local guides met them and led the groups to a prearranged meeting spot on the Mekong River.

The entire rescue—train fares, hotel rooms, food, and bribes—cost about $20,000. That worked out to $625 per person.

All in all, the rescue had to be deemed a resounding success, and so when Pastor Yoon's cellphone rang that evening at the tourist hotel in Chiang Saen, he was not mentally prepared for the news he was about to receive. The caller did not identify himself, but Pastor Yoon recognized the voice as that of a colleague in Yanji City. The message was brief. The caller warned him, "Do not come home." Chinese police had raided the pastor's apartment in Yanji City and found a photocopy of his American passport. His identity was compromised. But that was not the worst news. There were nineteen refugees staying in Pastor Yoon's apartment at the time. They were all arrested during the raid and were now in a detention center, soon to be repatriated to North Korea.

Pastor Yoon's original plan had been to drop off the thirty-two refugees at the South Korean Embassy in Bangkok and then fly back to Yanji City; he would then repeat the entire journey he had just completed, this time with the nineteen refugees who had just been arrested in his apartment. But returning to China was not an option now. Instead, he went home to Seattle to regroup.

Pastor Yoon was born in 1938 in what was then Japanese-occupied Korea and is now the Democratic People's Republic of North Korea. He was twelve years old when the Korean War broke out. His parents ordered him, his older brothers, and a sister to flee to safety in the South. They would follow later, they promised. He never saw his mother and father again. Many years later, his daughter Grace Yoon Yi attributed her father's compassion for North Korean refugees in China to his wartime experiences as a child. The North Korean refugees' experiences of starvation and divided families recalled the tribulations of his boyhood, she said.

In South Korea, the young John Yoon lived in a home for war orphans. When he turned eighteen, he was drafted into the army. After his military service, he entered college on a scholarship financed by an elderly Christian woman. He obtained an undergraduate degree in theology, went on to get a master's degree and was ordained in 1970 as a minister in the Korean Assemblies of God church, a Pentecostal denomination. In the early 1980s, he was invited to serve as the pastor of a Korean-American church in Fairbanks, Alaska. He became an American citizen in 1992.

Not long after that, the Korean Assemblies of God sent him and his wife on a mission to Siberia. His assignment was twofold: Set up a small seminary for thirty Russians who were training to be pastors, and minister to the growing community of South Korean businessmen who worked in Siberia. Trade between South Korea and Russia was growing apace in the wake of the diplomatic ties established in 1990, and South Korean companies had sent representatives to Siberia to buy timber and minerals. The Korean businessmen were usually there without their families, and Pastor Yoon's church functioned as a home away from home for them, a place where they could go to speak Korean and eat familiar food. Some of the businessmen were Christian, drawn by the prospect of Sunday worship. Others were open to Pastor Yoon's Christian message and in some cases became converts.

In the Far Eastern Russian port of Vladivostok, Pastor Yoon was less than a hundred miles from North Korea. Sometimes he would visit Khasan, a tiny border town south of the Vladivostok and the terminus for trains from North Korea. He would walk down to the Tumen River and gaze over the frontier to North Korea in the distance. Then he would say a prayer and think about the day when he would be able to visit his hometown again and reunite with relatives who might still be living there. He never expected that his mission in Russia would include ministering to North Koreans.

Not long after he arrived in Russia, he began to hear stories about timber camps deep in the Siberian woods where North Korean loggers were working under an arrangement worked out between the Russian and North Korean governments. His first sight of the loggers was on the train platform in Khabarovsk, where a group of two hundred young North Korean men were waiting to board a train that would take them farther north. They had just disembarked from the train from North Korea and were looking around them, their eyes drinking in the unfamiliar sights—the Cyrillic letters on the signs, the well-dressed Russians, the private vendors selling hard-boiled eggs and other snacks. The men were dressed identically in government-issued dark blue suits and wore identical ties. Pastor Yoon remembers his sadness at seeing the excited, hopeful looks on their faces. "They had nice suits," he said. "They had all this fancy stuff they never had before. So they were really happy." He knew the privations that were waiting for them at the logging camps, and he knew that their hopes of earning enough money to buy luxuries for their families were going to be dashed.

Pastor Yoon expanded his mission in Russia to include helping North Koreans who escaped from the logging camps. He set up food kitchens and shelters in Khabarovsk and Vladivostok to serve loggers. He also helped several loggers make the four-thousand-mile journey to Moscow to seek asylum in the South Korean Embassy. The embassy turned almost all of them away. He sent other loggers to China with introductions to missionaries there. A few of the loggers he assisted eventually reached South Korea, including a man who married a South Korean woman and set up a successful dental practice. Years later, the two met up again in Seoul, and the grateful dentist fixed Pastor Yoon's teeth.

It wasn't long before Pastor Yoon began to hear disturbing reports about life in North Korea from the loggers who showed up at his church looking for assistance. They spoke of widespread food shortages back home, even starvation. His fellow missionaries in northeast China were hearing similar stories from the North Korean refugees who crossed the river into China looking for food. Pastor Yoon decided he had to help.

The pastor's comparative advantage was his knowledge of the Korean-American Christian community and his web of contacts in the United States. So he made the decision to return to the United States to raise money for food assistance for North Korea. He traveled around the country, preaching at Korean-American churches and raising relief funds.

"North Korean government rations have stopped," he would tell the congregations, "and people are living off grass." He passed along information he had learned from his sources in South Korea who had visited the North. The most terrible reports were of cannibalism. At first he could hardly believe such stories, but his sources were excellent and he trusted them. "The starvation is so intense," he told the Korean-Americans, "that some of those who are hungry begin to hallucinate and see children and adults as animals to eat."

Pastor Yoon was a charismatic and persuasive speaker, and the congregations opened their wallets in response to his appeals. He raised enough funds to ship 150 tons of flour and rice to North Korea, along with seventy tons of fertilizer. He often gave thanks to God for the generosity of the Americans who were helping to save the lives of the starving people of North Korea.

And then he went there.

In 1997, Pastor Yoon joined a humanitarian mission to North Korea to visit a noodle factory supported by the donations he had raised. He was astounded at what he found. The suffering was worse than he had imagined, far worse than anything he had seen as a child in war-torn Korea. Children, in rags, were patrolling the streets, begging for food or picking up crumbs that had fallen to the street. The bodies of the dead were piled up outside the train stations, he was told over and over again.

Worst of all, he found evidence that the government was stealing some of the international food donations. Instead of reaching the starving civilians for whom it was intended, the aid was diverted to the military or given to the well-off elites of Pyongyang. International aid organizations that worked in North Korea were aware of the corruption. A few humanitarian groups, such as Doctors Without Borders, pulled out, refusing to operate under such circumstances. As one worker put it, "the [aid] teams realized that the government fabricated whatever they wanted aid workers to see: malnourished children in nurseries when more food air was desired, and well-fed children when donors needed reassurance that food aid was doing good."[2] Some of the North Korean refugees this worker interviewed in China said they had heard of the aid, and others had seen it for sale on the black market, but none had ever tasted it.

Other aid groups saw the leakage as a cost of doing business. They figured, probably correctly, that if the regime did not get what it presumed to be its share, it would expel the humanitarian workers. From the aid workers' point of view, it was necessary to overlook the regime's theft—even to the extent that they suppressed knowledge of the theft to international donors—in order to keep the aid flowing into the country. Yes, much of the aid was stolen, but they reasoned that a small percentage reached needy people who would otherwise die.

Pastor Yoon was outraged. He had always opposed the Communist government of North Korea. As a Christian, he deplored the regime's violent repression of the North Korean people. But he had not realized the lengths to which the regime would go to keep its hold on power—even to the extent of pursuing policies that led to the deaths of millions of North Koreans. He began to see the international relief efforts as a means of perpetuating a regime whose policies were responsible for the murder by starvation of a million or more North Koreans. Kim Jong Il was killing his own people, he said, and "those of us on the outside world were not aware of this killing because it was done within the secrecy of a closed society."

He decided to join the effort to help North Koreans escape. As he put it: "If you see someone who is drowning in the river, wouldn't you reach out and help that person? That was what was in my heart."

From that moment, he resolved to dedicate his life to helping North Koreans reach free countries. He saw the oppressive Kim family regime as beyond any hope of change; it was his duty, he believed, to help overthrow the regime. Help one person escape, he reasoned, and that person will get word to his family back home about the freedom that awaits them on the outside. Others will follow, and the regime will implode.

In the late 1990s, Pastor Yoon relocated his mission to China. Unlike his years in Russia, this time he couldn't operate openly as a missionary. Instead, he went into China on a business visa, with a cover job as the manager of a gravel factory. Using as a model the work he had done in Siberia and the Russian Far East, he began to set up an underground network of assistance for North Korean refugees. He and his wife, Sunja, rented apartments in several cities and turned them into shelters for North Koreans on the run. The shelters were temporary abodes where refugees could stay until they found jobs in the underground economy or decided to risk riding the new underground railroad to South Korea. The Yoons provided newly arrived refugees with stylish clothes to help them blend into Chinese society. Mrs. Yoon gave the women instruction in how to style their hair and apply makeup.

Pastor Yoon believed in the principle that work was essential for human dignity, and he came up with the idea of starting handicraft studios in his safe houses. His wife taught refugees how to do cross-stitch embroidery. The refugees stitched both enormous religious pictures and tiny crosses attached to key chains. The pastor would lug the handicrafts back to the United States in bulging suitcases to sell to the congregations he visited. He used the proceeds to pay wages to the refugees.

News of the Yoons' generosity spread among the refugee community. Soon the pastor had more North Koreans knocking on his door than he was able to handle. "When I helped a refugee, he would tell a friend, and that friend would tell his friends," he said years later. People would line up outside his apartment, waiting to talk to him. Some wanted money, some were looking for a meal or a place to live, and others wanted help in contacting a conductor on the new underground railroad. He sometimes became frustrated with his inability to help everyone as fully as he wanted to, and he took it out on the refugees.

"Sometimes I felt overwhelmed and would say: 'No, I can't help you. Go to your father Kim Jong Il and ask for help.' Then they would leave, and I would feel really bad. I would run after them—I'd yell, 'Hey, wait, wait, wait'—and give them money or whatever else they needed."

For security reasons, Pastor and Mrs. Yoon changed their own apartment every three months, sometimes even moving to a different city. If they stayed in any one location too long, they feared that a neighbor might become suspicious of the activity in their home and report them to the police. Local police routinely checked up on foreigners living in the neighborhood, sometimes stopping by unexpectedly, so the Yoons made it a rule not to answer the door if there was a North Korean in the apartment with them. They would sit quietly until the knocks on the door ceased and the policemen went away.

They didn't talk about it much, but the Yoons also feared for their own safety. In Russia, the couple knew missionaries who had been harassed by North Korean security agents. A South Korean minister had been murdered under suspicious circumstances. The murder was officially unsolved, but rumor had it that North Korean agents killed the missionary because of his work helping escaped loggers. Pastor Yoon believed it. In China, refugees told the Yoons stories of North Koreans who pretended to be refugees while they were really spies for the North Korean government. One of the spies' jobs was to report back to Pyongyang about foreigners who were working as conductors on the new undergound railroad.

Pastor Yoon's fears were not unfounded. Years later he received a phone call in Seattle from a prosecutor in South Korea. The prosecutor was calling to ask him about a North Korean woman who was under arrest in Seoul for spying for Pyongyang. The woman, who had reached South Korea by posing as a refugee, told the prosecutor that several years earlier, in Yanji City, she had been ordered by her superiors in Pyongyang to kidnap Pastor Yoon and take him to North Korea. Her orders were to befriend Pastor Yoon, learn as much as possible about his rescue operation, and obtain information about the refugees he was helping.

Pastor Yoon remembered the woman well. How could he forget? She was associated with one of the most painful incidents of his years in China. During the time he knew her in Yanji City, the Chinese police arrested and repatriated a group of refugees he had been helping. It was a group of about thirty men, women, and children. The North Koreans had crammed into his apartment one evening for a jovial dinner of beef soup and rice followed by a worship service. Later that night, after they went home, the refugees were arrested by the Chinese police in coordinated raids on the safe houses where they were living. The woman who was later arrested in Seoul told the prosecutor that she was the informant who had turned them in. Not long after that incident, the Yoons packed up and moved again, a decision that probably saved the pastor's life. If he had stayed, the plot to abduct him and take him to North Korea might have succeeded.

Another North Korean informant was responsible for the arrest and repatriation of the nineteen refugees in Pastor Yoon's Yanji apartment while he was in Thailand. This time the snitch was not an agent of the North Korean government but a disgruntled refugee who betrayed the other refugees to the Chinese police. Pastor Yoon said the informant was angry that the pastor had not included him in the group of thirty-two refugees who made their escape on the previous trip.

Years later, Pastor Yoon still found it painful to talk about this incident. The arrest of the nineteen North Koreans in his care was heartbreaking, he said. At the time, though, the emotion that overwhelmed all others and carried him through was anger. He resolved to find a way to return to China and continue his work. Back home in Seattle, he turned the problem over and over again in his mind.

Finally, he had an inspiration. John Yoon was barred from returning to China. China would never grant him a visa. But what if John Yoon was not the man applying for a visa? He consulted a lawyer about how to legally change his name. Within a few months, John Yoon, the name he was born with, was dead; Phillip Buck was born. He chose the name "Buck" because it was an unusual transliteration of a common Korean name usually written in English as "Park." He obtained an American passport under his new name and applied for a Chinese visa. He soon was back in Yanji City, and his branch of the new underground railroad was up and running again.

The first priority of the newly named pastor was to find out what happened to the nineteen refugees whom he had failed. Among the nineteen was a family of four—a mother and three sons. He eventually was able to piece together their story. He learned that the repatriated family was sent to prison, where the oldest son contracted tuberculosis and died. The rest of the family survived and eventually was released. The mother, unable to feed her family, crossed into China again. This time she hooked up with a broker, who sold her as a bride to a Chinese man. One day she managed to get to a telephone and call one of Pastor Buck's missionary colleagues, who told her to leave her "husband" and come to Yanji City. Within two days of her arrival, Pastor Buck arranged for her to go to South Korea, this time using an escape route through Mongolia. He then hired a broker to go into North Korea and bring out the woman's two surviving sons. They eventually were reunited with their mother in Seoul. The pastor was able to help six more of the nineteen North Koreans who had been arrested in his apartment when he was in Thailand. Of the remaining nine, he managed to track several to prison camps in North Korea, but after that the trail went cold. He was not able to find out what happened to them.

Pastor Buck continued his work in Yanji City until May 9, 2005, when he was arrested for the crime of helping illegal immigrants. His trial began on December 31 of that year and continued for several months. During the trial, he had a chance to address the judge who presided over his case. Months in prison had not quelled his anger: "You should not try me," the pastor scolded the judge. "The one who should be tried is Kim Jong Il for the murders he committed against his own people. I have only rescued them from drowning."

The Chinese court convicted Pastor Buck under Criminal Law 318 for the crime of illegally transporting people out of China. The crime carried a sentence of two to seven years, but he was deported before he could be sentenced. He had spent fifteen months in jail. He arrived home to a hero's welcome at Seattle-Tacoma Airport on the evening of August 21, 2006. Under the terms of his deportation, he is permanently barred from reentry into China.

PART IV

STOCKHOLDERS

Thee may take Harry Craige by the hand as a brother, true to the cause; he is one of our most efficient aids on the Rail Road, and worthy of full confidence.

—LETTER FROM THOMAS GARRETT,
A QUAKER, OF WILMINGTON, DELAWARE
THE UNDERGROUND RAILROAD RECORD
MARCH 23, 1856

LET MY PEOPLE GO

The story of the new underground railroad would not be complete without a look at the people outside China who help make it run. These are the funders, PR people, and political activists who shore up the rescuers working in China. Call it the railroad's back office.

With its traditions of grassroots political activism and private charity, the United States is home to many outspoken and effective advocates in behalf of the North Korean refugees. It is also home to many of the money men. A large number, though by no means all, are Korean-American. American activism in behalf of North Koreans took off in the mid-1990s as refugees started to pour into China and word of their plight began to seep out. The backers of the original Underground Railroad were called "stockholders." Today, we'd change three letters of that word and call them "stakeholders."

As with the nineteenth-century abolitionists who supported the Underground Railroad, much of support in the United States for the new underground railroad centers on churches. The Korean-American churches take their moral authority from the Bible, and God's exhortation in the Book of Exodus: *Let my people go.*[1]

One such congregation is Hana Presbyterian Church in Beltsville, Maryland. It is an example of a congregation of Korean-Americans who are committed, engaged, and political. The members of the congregation demonstrate their commitment in two ways: providing personal support to North Korean refugees who have received political asylum in the United States and engaging in awareness-building activities in nearby Washington, D.C.

Hana Presbyterian is a small, steepled church perched atop a gentle hill in a suburban community an hour's drive from Capitol Hill. It's set in a prosperous residential area, surrounded by spacious houses positioned on generous lots. On a snowy December Saturday, the neighborhood is quiet except for the traffic turning in and out of the church parking lot.

Hana Presbyterian is a Korean-American church, but on Saturday mornings the church makes its sanctuary available to a congregation of Philippine-Americans who lack their own house of worship. When I arrive at a side door, the Filipinos' worship service has just ended and the congregants are jostling each other in a narrow back hallway as they head to the fellowship hall for a potluck lunch that the ladies are laying out. A cheery gentleman formally attired in a three-piece suit waves me in the direction of the church office. "Pastor Lee is waiting for you," he tells me.

Heemoon Lee greets me with a smile and a handshake. He is not wearing a traditional, stiff clerical collar, but a more up-to-date collarless shirt—the kind that men older than he is will remember as Nehru shirts. Unlike many South Korean men his age, Pastor Lee does not dye his hair, which is abundant, wavy, and silvery.

The pastor was born in South Korea in 1958 and arrived in the United States in 1986, when he joined a sister who had settled in Minneapolis. Like many Korean families, his was divided by the Korean War. In his case, the physical division of the family was due to an ideological rift. During the Korean War, Pastor Lee's father renounced his family because he did not share the Communist beliefs of his older brother, Pastor Lee's uncle. That uncle, along with other members of the extended Lee family, were killed by South Korean soldiers during the war because of their support for Kim Il Sung and his Communist ideals. Pastor Lee's father did not reveal this family history to his son until after the boy had graduated from high school. The knowledge of that bloody event and that people in his own family had supported the enemy was too big a burden, Lee's father felt, to place on a child.

Pastor Lee's family history explains in part his decision to focus his work on North Korea. "I made up my mind to become an instrument of unification," he said. "I was called by God to work for unification and help the North Korean people."[2]

The church's name reflects that goal, and the flock he leads shares their pastor's work. Pastor Lee explains that *hana* is the Korean word for "one." In the context of the church's name, the word carries two meanings: First, the members of the church are one people, joined together to worship in the name of Jesus Christ. Second, the congregation is working toward the day when the divided nation of Korea once again will be one country. The church's eloquent, succinct mission statement says it all: "Rescue. Help. Mission. Educate."

Pastor Lee himself does not work on the new underground railroad, but he is well acquainted with many Americans and South Koreans who do. Under his leadership, Hana Presbyterian's congregation raises money to support specific rescue missions in China. The church is also active in raising awareness at home. It works to educate Korean-Americans and the American public at large about the plight of North Koreans in China. The church is a member of the North Korea Freedom Coalition, of which Pastor Lee has served as vice chairman. The coalition, run by a Washington, D.C., dynamo, Suzanne Scholte, was established in 2003 to promote policies in Washington and Seoul that will aid North Korean refugees in China and shed light on the human rights abuses perpetrated by the Kim family regime. It lobbies on Capitol Hill, and it hosts an annual weeklong conference that brings together activists for rallies, networking and public-information sessions.

The coalition, with Pastor Lee, helped organize Korean-American support for the North Korean Human Rights Act. That legislation was passed by the U.S. Congress in 2004 and signed into law by President George W. Bush. Members of Hana Presbyterian keep up the drumbeat through letter-writing campaigns to the White House, members of Congress, and the United Nations. Like many Korean-Americans, Pastor Lee and Hana's congregation are dissatisfied with the imperfect implementation of the North Korean Human Rights Act. They especially want to see more North Korean refugees admitted to the United States.

Hana Presbyterian's most immediate ministry is the intensive, day-to-day assistance it provides to a small number of North Koreans who traveled out of China on the new underground railroad and who have received political asylum in the United States. One hundred twenty-eight North Koreans settled in the United States between 2006 and early 2012. Eight are parishioners at Hana Presbyterian, and the church has helped several others who have now moved on. The North Korean refugees rely on the church for everything from housing to jobs to personal counseling. Church members offer the refugees an array of services. Members provide English lessons, drive the refugees to and from work, and advise them about coping with everyday tasks that can be bewildering to newcomers, such as grocery shopping and operating a washing machine. Next door to the church, on the other side of the parking lot, is the mission house. It is a split-level home that has been divided into private living spaces for the North Koreans.

The Jo family—a mother and two daughters—has agreed to meet me, and Pastor Lee escorts me to the mission house. We go out the church's back door and forge a path through the snow-covered parking lot as we walk the few steps to the house. The Jo women are living in a room at the back of the house that looks like it originally served as a family room. It is large, wood-paneled, and cheerful. Before entering, we take off our shoes, Korean-style, and put on slippers that the Jos have put out for us.

Their room is warm and inviting. Three single beds along the walls are made up with spreads and cushions to serve as sofas. There is a TV perched on a cabinet. A crimson-and-white Harvard banner is placed at a jaunty angle on a wall next to a bookshelf. The room appears not to have a closet, and the women's clothing hangs from a line strung neatly across one corner of the room. As we sit down, the mother asks her younger daughter, Grace, to bring us coffee.[3]

The Jos were originally a family of eight. The mother, Han Song-hwa, and her two daughters are the only three who survived. Another daughter disappeared one day when she was walking to the market in their hometown in North Korea; the family fears she was kidnapped and sold as a bride in China. The father died in a prison camp, where he was interned after being arrested in China and repatriated to North Korea. Mrs. Han's mother, who lived with the family, died of starvation. So did the Jo family's two small sons. One boy was five years old at the time of his death; the other was two months old. The baby died in the arms of his sister Grace, who was eight years old at the time. After the baby's death, Mrs. Han took her surviving daughters and fled to China, where they lived for ten years. In China, they were arrested and repatriated twice. In both cases, they survived prison terms in North Korea and then returned to China. An American pastor helped them reach the United States.

For all their past hardships, the Jo family seems to be thriving in the U.S. Their new life is hardest on Mrs. Han, who has health problems and spends most of her time at home and at the church next door. She seems worn out after her years of working to preserve her family in North Korea and China. Building a new life in the United States may be beyond her capabilities.

But her daughters are flourishing. The older girl, Jin-hye, is in her early twenties. She is studying English, working part-time at a local video store, and doing outreach work with the North Korea Freedom Coalition. She is energetic, outspoken, and impassioned. Not long after we met, she gave a speech to a group of Korean-American students at Princeton University. She urged the students to speak out about North Korea's abuse of its citizens. "When older people hear about tragedies, they cry because they do not have the ability to do something," she said. "When younger people hear, they think about what they can do." *Say* something, she implored the Princetonians. *Do* something.[4]

Grace is still a teenager and in high school. Her English-language skills already are excellent, and her grades are good. The Harvard pennant hanging in the family's quarters reflects her ambitions. In aspiring to an Ivy League education, she is much like Korean-Americans her age. Jin-hye was not able to attend school when the family was hiding in China and received little formal education. She seems proud of Grace and envious of the educational opportunities open to her sister.

Pastor Lee calls the Jo sisters exceptional and gives them a high compliment by comparing the girls to himself when he was a young newcomer to America. Most North Koreans have a far more difficult time settling into life in the United States, he says. But he puts the Jo sisters in the category of immigrants who are likely to succeed. He attributes their ease in fitting into American society to the fact that they lived for so many years in China, where they acquired personal skills that helped prepare them for life in the United States. North

Koreans who arrive directly from North Korea after only brief stays in China have a harder time adjusting to the freedom of choice available in every aspect of American life, he says. They also tend to lack initiative. They just want to be told what to do.

That can pose a problem for Hana's congregation. The Americans have to guard against providing too much help for the new arrivals. Independence and self-sufficiency, not permanent dependence on the good folks of Hana Presbyterian, are the optimal goals. The North Koreans "have to learn to do it by themselves," the pastor says. "I tell them, we can provide housing, but you have to help yourself. I share my experience. When I first came to this country, I had to take two buses to work. Five hours. Two and a half hours each way. I received just $4.25 an hour in pay."

Hama Presbyterian is not unique among Korean-American churches in the depth of its commitment to a free North Korea. Nor is it unique in the time and energy its pastor and congregation devote to helping the North Koreans who have settled in the United States. Other Korean-American congregations are similarly devoted to the cause. They assist refugees who live in their neighborhoods and conduct awareness-raising activities.

Churches are also a significant venue for raising money for the new underground railroad. They generally do so in response to specific appeals to help North Koreans who are on the run. Typical is Lee Jun-won, a small businessman who owns a hair salon in Queens, New York. Lee is not a rich man, but he donated $10,000 from his personal savings to rescue the Seo family of four when a member of his congregation issued a plea for help.

Thanks to Lee's assistance, the Seos eventually made it to the United States through China and then Vietnam. When I visited the Seos's apartment in upstate New York, I noticed a large framed photograph hanging on the wall of their living room. It was a picture of the hairdresser welcoming the family at JFK Airport in New York City. One of the Seo sons called my attention to the picture on the evening I visited the family. He cited it as an example of the difference between the United States and North Korea. In North Korea, he said, every household is required to hang official portraits of Kim Il Sung and Kim Jong Il on their walls, where they serve as objects of daily veneration. In America, he said with pride, he and his family can choose for themselves how to decorate their living room. They can even put a photograph of themselves and their friends on their walls if they wish. For this young man, the hairdresser's photo on the wall of his home was a significant statement—a symbol of his liberation.[5]

Some Korean-American churches sponsor missionaries who work covertly with North Korean refugees in China. The missionaries often are members of their own congregations. Some of the missionaries move to China to run shelters. Others serve as escorts on the new underground railroad. A few run small nonprofit organizations on the Chinese side of the Sino-Korean border that send food and medical supplies into North Korea.

Such efforts are separate acts of outreach by individual churches and individual parishioners. They are not the result of any organizational effort by the Korean-American community at large or by an umbrella group of churches. Rather, they are the result of a pastor or church member who is passionate about helping North Koreans and willing to take the lead.

These discrete efforts are linked by a shared commitment to helping the North Korean people directly, bypassing the government in Pyongyang. I. Henry Koh, a pastor in Georgia, put it this way: "Helping North Korea directly is absolutely useless," he said, making a distinction between the country and the people. "It only perpetuates the North Korean regime. During the years of the Sunshine Policy, South Korea poured billions of dollars into North Korea with the aim of helping. What happened?" He answered his own question: "They developed nuclear weapons."

Like other denominations, Pastor Koh's denomination, the Presbyterian Church in America, does not have a program focused on North Korea or the refugees in China. Individual churches provide help as they choose. Pastor Koh's congregation has sent three missionaries to work with North Koreans. Two went to North Korea; one went to China. "They were disguised, of course," he explained. That is, the missionaries' visas said they were businessmen or teachers, as indeed they were. But their primary aim was to teach the Christian message either by proselytizing or by example. Pastor Koh himself has traveled to China three times to perform baptisms and preach at an underground seminary in Beijing. A North Korean refugee who was traveling around the United States on a speaking tour stayed at his house for a week.

Not all Korean-American churches want to get involved with helping North Korean refugees in China. Within the Korean-American community, support of the new underground railroad can be controversial. Some churches eschew such work, deeming it unnecessarily provocative to the Kim family regime. They prefer to work with aid organizations that operate inside North Korea with the approval of the North Korean government, even if it means that some of the assistance they send will be diverted to the military, the Pyongyang elite, or other government uses.

The United States is home to 1.7 million people of Korean heritage, according to the 2010 Census. They are a wealthy, well-educated community. Like American Jews and also like other Asian-Americans, they are often referred to as super-immigrants. The 2000 Census put the median household income for Korean-Americans at $55,183, compared with $52,209 for the U.S. population overall.

Thirty-two percent of Korean-Americans have bachelor's degrees and 16 percent have graduate or professional degrees, compared with 17.5 percent and 10.2 percent of the American population at large.

About three-quarters of Korean-Americans are Christian,[6] and 2,800 churches can be called Korean-American, which is to say they have majority Korean congregations and a mostly Korean staff. The United Methodist Church identifies three hundred of its congregations as Korean-American. The Presbyterian Church USA is home to four hundred Korean-American congregations.

The Korean-American focus on helping North Koreans in China and on human rights in North Korea is relatively recent. It is a by-product of the information that is now available about North Korea thanks to the surge of refugees who have fled to China. Before the 1990s, the only way to help North Koreans was through aid organizations that worked directly with the regime, a route many Korean-Americans did not trust and refused to use.

Another reason for the recent surge in interest in helping North Koreans is generational. South Koreans who emigrated to the United States in the 1950s and '60s—the so-called first generation—were busy establishing themselves in their new country. Like other first-generation immigrants in American history, their focus was on finding jobs, building businesses, forming families. They were looking toward the future, not the past. This generation was also fleeing the turmoil of war and its aftermath. The Korean War was fresh in their memories, and they wanted to leave it behind. North Korea was often the last thing they wanted to think about or discuss with their children. "My parents never talked about the war," is a comment one often hears from the children of Korean-American immigrants.

Donald Sung, a second-generation Korean-American, born in 1966, recounted a personal experience that reinforced this point. It was not until he had become an adult, he said, that he saw his father without socks. When he finally glimpsed his father's naked feet, he was astonished to discover that the older man was missing several toes. When pressed, his father told him that he had lost his toes to frostbite when he was fleeing Kim Il Sung's forces during the Korean War. The elder Sung, then a teenager in South Korea, had been abducted in the South by the invading North Korean forces and conscripted into the North Korean army. When the older Mr. Sung related this story to his son, it was the first time the young man heard of his father's escape from North Korea. His father had kept silent for years. He wanted to leave his unhappy past behind him as well as spare his young son the knowledge of the suffering he had endured.[7]

For many Korean-Americans, the crucial factor in deciding whether, or how, to help North Koreans is trust. Korean-Americans, especially those of the first generation, tend to be suspicious of people and organizations that say they are helping North Korea, said Michelle Park Steel. As vice chairman of the California Board of Equalization, a state tax commission, she is one of the highest elected Korean-American officeholders in the United States. She and her husband, Shawn Steel, a lawyer and former chairman of the Republican Party of California, are active in helping North Koreans in China through their family's church. One of their daughters spent a summer working for an aid organization in China's Tumen River area.

"Many Korean-Americans, especially the first generation, just assume that the money will go to the regime," Michelle Park Steel said.[8] "They think that the North Korean government will get its hands on it. How do we know whom to trust? It's the biggest problem. There is a lot of doubt about whether the money they give will be used correctly." In her experience, the first generation gives money to people they know—members of their church who move to China as missionaries, for example—but they are reluctant to support organizations or to give money to strangers.

Some Korean-Americans are also reluctant to speak out publicly about the abuses of the North Korean regime. Incredible as it may seem in twenty-first century America, almost sixty years after the end of the Korean War, some Korean-Americans still fear reprisals against family members who may be alive in North Korea. They also worry that North Korea will attempt to shake them down for money in exchange for the safety of their loved ones. More than one hundred thousand Americans are believed to have relatives in North Korea.[9]

Michelle Park Steel cites an incident in her own family. She had a great-aunt, now deceased, who tried for years to get information about her first-born son, from whom the aunt had become separated in North Korea during the war years. North Korea finally granted a visa to another son to visit the older brother he had never met. The second son flew to Pyongyang. After a few days of waiting at the hotel to see his elder brother, the second son met with government officials who told him that his brother had died. Instead, the officials introduced him to a man they said was the son of the dead man. But the visitor smelled a rat. His so-called nephew looked too old to be who the officials said he was. The second son suspected that he was an imposter and that the officials were trying to trick him into giving money to his supposed relative, from whom they would confiscate the cash. When he got home, the second son's suspicions were confirmed when he received a letter from the "nephew" imploring him to send $2,000 immediately or he would be sent to a political prison.

Other Korean-Americans tell stories of being targets of shakedowns from Pyongyang. A California millionaire paid an exorbitant sum to buy his brother out of the country. A businessman had a sister who was permitted to live in the relative comfort of Pyongyang so long as her brother in America kept sending (through China) medications, luxury goods, and money. The businessman assumed that the regime siphoned off most of the gifts.

Helie Lee, a Los Angeles writer, wrote a book about how her Korean-American family rescued her uncle and some members of his immediate family from North Korea in the late 1990s. They had the help of a South Korean guide, Chinese-Korean gang members, and a Christian missionary. The family later learned that in-laws who had been left behind in North Korea disappeared, presumably into prison. The author applauds the courage of her North Korean relatives, who were seeking better lives for their children. But she also is appalled that her uncle was willing to leave behind family members whom he knew would be doomed by their association with him, a relative deemed to have betrayed the fatherland by his departure. "I felt both sympathy and disgust," she wrote of her uncle's position. "A family is a high price to pay for freedom."[10]

The Korean Church Coalition is an umbrella organization of 2,500 Korean-American pastors. According to its mission statement, the coalition was formed in 2004 "to bring an end to the sufferings endured by our brothers, sisters, and orphans in North Korea as well as China and other parts of the world, through non-violent means."[11]

The KCC started as a prayer movement. Since its beginnings it has held dozens of prayer vigils that have been attended by thousands of Korean-American pastors and members of their congregations. The coalition has done a good job of raising awareness in the Korean-American community, and it is an authoritative voice on the abuses perpetrated against North Koreans in North Korea and China. But when it comes to political influence, by its own admission it could do better.

Executive director Sam Kim offered a blunt assessment: "We have to speak out more forcefully," he said. As Exhibit A, he pointed to the 2008 decision of the George W. Bush administration to remove North Korea from the list of terror-sponsoring nations. "Everyone knew that we opposed delisting," he said, referring to the leaders of the coalition. It was a "terrible mistake," he said. "I let a lot of people know that in many one-on-one meetings in Washington." Yet when the Bush administration went ahead and delisted North Korea despite the recommendation of the KCC, the coalition made no public statement. It did not issue a press release opposing the delisting. It was too difficult to reach a consensus among its members, Sam Kim explained. Some of the pastors supported the delisting; others thought it was an inappropriate subject for the coalition to address. Keeping silent was a mistake, Sam Kim said.[12]

The Korean Church Coalition was a critical force in winning passage of the North Korean Human Rights Act of 2004. The legislation authorized the United States to accept refugees from North Korea. It increased the number of hours that Voice of America and Radio Free Asia broadcast to North Korea. And it established the part-time position of a special envoy on human rights in North Korea, a job that subsequently became full-time when the law was reauthorized in 2008. Then Senator Sam Brownback, a Republican from Kansas, proposed the original legislation in response to what he termed "one of the worst human rights disasters in the world." It was passed unanimously by both houses of Congress and signed into law by President George W. Bush on October 18, 2004.

Congressman Ed Royce, a Republican from Orange County, California, was another early backer of the North Korean Human Rights Act. Royce is a longtime activist on behalf of North Korean refugees in China, North Koreans imprisoned in their country's gulag, and human rights issues overall. Royce attributes his interest in North Korea and other repressive regimes to his father, who was one of the American soldiers who liberated the Dachau concentration camp in Germany in 1945. The elder Royce had a camera with him and took photographs that have haunted the congressman since his boyhood. "My brother and I opened my father's chest from World War II and found the pictures he had taken at Dachau," Royce said. "It had a profound effect on me." When he looks at photos of North Koreans today, he said, the people in the photos have the same look in their eyes as those in his father's snapshots. "They reflect the same level of abuse." In 2002, Congressman Royce held a Congressional hearing on the subject of human rights in North Korea. "I had a defector draw a map of one of the prison camps," he said. The hearing set the stage for the legislation that Congress passed two years later.

From his perch at the Hudson Institute in Washington, Michael Horowitz was one of the loudest, most effective voices advocating passage of the legislation. Several senators initially were fearful that the proposed legislation was too strong, Horowitz said. They worried about antagonizing China and making North Korea even more recalcitrant than it already was. "Then the KCC held its first convention in California, and one thousand–plus pastors showed up,"[13] Horowitz said. "The politicians got nervous." It was an election year, and it looked like Korean-Americans were finally waking up to their potential political clout.

Passage of the Human Rights in North Korea Act was the Korean Church Coalition's finest hour, Horowitz said. Congressman Royce agrees that the Korean Church Coalition was helpful in winning support for the law. Pastors from three hundred churches came to Washington, where they made congressional visits and held rallies, he remembers. It was a kind of coming-out party for Korean-American activism in the nation's capital.

Since the passage of the North Korean Human Rights Act in 2004, it is hard to point to any political achievement on the part of the KCC or any other Korean-American organization. Royce cites South Korea's Sunshine Policy as one reason for Korean-Americans' inaction. Many Korean-Americans take their cue on North Korean affairs from the South Korean government, and the Sunshine Policy of engagement with Pyongyang, which was the South Korean government's policy from 1998 to 2008, effectively signaled that human rights didn't matter. The Sunshine Policy belied its name, Royce said. It shone "no light" on the North Korean gulag or on the everyday brutality of life in North Korea. In Royce's words, the South Korean government "kept a lot of what was happening in North Korea in darkness."[14]

In Michael Horowitz's view, individual Korean-Americans work hard on North Korean issues, but no one wants to get out in front. That is partly cultural, he argues. Koreans traditionally have a high regard for hierarchy, and they show great deference to elders. But such attitudes serve them poorly when it comes to the rough-and-tumble of American politics. In Horowitz's words, "Korean-American leaders think they have made progress when they get a photo-op with a political leader or a letter from a politician saying, 'I feel your pain.'"

It is notable that the go-to activist in Washington on the issue of human rights for North Koreans is not of Korean ancestry. She is Suzanne Scholte, who, as her name suggests, is European-American. Scholte has been promoting awareness of North Korean issues since the mid-1990s. In 1996, she initiated a program to bring North Korean refugees to the United States to speak out about the North Korean regime. The visitors have ranged from high-ranking defectors to average citizens from all walks of life. They have included survivors of the political prisons, professors, engineers, military leaders, state security agents, and government workers. She has organized speakers for numerous Congressional hearings.

In 2004, Scholte organized the first North Korea Freedom Day in Washington, D.C. One thousand people gathered on the steps of the Capitol to rally in support of human rights for North Koreans. North Korea Freedom Day expanded to an annual North Korea Freedom Week, when activists, scholars, politicians, and refugees come together in Washington or Seoul for a week of information gathering, networking, and public outreach. Scholte is a familiar figure outside the Chinese Embassy in Washington, where she has led protests against China's mistreatment of North Korean refugees. In 2011, when President Hu Jintao's motorcade pulled up at the White

House for a state dinner, he was greeted by protestors organized by Scholte who were rallying at Lafayette Park. The demonstrators carried a coffin to symbolize the North Koreans who died when China repatriated them.

The South Korean government recognized Scholte's activism in 2008 with the Seoul Peace Prize, an honor that also has gone to Czech President Vaclav Havel, United Nations Secretary General Kofi Annan, and other international figures. The citation read: "At a time when countries are purposely neglecting the human rights conditions in North Korea for their political interests, Scholte has taken the lead in raising awareness of the miserable plight of North Korean refugees and encouraged the refugees who are seeking freedom."[15]

After the Holocaust, Jews vowed, never again. American Jews kept that promise during the Cold War, advocating in Washington, D.C., on behalf of persecuted Jews in the Soviet Union and demanding that Moscow allow Jews to exit the country.

This example is not lost on the second and third generations of Korean-Americans. These young people increasingly are taking up the issue of North Korean human rights and beginning to organize on campuses and elsewhere. The U.S.-born activists were raised on American values of personal liberty and respect for the rule of law. "Things are changing now, especially among younger Korean-Americans." Congressman Royce said. "They look at the Jewish community and see what it was able to accomplish during the Cold War."

There is one lesson in particular from that era that Korean-American activists would be smart to emulate. The movement to free Soviet Jews began as a grassroots effort far removed from the elites of Jewish society. It started in 1963 not with national Jewish leaders or even with rabbis. Instead, it began with a petition organized by two Jewish laymen in Cleveland, Ohio. The men were looking for ways to call attention to the deteriorating plight of Soviet Jews. In time, the struggle to help Soviet Jews attracted supporters from every part of Jewish life—religious leaders, politicians, businessmen. But the salient fact is that it began with ordinary citizens who were outraged enough to take action.[16] This kind of bottom-up approach will not come naturally to Korean-Americans brought up in a culture that reveres age and experience.

Korean-Americans face the challenge, too, of boosting awareness of the plight of North Koreans among fellow Americans of many different ancestries. George W. Bush used the bully pulpit of the American presidency to draw attention to the refugee crisis in China. He met with North Korean refugees several times during his term in office. Secretary of State Hillary Clinton and First Lady Michelle Obama had their picture taken with Lee Ae-ran the first North Korean woman to earn a Ph.D. in South Korea. Presidents Bush and Obama both have raised the refugee issue with their Chinese counterparts.

But North Korea does not have the status of an "Asian Darfur," as more than one activist has ruefully pointed out. Darfur activists have film star Mia Farrow as their spokeswoman; the free Tibet movement has actor Richard Gere. No celebrity has stepped forward as a champion for the North Koreans.

Washington activist Michael Horowitz has a suggestion for how to begin to educate Americans about what is happening in North Korea. Every Korean-American church, he says, should place a sign on its front lawn that quotes the Book of Exodus: *Let My People Go.*

BE THE VOICE

Angel Chung Cutno stood on the stage of the theater at the University of Connecticut's student union and recounted the story of how she became an advocate on behalf of North Korean escapees. She has told the story countless times at college campuses up and down the Eastern Seaboard.

With her halo of curly hair and luminous brown eyes that angle upward, Angel cuts a striking figure. She is biracial, the daughter of a South Korean woman and African-American man. Her parents met in the 1980s when her father was in the Army, one of thirty thousand American soldiers stationed in South Korea. She grew up in Louisiana. In college she became involved in North Korean human rights issues. Her commitment is demonstrated by the tattoo she wears on the inside of her left wrist. It is the red and blue flag of the Democratic People's Republic of Korea. Above the flag are tattooed the words, "Be the Voice."[1]

Angel represents a new generation of Korean-American activists. They are angry, fervent, and plainspoken. Unlike their immigrant parents and grandparents, they want to address the issue of North Korean abuses head-on. Nor do they have the regional prejudices and other cultural baggage that afflict the older generation. This younger cohort, now in their twenties and thirties, is outraged and driven. Kevin Park, a Korean-American from Seattle who became an activist on North Korea when he was a student at Pepperdine University, says older Korean-Americans have chastised him: You're "wasting your time," they say. The younger generation is different. "I've never met a second-generation Korean-American who said, 'I don't care about it,'" Park states.[2]

Raising awareness is a primary goal, and student activists are doing so on a growing number of campuses, where North Korea is becoming an increasingly popular concern. It is not up there yet with Darfur and Tibet as campus causes, but events about North Korea are turning up with increasing frequency on bulletin boards in student unions. The awareness campaigns aim to increase student understanding of life in North Korea and the atrocities that the Kim family regime is committing against the North Korean people. Many American students are ignorant about North Korea's totalitarian system. Their knowledge of the country may not go beyond *Team America*, the cult comedy film that lampoons Kim Jong Il, the easily lampoonable late dictator.

Kim Ju-song, an alias for a high-ranking North Korean military defector, spoke at a student forum at Yale University. He opened his remarks by imploring his listeners to shed their preconceptions. North Korea is nothing like anything any American student has experienced, he told them. "If you do not abandon your knowledge of the place where you are living right now, if you do not abandon your way of thinking, you will not be able to understand how North Korea works," he said. "I have visited a lot of countries. There is no country in the world that is like North Korea. The regime controls and represses its people."

When a Yalie asked the defector what his trial had been like in North Korea before he was sent to jail, the defector looked at him as if he were crazy. There was no trial, he told the student. That's not the way the system works in North Korea. "You need to think outside of the system you grew up with here," he repeated. "It's different in North Korea. If the government wants to arrest you, it will." The reason Kim Ju-song was able to make the decision to leave North Korea, he said, was that he was privy to information about what life was like outside his country. He knew that an alternative existed.[3]

At the University of Connecticut gathering, Angel picked up a microphone and explained to the assembled students how she had become the voice of the voiceless North Koreans. By telling her personal story, she hoped to encourage other young people to support the same cause. "I'm from New Orleans," she began. "I went to Louisiana State University. In the summer of 2008, I worked in Seoul at a school for refugees."

Every summer she was in college, Angel went on a service trip to a different place in the United States or another country. She would find the placements through the international mission board of the Southern Baptist Church. In early 2008, as she was researching her choices for the coming summer, she heard about an opening on a mission to South Korea. The job was working at a school for refugee youth from North Korea. Angel thought it would be interesting to spend a couple of months in her mother's native country and visit members of her extended family. "At the time I didn't know much about the issue of North Korea at all," she said. "I went in blindly."

The students at the school for refugees were around her age or a few years younger. "They were young and vibrant," she said. "They seemed just like me," she said, "until I started to get to know them and to hear all their stories." Then "it was heartbreak after heartbreak."

As she heard more about life in North Korea, Angel was surprised and outraged by what she learned: "the human abuse, the famine, the food issues, how strict Communism was." This was not something that her Korean relatives talked about or that she learned at school in the United States. Most of the North Korean students she worked with were alone in South Korea, having escaped from China on the new underground railroad without family members. Their parents were either dead, still living in North Korea, or they had been caught in China and repatriated and were now presumably serving terms in prison. A few students had parents hiding in China. One fortunate boy had a brother with him in Seoul.

There was an enigmatic girl who especially tugged at Angel's heartstrings. The girl was fourteen years old and had severe emotional problems. If Angel moved close to her or tried to hug her, the girl would push her away and sometimes even bite. Her back was covered with scars, and it was obvious that she had been abused. Yet no one knew her story. She appeared to have no family. The girl had been hiding in China for nine years and had forgotten how to speak Korean, so it was difficult to communicate with her. When she was asked, through an interpreter, what had happened to her parents, she refused to answer. She just looked down at the floor.

Angel told this story to the university audience, but then, to end on an upbeat note, she closed with an anecdote about a boy to whom she had taught English. At the conclusion of her summer in South Korea, when she was about to return home to the States, the boy came up to her and said shyly in English, "Very thank you." Angel gave a little laugh as she told that part of her story, and the audience laughed along with her. As she finished, someone in the audience shouted out, "Very thank you."

Angel was traveling the country as a volunteer spokesman for the nonprofit, grassroots organization, Liberty in North Korea. LiNK has run many missions on the new underground railroad—including the aborted Shenyang Six escape in 2006, when six North Koreans and three LiNK activists landed in jail. LiNK is dedicated to two goals: raising awareness on college campuses about the humanitarian crisis in North Korea and helping the North Korean refugees in China. It was founded at Yale University in 2004 by two Korean-American students who were appalled by the plight of North Koreans in China and outraged at the silence of the Korean-American community. Today the organization has one hundred chapters on American campuses along with a chapter in South Korea and several in the United Kingdom. It dubs its spokesmen "Nomads," because they wander from campus to campus. LiNK is nonsectarian, but, like Angel, many of its members are Christian, inspired by their faith to help North Korean refugees. It does not proselytize.

LiNK is a results-oriented organization. Part of its appeal to college students is that their contributions and volunteer work will have direct results. LiNK workers shelter North Koreans hiding in China, guide them on the new underground railroad to third countries, and help them arrange for permanent resettlement in South Korea or the United States. It runs a shelter in Southeast Asia for refugees who are waiting to be processed for exit visas. In the United States, it operates an outreach program to assist North Korean refugees who are trying to establish new lives there.

Like many humanitarian organizations operating in China, LiNK utilizes a network of partners on the ground, including brokers. LiNK volunteers, many but not all of them Korean-American, do much of the guiding themselves.[4]

Also unlike most of the humanitarian organizations that assist North Koreans in China, LiNK is not publicity-shy. Just the opposite. It's up front and vocal about its rescue missions, although it is careful not to reveal operational details. It has a robust website, and—in an effort to reach its college-age target audience—it's active in social media such as Facebook and Twitter. Several of the refugees it has rescued now speak out on LiNK's behalf to student and church groups in the United States and appear at fund-raisers. Hannah Song, LiNK's PR-savvy president, left a high-profile job in advertising in Manhattan to work for the nonprofit.

In 2009, LiNK launched the Hundred Campaign, with a goal of rescuing one hundred North Koreans hiding in China. Each rescue costs an estimated $2,500, and LiNK challenged every chapter to raise enough money to pay for one North Korean refugee to escape from China. As part of its fund-raising effort for the Hundred Campaign, it produced a short documentary film that chronicled the actual rescue of five refugees in China in August 2010. The film, called *Hiding*, was shot in China with hidden cameras. It follows LiNK's vice president, Justin Wheeler, as he prepares the refugees for the trip and then guides them across China to an unspecified country in Southeast Asia. It features interviews with North Koreans hiding in China, including a wrenching one with a twentysomething woman who had been pressed into service in a brothel. Her face was obscured, but you could see her hand moving up to her eyes every once in a while to wipe away tears. She declined Wheeler's offer to help her escape on the new underground railroad. She was too scared. She couldn't take the risk of being repatriated, she explained. Life in North Korea was too awful.

As a LiNK Nomad, Angel spent the autumn of 2010 spreading LiNK's message at events at colleges and universities from Maryland to Maine. She was a member of a three-person team, which included Lindsay Capehart from Kansas City, Kansas, and Stefan Hutzfeld from Dusseldorf, Germany.[5] The three Nomads traveled in a white van on which the yellow-and-black LiNK logo was painted in big, bold letters. They carried sleeping bags with them, and their hosts provided overnight accommodation, which usually meant a space on the floor of someone's dorm room. If there wasn't a LiNK chapter on campus, the Nomads' visits were sponsored by the local Korean Students Association, Asian-American Students Association, or a charitable organization. In three months on the road, the Northeast Nomads made dozens of presentations.

Neither Lindsay nor Stefan is of Korean heritage. Lindsay first heard about the North Korean refugees in China when she was a student at Manhattan Christian College in Kansas and read about then Senator Sam Brownback's efforts on the refugees' behalf. "I was really confused about what Brownback was talking about," she said. "I had only heard about the security situation in North Korea. So I did some research on it, and I started seeing facts about what was happening. I was blown away. I was really flabbergasted by that—that I didn't know—because I consider myself aware."

Stefan heard about North Korea from his older brother, who collected postage stamps and showed him some stamps from North Korea. Stefan learned from his brother that North Korea was a closed country, but he had no inkling of what that meant beyond the fact that mailing a letter there was impossible from most countries. Then he saw a video that a friend posted on Facebook, and he was shocked to discover that North Koreans were so oppressed. The online conversation about the video with his Facebook friends led him to LiNK. As a German, Stefan also was touched by the fact that Korea is a divided country. Many Korean-American students ask him about his German background and how it relates to his work on behalf of North Koreans. "I was born in 1989, the year the Berlin Wall fell," he said. "My parents always told me about how it was when Germany was divided, but I never saw it. I never got to experience it. For me, Germany was always a united country. But in school we saw documentaries that showed how people were overwhelmed with happiness that Germany was united again. I thought it was something beautiful. If Korea could unite, there would be a lot of joy."

Twenty-five students attended the LiNK meeting at the University of Connecticut. As is typical at many LiNK functions, most were Korean-American or foreign students from South Korea. Several students said that they attended because they knew little about North Korea and wanted to learn more. Even though they were South Korean or Korean-American, they explained, their families had never discussed the issue with them. A student from South Korea said he had learned more about North Korea from the Nomads' hour-long presentation than from all his years growing up in Seoul.

One young man, born in the United States, said LiNK's movie *Hiding* opened his eyes. Another man, born in South Korea, said he was shocked at what the film showed of China's mistreatment of the refugees. A Korean-American woman also expressed her astonishment. "You [would] think someone would do something about it," she said. Such reactions are typical, the Nomads told me. It's hard for people to grasp that such atrocities are taking place, Lindsay said. "They feel like everyone should know that something like this is happening. They ask, 'How could the world not know?'"

After the screening of *Hiding*, Angel went back onstage and talked about the ways students could get involved. Become a member of LiNK, she urged. Give us your email address. Start a LiNK chapter at UConn. Ninety percent of LiNK members are our age or younger, she informed the audience. Tell your friends about us. Angel urged students to buy LiNK T-shirts, which she would be selling at a table outside the theater after the conclusion of this event. "It's hard to go up to someone and just start talking about LiNK," she said. "But wearing one of our T-shirts will help provoke a conversation and give you an opportunity to talk about LiNK."

While Angel was speaking, two donation boxes circulated through the audience. Angel, Lindsay, and Stefan had set a fundraising goal of $10,000 for their tour, the sum needed to rescue four North Korean refugees in China. When we had met earlier in Washington, D.C., near the start of their campus tour, they had raised only $300. A month later, when we met in Connecticut, they had collected more than $4,000.

The three Nomads were now past the halfway mark of their tour. After the University of Connecticut, they would move on to Rhode Island, where they would be making their presentation the next night at Roger Williams University. Then on to Massachusetts, New Hampshire, Vermont, upstate New York, and Pennsylvania. They would work through Thanksgiving week, which they would spend in Canada, which does not celebrate the American holiday. Their last scheduled stop was Carnegie Mellon University in Pittsburgh in early December. Then they would head back to California to meet up with the Nomads from other sectors of the country and exchange notes.

Meanwhile, friends could follow their progress on Facebook. The three Nomads posted photos and videos from their tour along with a link to their blog. Their Facebook home page displayed a statement that served as a kind of one-line credo for their work of raising awareness of the plight of North Koreans:

"*Where* you live," they wrote, "shouldn't determine *whether* you live."

PART V

LEARNING TO BE FREE

They were adults, looking as though they could take care of themselves very easily, although they had the marks of Slavery on them. It was no easy matter for men and women who had been ground down all their lives to appear as though they had been enjoying freedom.

—THE UNDERGROUND RAILROAD RECORD
APRIL 1856

ALMOST SAFE

Somewhere in the Gobi Desert stands a cross in the sand. It marks the grave of Yoo Chul-min, a ten-year-old North Korean boy who died while walking across the Chinese border to Mongolia.

Chul-min was traveling with five other North Korean escapees when the group lost its bearings for more than a day somewhere near the Mongolian frontier. The terrain is harsh there, and the temperature drops precipitously at night. A healthy boy his age might have survived. But years of malnutrition in North Korea had weakened Chul-min, and he died of exhaustion and exposure. His companions carried his body across the border when they finally oriented themselves. The Mongolians buried the child. His father, Yoo Sang-jun, a Christian, flew to Ulan Bator from Seoul to pray at his son's grave. Chul-min's story is a reminder that not every North Korean who makes a bid for freedom is successful.

For North Koreans trying to escape, the route across China is a life-and-death game of hide-and-seek. There are two ways to win: They can gain entrance to a consular facility in China, which is technically foreign ground; or they can cross the Chinese border and touch the soil of a third country. After that, it is a waiting game. They must wait for South Korea to agree to take them, and they must wait for China or the third country to grant them permission to depart. The process can take weeks, months, or even, in a few cases, years.

It is unusual today to hear about North Koreans who are turned away at the door of a South Korean consular facility in China or elsewhere. But that was not always the case. During the presidencies of Kim Dae-jung and Roh Moo-hyun, from 1998 to 2008, rescue workers complained bitterly about what they saw as the South Korean government's abandonment of the North Koreans despite its constitutional obligation to accept them. South Korean consular facilities in China or third countries sometimes turned away North Koreans who appeared on their doorsteps. A partial explanation for South Korea's shameful actions, though no excuse, was that it was unprepared for the flood of refugees escaping from China.

The core problem, however, was the underlying political situation. The North Korean runaways put the South Korean government in an embarrassing position vis-à-vis the Sunshine Policy then in place of building bridges to the North. If North Korea was such a reasonable place, why did so many of its citizens want to get out? It was an awkward question for a South Korean government that was seeking reconciliation with the North, one that it preferred not to address. Kim Dae-jung and Roh Moo-hyun usually refrained from publicly raising the issue of the North Korean fugitives for fear of antagonizing Kim Jong Il's regime. If circumstances forced South Korea to help North Koreans on the run, it would. Otherwise, the refugees were a low priority.

The experience of one high-ranking defector illustrates this attitude. In the early 2000s, this man turned up at the South Korean Embassy in the city where he'd been posted and announced that he wanted to defect. The defector was what intelligence agencies call a walk-in. The receptionist told him to go away. It was left to the astonished would-be defector to remind her that the constitution of her country required the embassy to accept any North Korean who requested asylum. The would-be defector insisted on speaking to a higher-ranking diplomat. That diplomat agreed to accept him. The next day the North Korean was on a plane to Seoul.[1]

In this case, the defector was highly educated, well informed, and in possession of information that would be valuable to the South Korean government. Any ordinary refugee is much more vulnerable. If a South Korean consular official told him to go away, he might not know enough to stand his ground. When put in such a position, many would do as they were told and leave. An untold number did just that.

In 2001, a group of humanitarian workers, angered by the Chinese government's treatment of the refugees and Seoul's reluctance to help, launched a public-awareness campaign. Their objective was to put a global spotlight on the plight of the North Korean escapees and shame Beijing and Seoul into treating them better.

They began by organizing small groups of refugees committed to taking high-profile actions in China. Under their direction, the refugees stormed past guards and into embassies, where they demanded political asylum. Over the next three years, North Koreans would jump over walls, knock down Chinese guards, and push past gates at embassies, consular facilities, and United Nations offices. Many of these dramatic scenes were captured on camera by foreign journalists, whom the organizers had tipped off in advance.

The protests were conceived of and organized by an international group of rescuers: Tim Peters, the Seoul-based American missionary; Kim Sang-hun, a lay Christian worker from South Korea; Hiroshi Kato, founder of a Japanese nonprofit group, Life Funds for North Korea; and Norbert Vollertsen, a German physician who had worked in North Korea. The four men sketched out their operations in a series of meetings over coffee at a McDonalds restaurant in Seoul. The German, Dr. Vollertsen, was the public face of the movement and its unofficial spokesman.[2]

With his tall, imposing physique and flowing blond hair, Vollertsen was a charismatic personality who believed that the refugees were the key to regime change in Pyongyang. The publicity campaign he and his colleagues devised had three objectives: gain global publicity for the plight of the North Koreans, force China to protect them, and shame South Korea into accepting them. Vollertsen and his friends aimed to trigger a larger outflow of North Korean refugees that would in turn destabilize the Kim family regime. As Vollertsen said at the time: "We hope to achieve something similar to what happened in 1989 when East Germans sought asylum in Hungary, which forced it to open its borders in a step that led to the collapse of East Germany."[3]

Vollertsen is another example of a humanitarian worker who underwent a road-to-Damascus conversion while working on the ground in North Korea. He spent one and a half years in that country as a representative of a German medical charity. The experience taught him that working with the Kim family regime was hopeless. He reached the conclusion that it was impossible to help North Koreans inside North Korea. He came to believe that the only way to alleviate the suffering of the North Korean people was to help some of them escape.

The doctor's conversion took place on the road, not to Damascus, but to Haeju, a city seventy miles south of Pyongyang. Vollertsen was traveling in a car with a German colleague, their North Korean minder, and a driver, when they saw a uniformed soldier lying along the side of the road. The Germans insisted that the driver stop the car. The soldier was dead. When Vollertsen examined the body, he observed that the man had suffered from malnutrition. The doctor also saw signs of torture. Police arrived, and an altercation ensued when Vollertsen tried to take photographs of the corpse. The incident prompted him to deliver a statement on human rights to the North Korean government. He was expelled from the country.

The first protest organized by Vollertsen and his colleagues took place in Beijing in June 2001. Seven members of a North Korean family entered the office of the United Nations High Commissioner for Refugees, requested asylum, and refused to leave. The incident had its desired effect: The world press covered the story aggressively; South Korea said it would accept the refugees; and three days later, China allowed them to depart. The family flew to Seoul via Singapore and Manila. In Seoul, the government of President Kim Dae-jung called a meeting of the national security council to discuss the impact of the asylum bid on intra-Korean relations. Vollertsen announced that there would be more rushes on foreign facilities in Beijing.

The next incident occurred in March 2002, when twenty-five North Koreans stormed through an open gate into the Spanish Embassy in Beijing. The North Koreans stood on the lawn outside the residence of the ambassador, raised their arms in a sign of victory, and passed out pamphlets in English and Korean expressing their desire to seek asylum in South Korea. The Chinese government allowed them to depart the next day for Seoul via Manila.

The rush was on. In the next few months, North Koreans forced their way into the German, American, Canadian, and South Korean Embassies in Beijing and into consulates in the northeast city of Shenyang, near the North Korean border. Invasions of more embassies followed, along with incursions into several foreign-run schools in Beijing.

Many of these incidents made international headlines, but none pulled more at the heartstrings than the story of an adorable two-year-old girl with pigtails. Her name was Kim Han-mee. In May 2002, Han-mee and her parents, grandmother, and uncle pushed past the Chinese guards and entered the compound of the Japanese Consulate in Shenyang. The guards went in after the family and manhandled them back into Chinese territory. Photographs showed Chinese security officers dragging Han-mee's mother out of the compound while Han-mee stood sobbing on the Japanese side of the entrance gate. The images aired worldwide and ignited a diplomatic spat between Beijing and Tokyo, which charged that Chinese soldiers had violated their consular ground by rushing in after the North Koreans. After spending two weeks in a Chinese jail, the family was released and sent to Seoul via the Philippines. President George W. Bush later invited Han-mee to the White House.

At first, China allowed North Koreans who invaded consular facilities to leave the country within days or weeks. In 2002, as the rushes on embassies proliferated, the Chinese Foreign Ministry began to take a tougher line. It announced that the North Koreans did not meet the legal definition of refugees. Embassies had no right under international law to grant them asylum, it proclaimed, and it demanded that the embassies hand over the refugees in their care. China's interpretation of international law in this regard was rightly seen as preposterous, and diplomats ignored its demands. Beijing then tried to bully the embassies into withdrawing their protection of North Koreans: We will let the current group of refugees go, it offered, so long as you promise not to give asylum to any more North Koreans. That tactic didn't fly either.

Eventually Beijing began to punish embassies for accepting North Koreans by delaying exit permits. Diplomatic facilities are unprepared to host refugees for any lengthy period of time. Having North Koreans to feed, house, and entertain for months on end was expensive and hugely inconvenient for the embassy staff, who were forced to share their space and help take care of them. As Tim Peters put it: "Caring for North Koreans takes an amount of sacrifice and forbearance. It affects the diplomats personally. It is way outside their comfort zone." In 2003, South Korea shut its embassy in Beijing for ten days, saying it was overwhelmed with refugees and could not accommodate more.

All in all, between seven and eight hundred North Korean refugees reached safety in the early 2000s through the tactic of invading diplomatic facilities in China. In the end, Beijing put a stop to the practice through the crude but effective technique of making the consular facilities inaccessible. It erected roadblocks on streets that were home to embassies, installed spikes and barbed wire on top of the walls surrounding diplomatic compounds, and dramatically increased the number of guards at the front gates. Embassy visitors now had to pass through two sets of Chinese security barriers, as well as the virtual no-man's land in between. A North Korean who attempted entry was almost certainly doomed to failure.

At the same time that some North Korean refugees were seeking asylum at embassies in China, others were fleeing to third countries.

Mongolia was a popular route on the new underground railroad in the late 1990s and early 2000s. Its principal advantage was its location next to the northeast region of China, where most of the North Korean refugees arrive. Escapes were routed through Heilongjiang Province and the Chinese autonomous region of Inner Mongolia, which shares a border with Mongolia. As the death of the child Yoo Chul-min in the Gobi Desert shows, the desert terrain along the Chinese-Mongolian frontier is treacherous, and crossing the border can be extremely perilous.

The government of Mongolia, which maintains good relations with both Koreas, has a history of treating the North Koreans humanely. Border patrols on horseback would pick up refugees crossing from China and arrange for them to be transported to the capital of Ulan Bator. From there the North Koreans would be issued exit permits expeditiously and allowed to travel to South Korea. As a Mongolian analyst put it in 2006, Ulan Bator was "trying to handle this issue in a careful and delicate manner."[4] There were reports, denied by the Mongolian government, that Mongolia might establish a refugee camp at a former Soviet military barracks to care for the North Koreans until they could be transferred to South Korea.

Like every country that hosts North Korean refugees, Mongolia was reluctant to release information about them, including divulging how many entered the country illegally. It was concerned both with the security of the refugees and with maintaining good relations with China, North Korea, and South Korea, none of which wanted a spotlight on the crisis. In a rare public comment on the subject, a Mongolian official said in 2003 that more than five hundred North Koreans had been resettled to South Korea from Mongolia since 1999.[5]

For a while, North Koreans were able to move around relatively inconspicuously in China's Heilongjiang Province, which is home to many Korean-Chinese. But sometime in the early or mid-2000s, as part of its overall crackdown on North Korean refugees, the Chinese government stepped up ID checks in the sparsely populated areas of that province and in the Inner Mongolia Autonomous Zone. They arrested so many North Koreans that the escape route through Mongolia virtually shut down. Some still got through, but the preferred escape route shifted to Southeast Asia.

North Koreans sometimes give idiosyncratic reasons for choosing a particular destination on the new underground railroad. Eom Myong-hui, who arrived in Seoul in 2002, selected Burma because she had heard that this was where, in 1983, North Korea tried to assassinate the visiting South Korean president, Chun Doo-hwan, in a bomb attack that missed the president but killed half the South Korean cabinet. Eom Myong-hui mistakenly assumed that the generals running Burma hated North Korea because of that incident and would therefore treat an escaped North Korean kindly. When she discovered, upon arrival, that she would be arrested and jailed for illegal entry, she made a beeline for neighboring Thailand, where she found a warmer welcome.[6]

Most North Koreans rely on their guides to make the decision about their destination country. The guides in turn base their decision on three factors: how easy it is to cross the border into a given country, how welcoming that country is to North Koreans, and how good the guides' contacts are in that country. Passengers on underground railroad routes through Southeast Asia have sought asylum in Burma, Cambodia, Laos, Thailand, and Vietnam.

Since President Lee Myun-bak took office in February 2008 under a pledge of doing more to help fleeing North Koreans, South Korea's policy toward the refugees has improved. Consular facilities worldwide are under instructions to help North Koreans who knock on their door. The United States has a similar policy regarding refugees from North Korea. Most North Koreans want to settle in South Korea, but if they prefer to go to the United States, they are welcome under the North Korean Human Rights Act of 2004.

Not all South Korean diplomats got President Lee Myun-bak's message, as seen in a September 2009 case involving nine North Korean refugees who had made their way to Vietnam. Tim Peters, the American activist based in Seoul, was one of the organizers of that rescue. "We went to the South Koreans initially," he said, referring to the South Korean Embassy in Hanoi. "But they would not let us in." His group made three separate inquiries at the South Korean Embassy. Each time, the embassy refused to accept the North Koreans.[7]

The group ended up at the Danish Embassy, which had to erect a tent in its garden to accommodate them. In Copenhagen, a spokesman for the foreign ministry announced that the North Koreans would be allowed to stay at the embassy. "We do not send people out who could face some kind of persecution," the Dane said. The international publicity probably helped the refugees. Seoul agreed to accept them. Vietnam gave them permission to leave the country, and they left for South Korea within the month.

The coalition of organizations that sponsored the mission had selected Hanoi as the destination for the nine refugees in part because the group hoped to reopen the Vietnam route on the new underground railroad. The flow of refugees to Vietnam had slowed drastically after a diplomatic incident in 2004 involving hundreds of North Koreans. Since that time, the government of Vietnam and the South Korean Embassy in Hanoi both had become less hospitable to North Koreans. A refugee who applied for asylum in Vietnam could expect to spend many months in uncomfortable detention before being permitted to go to Seoul. The rescuers hoped to spur the South Korean government to become a better advocate for the refugees. They also hoped to press Vietnam to improve its treatment of arriving North Koreans.

But the shadow of the 2004 incident still lingered. In 2004, the South Korean government had secretly chartered a plane and flown out 468 North Koreans who had sought asylum at its embassy in Hanoi. The South Korean Embassy had been support-ing the refugees for months either in its own facilities or in private shelters run by South Korean citizens. The refugees were living in cramped conditions, one man reportedly tried to commit sui-cide, and the South Korean officials were worried that the refugees might despair and become violent. "The situation was not manage-able," an official of the South Korean Foreign Ministry was quoted as saying.[8] In an effort to minimize the damage to what it saw as its improving ties with North Korea, South Korea tried unsuccessfully to keep its rescue mission secret. When news of the airlift got out, as of course it was bound to do, government officials refused to release the name of the country where the refugees had been stay-ing. They said only that the North Koreans had arrived in Seoul from Southeast Asia.

North Korea, however, had no such reticence, and it used the incident to try to intimidate South Korea into reducing assistance to North Korean refugees in China and elsewhere. It issued a belligerent statement outing Vietnam as the country from which its citizens had been "lured" by South Korea. It described the airlift as a "criminal" act, a "heinous crime of terrorism." By its "enticement and abduction" of North Korean citizens, the statement said, South Korea had pushed inter-Korean relations into a period of "acute confrontation."

By letting the North Korean refugees depart, the Vietnamese government, for its part, took sides against North Korea, an ideological ally, in order to preserve good ties with South Korea, which was making significant investments in Vietnam's developing economy. Several weeks after the airlift, South Korea announced a $21 million loan to Vietnam on favorable terms. The timing of the deal may or may not have been coincidental. Several months later, South Korea announced that it would never again attempt a large-scale rescue of refugees. North Korea's intimidation apparently had worked.

The popularity of other Southeast Asian countries as destinations on the new underground railroad ebbs and flows. Guides became wary of Cambodia in 2009 after that country sent twenty Uighur refugees back to China at the request of Beijing. They feared that Cambodia might adopt the same policy vis-à-vis North Koreans and send them back to China if Beijing made a similar demand. Another factor militating against the Cambodia route is Phnom Penh's history of good ties with Pyongyang. Kim Il Sung, the late founder of North Korea, was a close friend of Cambodia's former King Norodom Sihanouk, who lived in exile in a sixty-room mansion in Pyongyang in the 1970s. The countries continue to have warm ties.

Thailand is another destination for North Koreans on the run. The kingdom does not border China; to get there, North Koreans first must pass through Burma, Laos, or Vietnam. Guides typically escort refugees across the Thai border and then say good-bye. Turn yourselves in to the police, the refugees are instructed. The police will feed you, give you a place to sleep, and then arrange for you to be taken south to the international detention center. "It's the fastest way to get to Bangkok," says an American who guides North Koreans out of China on the new underground railroad. It's also the fastest way for a refugee to get to Seoul. The journey—from the day a North Korean arrives at the international detention center in Bangkok until the day he gets off the plane at Incheon Airport in South Korea—takes about one month.

Phil Robertson is deputy director of the Asia office of Human Rights Watch and an expert on refugees in Asia. Thailand does not want to repeat its difficult experience during the Vietnam War, when it was a magnet for refugees, he said. The Thai government takes a tough position regarding people who enter the country illegally. The North Koreans are an exception, Robertson noted. But even then, the government requires that they be dealt with in accordance with Thai law. The North Koreans must pay fines for entering the country illegally and serve a term in detention before they are permitted to depart for Seoul under the supervision of South Korean officials. The Thai government takes the position that it is "deporting" North Koreans back to their home country of "Korea." The geographic distinctions between North and South Korea are "conveniently blurred," explained a classified diplomatic cable from the American Embassy in Bangkok, as disclosed by Wikileaks. The cable also noted that South Korea is "an important trade partner and market for Thai labor."[9]

"Thailand does not lose anything by helping the North Koreans," Robertson, of Human Rights Watch, observed. It might even gain something in terms of the goodwill it earns from South Korea and the United States for its humane treatment of the North Koreans. He pointed out that unlike the tens of thousands of Burmese who have crossed into Thailand and are living in refugee camps along the border, the North Koreans all have a guaranteed place to go: South

Korea. Nor are they a burden on the Thai economy. South Korea helps pay for their care while they are in Thailand, and it also pays their fines for entering Thailand illegally. [10]

South Korea's proactive approach to helping North Koreans in Thailand is a change from as recently as 2007, when four hundred refugees went on a hunger strike at the international detention center in Bangkok. The North Koreans were protesting cramped accommodations and poor sanitary conditions at the detention center as well as delays in their resettlement in South Korea. The improvement in their treatment is probably due to the change in government in South Korea in 2008, when President Lee Myung-bak took office. His government has pushed for better treatment of North Korean refugees.

Thailand has become an increasingly popular way station for North Koreans traveling on the new underground railroad. According to the Thai national police, only forty-six North Koreans were arrested and detained in Thailand in 2004. By 2010, that number had increased many times over. That year, the number of North Koreans who entered Thailand illegally was reported to be 2,482. [11]

Southeast Asia is where most North Koreans get their first taste of freedom, and there is bitter to go along with the sweet. Refugees usually experience a sense of elation at having reached safety. But that can be coupled with feelings of frustration and boredom when they must wait weeks or months before leaving for their new homes. They also worry about what will come next. [12]

Sarah Yun is a young American who manages a shelter for North Koreans in a Southeast Asia city that she wishes to remain unnamed. The shelter is sponsored by Liberty in North Korea. LiNK's shelter is a large, two-story house built around a sunny courtyard that is home to a few potted plants and a basketball hoop. The kitchen, living

room, and dining room are all common spaces. There are two dor-
mitory-style bedrooms—one for men, one for women—each with
beds on the floor, Korean-style, covered with cheerful coverlets. Yun
and another house manager share the third bedroom. The fourth
bedroom serves as their office. A tiny fifth bedroom is filled with
boxes of clothes and shoes, and the residents may help themselves to
these. Many of the North Koreans arrive at the shelter with little or
nothing other than the clothes on their backs.

Refugees relax in the LiNK shelter for a few days before turning themselves in to the local authorities or at a South Korean consular facility. Soon after their arrival at the shelter, they are briefed
about what to expect from the local government and from the South
Korean diplomats who will interview them. They receive tips about
how to handle themselves in a range of possible situations, including
run-ins with the police or other government authorities. They get
advice about their rights under local law—a concept that is foreign
to most of them. The shelter also sets up video conferences with
North Korean refugees who recently have settled in South Korea.
The new arrivals have an opportunity to ask questions of people who
have had experiences similar to theirs. Most of the refugees move on
after a few days, but a few stay in the shelter for longer periods of
time. North Koreans who decide to seek asylum in the United States
typically spend several months there while officials are processing
their applications.

On the day I visit, the clients the shelter is hosting include two
sisters who are waiting to join their father in the United States. The
sisters haven't heard yet whether the State Department has approved
their application for asylum. They already have had their initial entry
interviews at the American Embassy. Those seemed to have gone
well, although on the day we meet, the younger sister is still brood-
ing over her failure to remember the name of Kim Jong Il's mother.
She knows the woman's name as well as she knows her own, she

says, but she was so flustered at the time of the interview that it popped out of her head. Like the World War II stories of strangers professing to be American—and asked who won the World Series to prove they weren't German spies—North Korean refugees typically must answer a range of questions about life in North Korea to ensure they really are from that country. There have been cases of Chinese nationals posing as North Korean refugees in order to receive South Korean citizenship.

Sarah Yun has her hands full making sure the house runs smoothly and keeping up the spirits of the residents. Everything is quiet at the moment, but new arrivals are expected in a few days. LiNK colleagues currently are guiding a half dozen North Koreans across China. They are scheduled to cross the border soon and make their way to the safe house. As Yun knows from experience, the entry of newcomers could upset the current equilibrium. Yun has a degree from Harvard, which gave her a good education on Korean history. But she acknowledges that Harvard did not prepare her for working with North Korean refugees. The group dynamics can be challenging. She sometimes wishes she had a degree in psychology.

The shelter is run under a strict set of house rules. Every resident is required to sign a pledge at the outset of his stay agreeing to abide by them. The rules are intended to ensure the security of the refugees and guard individual privacy: Do not disclose any information about anyone other than yourself. No personal cellphones. No email. Do not leave the house without permission. Yun enforces a three-strikes policy. If a resident breaks three major rules, he must leave the shelter. She turns him over to the local immigration authorities.

Yun notices a difference in attitude between North Koreans who arrive directly from North Korea after having spent only a few days or weeks in China and those who have lived in China for extended periods. "Those who come straight out are pampered," she said. It's an odd word to use to describe people who have just left the world's most repressive state. She puts it another way: Many North Koreans go through a version of adolescence once they reach a free country, she says. They are used to having decisions made for them in North Korea. Now, for the first time in their lives, they are expected to take control of their own lives. They don't understand how to handle their newfound independence, she says, and they can be overwhelmed with choices and responsibilities. Life in North Korea has left them with few problem-solving skills. They go through a period of trial and error that can be very frustrating to them. The Americans who work at the shelter provide structure and support but try not to be too nurturing. They understand that the North Koreans must learn to make it on their own.

North Koreans who stayed in China for extended periods of time have different kinds of adjustment problems. They lived a kind of half-life in China, Yun observes. "They were always worried about deportation in China. They had no rights. They were exploited." Once they reach a third country, the anxieties they've been living with don't simply go away. It takes a period of adjustment. At the same time, she says, North Koreans who have lived in China have a better understanding of the meaning of their new freedom and a better appreciation of it. "Everyone expresses huge gratitude and is very cooperative," she says. "I don't have to remind them to do chores. They appreciate the fact that they can trust someone."

A few days after we meet, Yun is scheduled to take part in her first rescue mission. She is driving to the border to meet the group of North Koreans who are now making their way across China. She and another LiNK colleague are to pick them up at a prearranged location and drive them back to the shelter. She is nervous. Will the group make it out safely? Will Yun and her colleague be able to find the correct spot and pick up the North Koreans as planned? "It's notable how well established the underground railroad has become over the past decade," she says, almost as if she were reassuring herself. "It's relatively easy to get someone out these days."

That said, she will be happier once the North Koreans are across the border, safely seated in her van and en route to the shelter. Escorting North Koreans out of China on the new underground railroad is someone else's job. Welcoming them to freedom is hers.

UNIFICATION DUMPLINGS

The story of a Chinese watermelon illustrates the difficulties North Koreans face adjusting to their new lives outside the closed, totalitarian state they fled. The watermelon in question belonged to a North Korean family hiding in the mountains of northeast China. They lived in a tent and ventured out of the woods only occasionally to look for odd jobs or to beg for food in the community. One day a local farmer took pity on them and gave them a watermelon from his field. Later in the week, the farmer dropped by and noticed that they hadn't touched his gift.

"Why haven't you eaten the melon?" the farmer asked.

One of the North Koreans replied, "We don't have a pot to boil it in."

Identifying fruits is of course the least of the problems that North Koreans encounter when they reach South Korea or the West. It is easy for a newcomer to learn what a watermelon is and how to eat it. It's far more difficult to learn how to thrive in a modern culture, a free-market economy, and an open political system.

The record is mixed. Many North Koreans progress painfully and achieve limited success in their new homes. Others move forward quickly and adapt to their new environments more easily. A few achieve a high level of success in a relatively short time—a college degree, a profitable small business, a well-paying job. The newcomer's age, level of education, length of time spent in China and whether he has relatives in his new country all are factors in determining how well and how quickly he is likely to adjust. The energy, persistence, and ambition that characterize a refugee's escape from North Korea and China don't always transfer well to life in a free society.

This holds true even in the one place where a North Korean might be expected to fit in relatively easily: South Korea. Most of the North Koreans who flee China end up in South Korea, where they receive generous resettlement benefits from the South Korean government. But government support isn't everything. Despite a shared language, history, and culture, refugees from North Korea often have a tough time in the South. On the surface, the statistics are discouraging: North Koreans in the South earn less than South Koreans do. Their rates of joblessness are higher. Their children are more likely to drop out of school. They suffer more from psychological and emotional disorders. A disproportionate number turn to drugs, alcohol, or crime. A tiny few are so unhappy that they actually have returned to North Korea.

But we need to put such statistics in context. Most of the North Koreans who live in South Korea have arrived since 2000. That is, they have been there for less than a generation. In 2001, there were only 1,357 North Koreans living in South Korea.[1] A decade later, there were 22,000. South Korea is one of the world's richest countries. It's unrealistic to expect immigrants from a place as poor and backward as North Korea to perform at South Korean levels in such a short period of time. As is typical with immigrants everywhere, full integration probably belongs to the next generation. The refugees' children are more likely than their parents to achieve comfort, wealth, and status in South Korea.

That said, the South Korean people could do a better job of welcoming North Koreans. Too many refugees encounter ignorance, apathy, and discrimination in their new home. Some South Koreans tend to perceive North Koreans as outsiders, even interlopers. Stereotypes characterize North Korean refugees as losers—lazy, uneducable, and uncooperative. The Northerners are aliens among brothers, as a pair of South Korean commentators have put it.[2]

An award-winning South Korean feature film, *The Journal of Musan*, portrays the discrimination faced by some North Korean immigrants in South Korea. A scene early in the movie shows a young man on his way to a job interview in Seoul. An older South Korean man gives him a piece of advice: "Don't tell him you're from North Korea, OK?"[3] The implication is clear: If the interviewer finds out that the job applicant is from North Korea, he'll be less likely to hire the young man.

It doesn't help that some South Koreans, especially young people, are profoundly ignorant about North Korea, sometimes even to the extent of not fully grasping the repressive nature of the Kim family regime. Everyone knows that North Korea is poor, but there is a tendency to compare it to the South Korea of the 1950s or '60s, when the South's economy was developing and its political system was under authoritarian rule. The younger generation of South Koreans don't have a good understanding of what life is like in North Korea, said Patrick Daihui Cheh, one of the producers of *Crossing*, a South Korean feature film about a father and son's escape from North Korea. "They know, but they don't really know."[4]

A former inmate at the infamous Yodok prison camp who now lectures in South Korea is stunned at the responses he receives from his audiences. After giving a speech to a group of South Korean soldiers, he told a reporter that no one in the audience was interested in learning more about the atrocities being committed against their fellow Koreans. Instead, the questions were trivial and reflected a lack of basic understanding about the nature of life in North Korea. One listener wanted to know how many vacation days a North Korean soldier received. Another asked whether North Korean soldiers were permitted to visit their girlfriends. Some South Koreans do not believe the gulag even exists, according to another prison-camp survivor who now lives in South Korea.[5]

South Koreans' ignorance and apathy can be laid in large part at the feet of former Presidents Kim Dae-jung and Roh Moo-hyun. They are unfortunate side effects of the now abandoned Sunshine Policy of engagement with Pyongyang. The Sunshine Policy was initiated by President Kim Dae-jung in 1998 and continued by his successor, Roh Moo-hyun, who held the presidency from 2003 to 2008. Kim and Roh wanted to win public support in South Korea for their efforts to engage Pyongyang, a path they believed would help open North Korea. They also wanted to avoid public statements that might ignite the fury of the Pyongyang regime. As a result, they deliberately glossed over the Kim family regime's human rights abuses. South Koreans who work on the new underground railroad often refer to the years of Kim Dae-jung and Roh Moo-hyun as the Lost Decade. For ten years, the South Korean government did its best to prevent South Koreans from having a full and accurate picture of the true nature of the Kim family regime. The Sunshine Policy made it easy for South Koreans to overlook the atrocities in the North. If their government did not seem to care, why should they?

The callous attitude of the two former presidents, both now deceased, is all the more peculiar given their personal histories as champions of the rights of the South Korean people. Kim Dae-jung was a prominent human rights activist before he became president, but he lost his voice when it came to the human rights horrors in the North. Roh Moo-hyun was a human rights lawyer before he took office, but human rights north of the DMZ were way down on his priority list during his presidency. Their silence about the suffering of the North Korean people was one of the great moral travesties of our time.

The Sunshine Policy was abandoned by President Lee Myung-bak, who took office in early 2008 on a promise of tougher policies on North Korea. His government began to speak out about the North Korean regime's atrocious treatment of its people. At the United Nations General Assembly in New York City that year, South Korea co-sponsored an annual resolution on human rights in North Korea. This was a reversal of the policy of the previous Roh administration, which not only had refused to join the European Union and Japan as a co-sponsor of the human rights resolution but had twice refused even to vote for it.[6] In 2009, the South Korean Human Rights Commission published a report on human rights in North Korea, the first time that it had offered a public assessment of the Kim family regime's abuses of its people.

The Lee Myung-bak administration appears to understand the future value of the North Korean refugees in a reunited Korea and has taken measures to prepare for that eventuality. In 2011, President Lee appointed a North Korean defector to head a new government-affiliated education center on what things will be like when the two Koreas reunite. It was the first time a North Korean had been named to a high-level government post in Seoul.[7] More than a dozen North Koreans now work at government agencies, and the Lee administration has introduced an affirmative action program to encourage government offices to hire more North Koreans. These are symbolic gestures, but they signal that the South Korean government considers the North Koreans living in South Korea worthy of respect.

Also on President Lee's watch, the South Korean government selected five North Korean students at South Korean universities to study in the United States under a joint American–South Korean program. That was a small but important step. If North Koreans are going to succeed in the highest ranks of business and government in

South Korea, they need to speak English. Speaking English is also an essential skill if they are going to be effective global spokesmen on North Korea. Right now there are few, if any, North Korean refugees or defectors who speak fluent, accent-free English.

The tiny number of defectors who arrived in South Korea from the 1950s through the mid-1990s received heroes' welcomes. They benefited from generous resettlement packages that included apartments and large sums of cash. That changed in 1999, when the annual number of refugees reaching South Korea exceeded one hundred for the first time and it became clear to the government that its lavish support of defectors was too unwieldy and expensive to continue. The new arrivals were more likely to be ordinary citizens than defectors bringing state secrets with them.

That year Seoul opened a resettlement center for the newcomers. Its official name is the Settlement Support Center for North Korean Refugees, but everyone calls it by its nickname, *Hanawon,* or "house of unity." Hanawon was shrouded in secrecy until 2009, when President Lee Myun-bak's administration invited journalists to tour the facility on the occasion of its tenth anniversary. The Kim Dae-jung and Roh Moo-hyun administrations had played down Hanawon's role. They did not want to risk upsetting Pyongyang by broadcasting how well South Korea treated refugees from the North.

Hanawon is an hour's drive south of Seoul set on a sprawling campus in the heart of the Korean countryside. The facility is surrounded by a fence that is topped with barbed wire and too high for intruders to scale easily. Armed guards inspect visitors' credentials at the entrance. But first you have to find it, which is no easy task. For security reasons, the Ministry of Unification does not publish the street address, and there are no road signs directing visitors to the facility, which is off a country road and nestled amid cornfields and tile-roofed farmhouses. Authorized visitors receive driving instructions, but on the morning of my visit, my driver had to stop several pedestrians to ask for directions and also make a phone call to the director's assistant before we finally located the entrance.

As we pulled into the parking lot, we passed several dozen young women strolling toward two buses that were waiting for them nearby. The women were dressed identically in gray athletic pants, sneakers, and puffy winter jackets in a metallic silver color. Slung over each woman's arm was a tote bag inscribed in Korean with an inspirational quotation from Helen Keller: "Hope is the religion that leads to success. Without hope, nothing can be accomplished." Foreign visitors are rare at Hanawon, and the women stopped to stare at me as I got out of the car. I guessed that I was the first Westerner some of them had seen. When I first lived in Asia in the early 1970s, this kind of reaction was not uncommon. But there aren't many places in Asia anymore where a white face, green eyes, and brown hair will stop someone in her tracks. Their stares are a measure of North Korea's isolation.

Hanawon is the second stop for North Koreans who reach South Korea. Upon arrival in the country, refugees are whisked away to a secure facility, where the National Intelligence Service interviews them. The aim of the debriefing is twofold: to weed out spies and to see if the refugee has information that could be useful to the South Korean government. Even ordinary people can provide useful information for South Korean researchers on life in the North. The information they impart can point the way to political or social trends that might prove to be significant. These intelligence debriefings can last from one to several months.

The refugees then head for Hanawon and a three-month crash course to prepare them for life in the South. Hanawon's curriculum is intensive: 420 hours of required course work, 80 hours of vocational training at off-site locations, and 386 hours of elective classes. Students rise at seven in the morning and are required to attend classes from nine to five. The mandatory curriculum includes courses in history, political science, and economics. A lot of time is devoted to unlearning what they were taught in North Korea. In North Korea, for instance, schoolchildren learn that the Korean War began when American troops invaded their country on June 25, 1950. At Hanawon, the refugees learn the truth: The war started when Kim Il Sung ordered his troops to invade the South.[8]

The North Koreans at Hanawon spend hours studying the Korean language as it is spoken in the South. They learn South Korean slang and the myriad English words that South Koreans have adopted into their vocabulary. North Koreans who have settled in the South often complain that they can't understand what their bosses or neighbors are saying, or that they can't read something seemingly as simple as a billboard or a newspaper ad. Similarly, South Koreans say they can identify someone from North Korea the moment he opens his mouth. The language study is both a practical necessity and a confidence builder for the newcomers.

Vocational training is aimed at preparing the students to work immediately after graduation from Hanawon. It focuses on factory work for men, and food preparation, hairdressing, and nurse's-aide jobs for women. The women I saw in the parking lot were boarding buses that would take them to their vocational internships. Hanawon also offers prep courses for the examinations for vocational licenses.

By far the most popular elective is computer training. The new arrivals' eagerness to become computer-savvy is a positive indicator of their determination to succeed in South Korea's wired society. Unless they became computer-literate while staying in China, most of the new arrivals will sit in front of a computer screen for the first time only after they reach Hanawon. The center has five sixty-seat computer labs. In the evenings, all are packed with North Koreans learning how to manipulate a mouse and surf the Web.

Students also take courses in the practical basics of everyday life in South Korea. They learn how to use an ATM, how to signal the bus driver that they want to get off, how to use a credit card, how to operate a kitchen stove and a hot-water heater. They take field trips to supermarkets, the subway in Seoul, and a local bank. They have a chance to go on a two-day homestay with a South Korean family. Nearly all the refugees are able to read, write, and do basic arithmetic, but many have had only several years of formal education. Hanawon offers remedial training to help them brush up such essential skills.

The hardest thing to teach new arrivals is South Korea's work ethic. "In South Korea, you need to work very hard," said an official at the Ministry of Unification. "Almost all the refugees complain that it is too hard to work in a South Korean company. It's too demanding."[9]

The director of Hanawon, Youn Mirang, explained: The North Koreans "don't understand the real meaning of competitiveness or competition," she said. Teaching such concepts is difficult. North Korean refugees are good at taking directions, but they are very passive workers. "They accept orders, but that's it," Youn Mirang said. "They don't have any initiative."

Given the culture they grew up in, that shouldn't be surprising, Youn pointed out. In North Korea, initiative and creativity are dangerous attributes. A worker who speaks up could face serious consequences. "It's safer to be passive." At her invitation, North Koreans who have settled successfully in South Korea give guest lectures at Hanawon and offer tips about how to behave in the workplace.

All this support is expensive for the South Korean taxpayer. Almost half of the Ministry of Unification's annual budget is devoted to the resettlement of refugees. In 2010, that amounted to $67.2 million, up 27 percent from 2009. In addition to the Hanawon training course, every refugee is entitled to an array of benefits, including a rent-free apartment for up to fifty years, medical care, job training, and educational assistance. Upon graduation from Hanawon, refugees receive a payment of $2,644, with additional payments of an equivalent sum in quarterly installments over the following year. Refugees used to receive their resettlement money in one large lump sum, but the South Korean government changed that practice after it found that too many refugees either went on shopping sprees or were taken advantage of by con men.

As an incentive to work, refugees are eligible for additional bonuses of up to $20,000 if they complete five hundred hours of job training and hold down a job for at least six months. To encourage the hiring of refugees, the government gives companies that employ a North Korean a subsidy equal to half that employee's wages for up to three years. Refugees are eligible for full tuition at public universities and half tuition at private universities. In 2009, the Lee government established a series of Hana Centers in communities around the country staffed by social workers and others. The Hana Centers provide support, counseling, and advice to refugees.

All this adds up to a generous package aimed at integrating North Koreans into South Korean society. Refugees are assisted, too, by dozens of nonprofit organizations, many run by churches, that provide a wide range of services, including job support, English classes, and personal counseling.

The government will support qualified North Koreans who want to set up small nonprofits or go into business for themselves, and it offers loans or grants to refugees with approved business plans. Choi Jung has done both and agreed to talk to me about her experiences opening a dumpling factory and establishing a nonprofit dance troupe. Both are located in Daegu City, south of the capital.

Mrs. Choi arrives at my hotel in Seoul in a whirlwind of pink. It is Saturday morning, and she stands out from the lunchtime crowd of fashionable Seoulites who are studiously dressed down for the weekend in designer jeans and leather jackets. In contrast, she is dressed to kill in a flamingo-hued dress. Her three-inch heels herald her arrival as she click-clacks her way across the lobby to greet me. She is impeccably coiffed and made up, and holds a cellphone in one hand and a handsome leather handbag in the other. It would be easier to mistake her for a businesswoman on her way to a meeting than for what she really is: a North Korean refugee who has made it big in a provincial city in the South.

Mrs. Choi is trailed by an entourage of fellow refugees, including her husband and three younger women. She greets me warmly. We have been introduced by Phillip Buck, the Seattle pastor who guided both Choi Jung and her future husband out of China. Pastor Buck calls her on her cellphone later to make sure we have connected. She would do anything for him. "It's not easy for us to talk about North Korea," she tells me later. But Pastor Buck asked, so she agreed.[10] After the introductions, Mrs. Choi takes charge. She has prepared a presentation for me and wants to go upstairs to my room to play two DVDs she has brought. The first DVD is a recording of a recent performance by her dance company at the Daegu City Center. The performers—dancers, musicians, drummers, comedians—are North Korean. They all have day jobs; dancing is a sideline.

As I watch the DVD, the lead dancer, a tall, slender, graceful woman, looks familiar. I realize that's because she is sitting on my couch. She is one of the ladies in Mrs. Choi's entourage. The dancer, who appears to be in her late thirties or early forties, tells me she is a graduate of an elite music and dance university in Pyongyang. She left North Korea after a friend threatened to expose her as an enemy of the state for watching a videotape of a South Korean TV show. The dancer had made the error of telling her friend that she believed what she saw and heard on the forbidden tape. Fearing arrest, she took a train to a city near the Chinese border and handed over all her savings to a broker to guide her across the river.

In South Korea, the woman is ecstatic to be dancing again. In North Korea, she says, she had been selected by the government when she was a child to be a dancer. But in South Korea, the government does not direct your future, she explains. She speaks emphatically. From her point of view, she is making a great revelation, and she wants to be sure that I grasp the importance of what she is saying. If someone in South Korea *wants* to pursue a career, she tells me, she can *choose* to do so. It is a matter of personal preference. "*That's* the difference between South Korea and North Korea," she announces. She adds that if she were still living in Pyongyang, she would no longer be permitted to perform. North Korean women are not allowed on stage after the age of thirty, she tells me. She then reveals another great truth she has learned about the South: In South Korea, dancers can perform as long as they are able.

Mrs. Choi's second DVD is about her dumpling factory. She started it in 2008 with a bank loan guaranteed by the government, investments from friends, and all the money she had in the world. She arrived in South Korea in 2003. She accumulated her savings from five years of working in a restaurant during the day and cleaning offices at night. She reels off a list of the factory's offerings— red pepper dumplings, scallion dumplings, vegetable dumplings, meat dumplings, kimchi dumplings, red bean paste dumplings. The dumplings have a distinctive North Korean taste, she tells me—very spicy and very delicious. She apologizes for not bringing me samples.

Mrs. Choi has another goal in addition to building a successful business. She wants to bring Northerners and Southerners together through food, by introducing traditional North Korean cuisine to the South. In honor of this attempt at dumpling diplomacy, she named her business Unification Dumplings.

Mrs. Choi describes the ups and downs of the dumpling business. "When I finished Hanawon, I was daydreaming about life in South Korea," she explains. "I thought that as long as I worked hard, I could accomplish anything. But there were a lot of difficulties." She goes through a long list of problems she had to solve before her factory could begin to operate: perfecting the recipes, finding suppliers, testing the market, devising a budget. Her biggest mistake, she says, was hiring employees before she had any work for them to do. She had to pay seven salaries for four months while she developed her product line. "I was thinking more about helping people than about my budget," she says. Today the Unification Dumpling factory has fifteen employees. Most of them are from North Korea. The factory has a daily production of fifteen thousand dumplings, which it sells largely to restaurants.

Mrs. Choi would much prefer to talk about her dance troupe and her dumpling factory than about her experiences in North Korea and China, but as our conversation draws to an end, she agrees to discuss her past a bit. She says she arrived in China "by accident." She was tricked to go there by the promise of a job, she says, and then unable to go home because she lacked money to bribe the border guards and pay the fines owed to her North Korean factory bosses for missing work without permission. It sounds as if there is more to her story than she is willing to tell.

Instead, she wants to talk about the good people and kind deeds she encountered in her flight to South Korea: the Chinese Christian who found a place where she could live and who introduced her to Pastor Buck; the Chinese policeman who raided her apartment and discovered her hiding in a closet but decided not to arrest her; and above all, Pastor Buck, who is at the top of her list of Good Samaritans. His first act of kindness was to give her a job while she was hiding in China. His second charitable act was even more profound: He personally led her out of China on the new underground railroad.

Mrs. Choi is an example of a North Korean refugee who is thriving in the South. She is a natural leader whose organizational and business talents have been liberated by the opportunities she enjoys in a free society. But the cost is dear. The smile disappears from her face when she mentions briefly the children she left behind in North Korea. "I had three daughters," she says. "They were four, six, and eight back then." She uses the past tense.

Later, the leader of the dance troupe attempts to explain the emotional pain that North Koreans carry with them to South Korea. Life is good in South Korea, she says, and North Koreans who make it there are rewarded with an abundance of material success. If you work hard, you can find a well-paying job, make money, create a good life for yourself.

"But the reality is devastating," she says. "You can't imagine how it is." North Koreans who succeed in building new lives in South Korea can never forget the families they left behind in North Korea or China. It is a burden every North Korean carries with him to the South. "There's one sky," she says, pointing to the dull, wintry sky outside the window. "We're all living under the same sky." The gray outside is a reflection of her somber mood. "For people like us, with children and parents still in North Korea, not a single day goes by without aching."

The dancer's concerns about her absent family are shared by virtually every North Korean who flees. Many of the North Koreans who make it to the South arrive alone, cut off from families still living in North Korea or China. They often see themselves as leading the way, blazing a trail for the spouses, siblings, parents, and children they have left behind. As they struggle to succeed in their new homes, the newcomers often share the same deep ambitions: Work hard, save money, obtain passage for their families on the new underground railroad.

LEFT BEHIND

The most effective means of control that the Kim family dictatorship exercises over the North Korean people is its policy of punishing the families of transgressors. Consider this North Korean joke that offers some black humor on the subject:

Kim Jong Il and Vladimir Putin are having a summit meeting in Moscow. During a break, they're bored, and they decide to take a bet to see whose bodyguards are more loyal.

Putin calls his bodyguard Ivan, opens the window of their twentieth-floor meeting room, and says: "Ivan, jump!"

Sobbing, Ivan says: "Mr. President, how can you ask me to do that? I have a wife and child waiting for me at home."

Putin sheds a tear himself, apologizes to Ivan, and sends him away.

Next, it's Kim Jong Il's turn. He calls his bodyguard Lee Myung-man and yells: "Lee Myung-man, jump!"

Not hesitating for a second, Lee Myung-man is just about to jump out the window when Putin grabs him and says: "Are you out of your mind? If you jump out this window, you'll die! This is the twentieth floor!"

Lee Myung-man tries to escape Putin's embrace and jump out the window: "President Putin, please let me go! I have a wife and child waiting for me at home!"[1]

The joke's humor, such as it is, requires the listener to grasp the utterly brutal nature of the Kim regime's control over its citizens. The first thought of each bodyguard is the same: how to protect his wife and children. But unlike Ivan, it does not occur to the North Korean bodyguard to ask for mercy. Vladimir Putin, a former KGB agent, may yet have a heart; Kim Jong Il does not. The North Korean bodyguard knows that the only way to save his family is to show total and immediate obedience, even if it means leaping to his death out the window of a skyscraper.

A top priority of North Koreans who escape is protecting their families back home. When they leave their country illegally, they know they are putting their loved ones in jeopardy. Even after they have permanently resettled in South Korea or elsewhere, many North Koreans refuse to use their real names or have their pictures taken, citing concern for their families still in the North. A survey of refugees in China found that an astonishing 99 percent of respondents feared for the safety or survival of their families in North Korea.[2]

The range of punishments meted out to the families of escaped North Koreans varies widely. The punishment can depend on the importance of the person who left, the political climate in Pyongyang at the time, and the often capricious attitudes of the local authorities. Some families are left alone or, at worst, called in to their local police station for a reprimand that may include some roughing-up. In other cases, families lose their homes and are banished to remote villages as punishment for their relative's escape. In still other instances, families simply disappear, taken away in the middle of the night to an unknown, presumably highly unpleasant, location. Families of political defectors have been known to end up in the gulag or suffer fatal "accidents." In early 2012, reports from news organizations and humanitarian groups with sources in North Korea told of families who were forcibly relocated to rural locations in the interior of the country as punishment for a relative's escape.

After reaching safety in South Korea or elsewhere, refugees, like immigrants everywhere else in the world, send regular remittances to their relatives back home. The difference is that a North Korean cannot walk into a bank or a Western Union affiliate and arrange to do so. There are no official channels through which to send money to an individual in North Korea. Refugees instead must seek out informal means, usually brokers who specialize in transferring money into the country. The initial point of contact is often a North Korean resident of South Korea who has gone into the business of helping new arrivals reach out to their relatives; such a broker often works with a network of helpers in China. Many of the South Korea–based brokers are refugees from the North who rely on the knowledge and skills they acquired while on the run in China. They typically employ Chinese citizens of Korean heritage. The brokers provide communication and financial services. They set up illegal cellphone calls with refugees' relatives, and they carry in cash.

Making a phone call to a relative in North Korea isn't a matter of flipping open a cellphone and punching in a long series of numbers. First, a refugee or his broker must hire a courier in China. The courier will cross the river, go to the relative's house in North Korea, knock on his door, and deliver a Chinese cellphone with prepaid minutes on it. The North Korean resident will be instructed to travel to a border town at a specified time, turn on the phone, and wait for a call from his relative. The cellphone captures a signal from China, not North Korea. It is illegal to possess such phones, so the owner must bury it or otherwise hide it until he needs to use it.

Mobile phone service was introduced to North Korea in 2008, when the Egyptian telecommunications company Orascom formed a joint venture with a state-run North Korean firm.[3] Service was limited to Pyongyang at first, then spread to other cities. By mid-2011, Orascom said that it had more than six hundred thousand subscribers. By early 2012, it was boasting that it had one million subscribers, or more than 4 percent of the North Korean market. Visitors to Pyongyang reported that their guides all seemed to be using mobile phones, and the government reportedly was encouraging cellphone use among officials.

The Orascom phones are useless, however, for communicating with the outside world. In keeping with Pyongyang's policy of closing off access to the rest of the world, phone service is limited to domestic calls. International calls are blocked. Nor can North Koreans make calls to foreigners inside North Korea. The phone numbers assigned to foreigners living in North Korea are different from the phone numbers assigned to North Koreans; it is impossible to make calls between them. In any case, the authorities can monitor phone calls and do so.[4] The government confiscates the cellphones of foreign visitors when they enter the country and returns them upon departure.

The process for sending money home to North Korea is labor-intensive. If the refugee is living in China, he will give cash to a broker, who will in turn hire someone to deliver it by hand to the relative in North Korea. If the refugee is living in South Korea or elsewhere in the free world, the refugee will arrange for the money to be transferred electronically to the Chinese broker's bank account. Next, a middleman, usually a Chinese citizen, will cross the border and deliver the money, in cash, to the designated recipients. If the recipient doesn't live near the border, the broker might hire a local courier to deliver the money elsewhere in the country. North Koreans who have settled in the South secretly send some $10 million a year to their families in the North, according to at least one estimate.[5] The broker's service fee is usually 30 percent.[6]

A survey conducted by a South Korean nonprofit found that 71 percent of refugees settled in the South have tried to send money to family members in the North.[7] "Tried" is the operative word. Many of the respondents said they believed the money did not reach their relatives. Sending cash through brokers is a risky business, and gullible North Korean refugees, often desperate to help their families, are easy prey for unscrupulous brokers. There are many stories of brokers who take a refugee's money and disappear.

If a remittance gets through, the recipients also receive something even more valuable than the money: information. A North Korean refugee identified only as "Kang" explained to a South Korean newspaper how the process works. "When we make remittances to our loved ones in the North, we talk to them over the phone to ensure the money was properly sent," he told the *Korea Herald*. "Through such talks, a wave of news about the capitalist society flows in and spreads there."[8]

Since the early 2000s, as an increasing number of North Koreans reached South Korea, the brokers' range of services has expanded beyond setting up phone calls and helping refugees transfer money to relatives. A new service has been added: people smuggling. One sub-specialty of brokers specializes in extracting North Koreans from their country and delivering them to China. Another sub-specialty focuses on getting North Koreans out of China on the underground railroad to a third country, from where they go on to South Korea. Many brokers work in tandem with Christians and other humanitarian workers.

Brokers are critical to the smooth operation of the new underground railroad. There are unscrupulous people in this business, to be sure, and nasty stories abound of brokers betraying their clients. But it would be wrong to tar all brokers as such. The best brokers understand that if they want to stay in business, they have to deliver what they promise. As with legitimate service businesses, reputation is the key to success. They are in the business of smuggling people, which means that they take risks. It also means they expect to make a profit. If they fail, the émigré grapevine will ostracize them and their business won't succeed.

"Brokers are a necessary evil." That statement is heard over and over again from refugees, humanitarian workers, and, off the record, from South Korean government officials. A Unification Ministry official concedes, "Without brokers, it would be almost impossible for North Koreans to bring their children here."[9]

The majority of North Koreans who reach the South today are women. If they are mothers, getting their children out of North Korea or China is often their top priority. This was the case with one woman, now settled in the South, who asked me not to use her real name. Ten years after "Ms. Lee" escaped from North Korea, her dearest dream came true. Her daughter joined her in Seoul.[10] The story of how Ms. Lee orchestrated her daughter's escape—first from North Korea and then from China—is typical of how such rescues work.

Ms. Lee is a businesswoman in her forties. She is well educated and possesses a generous share of street smarts. She approached her daughter's escape in the same way that she would approach an important business deal, giving it her full attention and checking and double-checking every detail. She was unlikely to be taken advantage of by any of the con men in the underground.

Before giving her daughter the green light to cross the river, Ms. Lee did her homework on the brokers and possible escape routes. The refugee network in Seoul helped her evaluate the reliability of various brokers and make decisions about whom to trust. So did her contacts among Christians who worked on the new underground railroad. An American who rescues trafficked women gave her an introduction to his network of helpers in China.

Ms. Lee had been praying for years to be reunited with her daughter. After her initial escape from North Korea in 1999, she had no contact with her husband and daughter for three years. She spent some of that period in a North Korean prison, where she was incarcerated after having been arrested in China and repatriated. When she was released from prison, she returned immediately to China.

In 2002, while in China for the second time, Ms. Lee saved enough money to hire a Chinese broker to track down her family's whereabouts and set up a phone call. The broker discovered that Ms. Lee's husband and daughter had been expelled from Pyongyang, where they had been living at the time of Ms. Lee's original departure, and assigned to live in a city in the undesirable far north of the country. Only ideologically pure citizens are permitted to live in the capital city, where they have better access to food, good housing, and jobs. That category does not include those who have a relative who left the country illegally. After the broker tracked down Ms. Lee's husband and daughter, he set up a phone call.

At the time of that first phone call in 2002, Ms. Lee tried to persuade her husband to let their daughter join her in China. But he refused: Crossing the river was too dangerous, and living in China was too full of risks. The girl was only thirteen. In China, she ran the risk of being sold as a bride or pressed into service in the sex industry. If she was captured and repatriated, she might not survive the inevitable stay in a detention center. The husband's fears were not without basis.

Once Ms. Lee reached South Korea later that year, she tried again to persuade her husband to let their daughter leave. He continued to refuse. So she gave up. "I was living my own life in South Korea, and she was living her life in the North," she said. She continued to send money to her daughter, and they would talk on the phone once in a while. But she did not again raise the subject of the girl joining her in the South.

One day in early 2009, she was surprised to answer the phone and hear her daughter's voice. The young woman, now nineteen years old, was calling from the home of the broker Ms. Lee had been using in North Korea to send money and arrange phone calls. Her daughter had traveled to the broker's house in a border town several times in the past to receive calls from her mother, and she had memorized the address. This time she went to the broker's house on her own initiative and asked him to place the call for her. She did not tell her father what she was doing.

Once she had her mother on the line, she made an announcement. "I want to go to South Korea," she told Ms. Lee. "What should I do?"

Ms. Lee sprang into action. She had been working with the broker in North Korea for a decade and believed she could trust him to get her daughter out of North Korea safely. With the help of her Christian contacts, she lined up another broker in Seoul who specialized in extractions from China. She gave the two brokers each other's phone numbers and instructed them to come up with an exit plan. The North Korean broker agreed to manage the girl's crossing into China. He would get her as far as Yanji City in China, close to the North Korean border. After that, a Chinese guide hired by the broker in Seoul would take over. The guide would escort the young woman across the country to Southeast Asia.

One of the decisions the broker in South Korea had to make, in consultation with Ms. Lee, was what third country the daughter should use as her springboard to South Korea. Ms. Lee's broker worked in three countries: Laos, Cambodia, and Thailand. They decided on Cambodia, where the broker had a reliable team and where, they believed, the political climate was welcoming at the time and the South Korean Embassy would not turn her away. The Chinese guide would see the girl to the Laotian border. She would walk across that border on her own and then meet up by prearrangement with a local guide. The Laotian guide would escort her to the Mekong

River and put her on a boat that would take her to Cambodia. At that point a local Cambodian guide would take over. He would take her to Phnom Penh and drop her off at the South Korean Embassy. The entire operation, from Yanji City in the northeast of China to Phnom Penh in south-central Cambodia, would take a week.

Bringing her daughter to Seoul was not cheap. The portion of the journey from North Korea to China would cost $2,000, Ms. Lee was told. The journey from China to Phnom Penh would require an additional $3,000. Ms. Lee did not blink at the costs. She had done her research and knew that these fees were in the normal range, in line with what others were paying for the same services. "There are set prices for getting people out of North Korea and for getting them out of China," she explained. "These are separate operations."

Although Ms. Lee had high confidence in the brokers handling her daughter's extraction, she knew that the trip was hazardous and that even with the best planning, something could go wrong. For the mother, the scariest part of the journey was the week her daughter stayed in China. "There was nothing to worry about in North Korea," she said with a dismissive wave of the hand, referring to the planned escape from that country. The corruption that infuses every aspect of life in North Korea provided her some measure of comfort in these circumstances. Just about everything in North Korea can be had for a price, she said. "As long as there is money, any problem can be solved in North Korea."

China was a different story. Ms. Lee knew from her personal experience that China is an extremely dangerous place for a North Korean refugee. You couldn't count on the corruptibility of Chinese officials. Many would accept bribes, but not all, and not all officials were corruptible. Money didn't always get you out of a fix. "My daughter could be caught and repatriated," she said. "I knew that as soon as she left China, she would be safe."

Her biggest fear was that her daughter would be arrested in China and repatriated. Springing someone from jail in North Korea was possible, but it cost a lot of money, it took time, and the prisoner might not survive. If her daughter were accused of a political crime—such as planning to go to South Korea—and sent to a political prison, it would be even harder to spring her.

Before the girl departed from North Korea, Ms. Lee gave her some advice. Trust the guides and follow their instructions completely, she told her. Second, get new clothes. The guides would probably give her Chinese-made clothes, but if they didn't, she instructed the girl to insist on them and to throw away her North Korean ones. She needed to be as inconspicuous as possible.

Ms. Lee had two conversations with her daughter during her week in China and one thereafter. The first call was from a safe house in Beijing—the girl used her guide's phone to call her mother. She placed the second call when she was about to cross the border into Laos. They had one final phone conversation before their reunion in Seoul—the daughter called right after arriving in Cambodia. She phoned her mother to say that she was safe.

After those three phone conversations, Ms. Lee had no word for seven months. She later learned that her daughter spent four months in Cambodia waiting for an exit visa and three months in Seoul being vetted by the National Intelligence Service. The daughter then was released to Hanawon, where she finally was reunited with her mother.

Ms. Lee's daughter was nine years old when they parted in 1999; she was twenty when the two met again in 2009. As Ms. Lee entered the large conference room where they were to meet, she looked at the sea of faces and had a sudden flash of anxiety that she would not recognize the young woman who had been a child when she last saw her. Then she spotted her daughter across the room, and her anxiety melted away in an instant. "I could tell from a distance that she was my daughter," Ms. Lee said. "And my daughter also recognized me."

Ms. Lee's daughter represents a new wave of arrivals in the South: North Koreans who arrive straight from the North after only brief stays in China. Their numbers are growing as more North Koreans settle in South Korea and save enough money to buy their relatives out of both countries.

According to Youn Mi-rang, director general of Hanawon, almost 30 percent of the North Koreans who reached the South in 2009 arrived within a year of leaving North Korea. She believes this is a record and predicts that the trend will continue.[11]

Many of these new-wave arrivals were the teenage or adult children of refugees who previously had escaped to South Korea. Their escapes were organized and paid for by relatives, usually their mothers. Women who set the goal for themselves of bringing their children to the South "have a purpose in life," Director Youn said. They often work harder than other refugees, with the objective of saving enough money to free their relatives.

In Youn's view, refugees who come straight from North Korea tend to exhibit fewer psychological problems than refugees who have spent time in China. About 25 percent of the refugees who reach South Korea suffer from post-traumatic stress disorder, she said. Women who were sold as brides or into the sex industry in China are especially vulnerable to lingering psychological disorders. Many refugees also have to cope with the guilt they feel about deserting their families in China or North Korea, especially if they left behind children. Hanawon has a psychiatrist on staff and also provides guidance in how to handle stress.

North Koreans who come directly to the South from North Korea, with only short stays in China, are less likely to display symptoms of post-traumatic stress disorder, according to Youn. Of course, some do suffer from lasting stress. "Some of them witnessed executions, or some might have experienced imprisonment or torture," and they have a hard time dealing with those memories, she said. But as a general matter, according to Youn, the shorter the period of escape, the less the disorder. Refugees in the new wave have another advantage if they have a family member to show them the ropes and provide emotional support in South Korea

Not everyone who works with displaced North Koreans shares Youn's view. Others observe that refugees who experience the relative freedoms of China before settling in free countries often fare better than those coming directly from the North. The North Koreans get used to making decisions for themselves in China, they say. This gives them an edge when they reach their final destination.

North Koreans who have made it to safety in South Korea or elsewhere do not always have an easy time persuading their family members to join them. Relatives can be reluctant to leave, said Lee Keum-soon, of the Korean Institute for National Unification, a government-sponsored think tank in Seoul.[12] In addition to fears of being shot, captured, arrested, or repatriated, they also are sometimes afraid of moving to South Korea or the United States. These countries are portrayed in venomous ways by the North's propaganda machine. Even though their relatives assure them otherwise, it's hard for some North Koreans to believe that the American "jackals" or their South Korean "lackeys" won't execute them after they arrive in South Korea. Making the decision to leave North Korea is not easy, even when a family member encourages the relative to depart, makes all the arrangements, and pays the bill.

The story of two sisters—call them "Sun-mi" and "Bo-mi"—is a case in point. I met the sisters in a safe house in Southeast Asia run by LiNK. They had escaped from North Korea three months earlier.[13]

The sisters, ages seventeen and nineteen, lived in a city in a northern province of North Korea. One day in the summer of 2010, they heard a knock on the front door. Sun-mi opened it to find a stranger who said she was an emissary from the girls' father, who had disappeared from home three years earlier. The girls assumed their dad had gone to China, but they had not been able to confirm this. They had heard no word from him since he left, and they didn't know whether he was alive or dead. He could be in China, or he could have been caught or killed while attempting to cross the river. Now, three years after his disappearance, the woman at their front door said their father was safe and wanted to talk to Sun-mi on the phone. The courier wanted to take Sun-mi to a location nearer the border so they could capture a Chinese phone signal and Sun-mi could place a call to her father.

Sun-mi refused. "I didn't trust her," she said. "I thought she was going to take me away and then I'd be kidnapped, taken to China, and sold to a Chinese man."

Five days later the woman returned, and this time Sun-mi's curiosity got the better of her. Maybe her father really did want to get in touch with them. The woman knew the sisters' names and seemed to know all about them. So perhaps she really was a messenger from their father. She decided to take the risk and go with the woman.

The woman turned out to be legitimate. She took Sun-mi to a town near the border and placed the call to her father. It was the first time Sun-mi had heard her father's voice in more than three years. He was as gruff and as blunt as she remembered. "Get off the phone and go to China," he ordered.

It took two more phone calls before Sun-mi was convinced. She finally agreed to go to China, and she promised her father that she would take her sister with her. Sun-mi knew that persuading Bo-mi to accompany her would take some doing. Bo-mi had a special terror of crossing the river, fearing she would be shot in the back by North Korean border guards. But Sun-mi calculated that the prospect of staying home alone without her older sister would be more terrifying to Bo-mi than crossing the river. She was right. Bo-mi reluctantly agreed to go.

Sun-mi had one more phone call with her father before leaving North Korea. In the final conversation just before the girls' departure, their father gave Sun-mi some last-minute instructions: The broker will handle everything, he told her. Just do whatever you're told. And by the way, he had something to tell her that he hadn't mentioned before. He was in America. In a place called Florida. The sisters were going to join him there.

Sun-mi couldn't believe her ears. America was the evil country she had learned about at school. Americans wanted to kill North Koreans. She remembered a poster on the wall of her classroom that depicted an American soldier bayoneting a North Korean baby during the Korean War. When she told Bo-mi that they were going to join their father in America, her little sister freaked out. There was no way she was going to America. Sun-mi had to resort to a lie before she could get Bo-mi to go along. We'll stay in China for just a few months, she promised, and then we'll return home.

The girls obeyed their father and went to China, where they spent less than a week. When I met them, they were in Southeast Asia, waiting to go to America to join their father in the place called Florida.

South Korea accepted a total of 2,927 North Koreans in 2009, according to the annual tally by the Ministry of Unification. Using Youn Mi-rang's estimate that 30 percent of that year's arrivals came directly to the South from North Korea, we can estimate that nearly nine hundred of the arrivals were new-wave refugees. Of those, most were North Koreans reuniting with family members.

The recent reunions of North Korean family members hold special poignancy when set in the context of the postwar history of the two Koreas, when about ten million Koreans were separated from relatives. Today, newly arrived North Korean refugees, working through unofficial channels, are able to reunite with their families, a goal that mostly has eluded an older generation of refugees for more than half a century. Most of the Korean War generation of refugees from the North do not even know whether the relatives they left behind in the North are alive or dead. The South Korean government estimated in 2011 that between four and five thousand elderly South Koreans with family members in the North are dying every year without having received news from their loved ones.

Over the years, the governments in Seoul and Pyongyang have permitted a limited number of brief reunions of families divided by the Korean War to take place under tightly controlled conditions. The first reunions were held in 1985, after thirteen years of negotiations. In that year, the governments of the two Koreas arranged highly publicized family meetings in each other's capitals under the auspices of the Red Cross organization of each county. Fifty family members participated from each side. North Korea canceled the family reunions in 1986 in protest over joint U.S.–South Korean military exercises.

Fifteen years passed before the next reunions took place in 2000. These reunions were a by-product of the historic summit meeting in Pyongyang that June between Kim Jong Il and South Korean President Kim Dae-jung. This time, one hundred family members participated from each side. In Seoul, seventy thousand family members applied for the one hundred slots, which were decided by lottery. In the words of one disappointed man, "This was like giving steak to only one hundred selected people, while a million others can't even eat porridge."[14] In Pyongyang, the selection process was not left to chance. The regime selected the one hundred participants.

Between 2000 and early 2011, seventeen rounds of family reunions took place along with seven rounds of video reunions. A total of 28,848 Koreans from 4,130 families met with relatives on "the other side." In 2008, the South Korean government completed construction of an expensive family reunion center at Mount Kumgang, a tourist site in North Korea developed with South Korean money for the use of South Korean tourists.

There is a special kind of cruelty in these family reunions, which are limited to a few days. South Koreans arrive with food and expensive gifts for their relatives, who may or may not be permitted to keep them. Watchers are always nearby and privacy is limited. The joy of seeing one's brother or sister or mother or father again is mitigated by the knowledge that the meeting is temporary and that this is probably the last time the family will be together. Lifetimes have to be recounted in hours, and at the end of the appointed time, the families must part again, with no assurance that Pyongyang will permit even an exchange of letters.

North Korea "fattened up" citizens selected for these reunions, according to a classified cable filed by the American Embassy in Seoul in 2009 and disclosed by Wikileaks.[15] North Koreans are chosen to participate in the reunions based on their loyalty to the state, the cable said. They are "transported to Pyongyang and then fattened up with regular meals and vitamins to mask the extent of the food shortages and chronic malnutrition in the North." The North Korean participants receive new clothing—suits for men, the traditional high-waisted Korean *hanbok* dresses for women—that they must return to the government after the reunions along with any cash they have received from their relatives.

For Pyongyang, separated family members are useful hostages in its dealings with Seoul. In the late 1990s and early 2000s, the administration of President Kim Dae-jung reportedly gave large donations of food and fertilizer to facilitate the reunions. The Mount Kumgang family-reunion center sits on twelve acres of land and consists of three buildings paid for by the South Korean government.

Pyongyang has also used separated family members to extract ransoms from wealthy South Koreans desperate to obtain information about their relatives. In 2000, South Korea's Unification Ministry reported that 525 South Koreans had succeeded in meeting their families in China after working with private agencies in that country. The middlemen for these private reunions were North Korean agents working in China or Japanese-Koreans with ties to Pyongyang. Family-reunion fees ranged from several thousand dollars to hundreds of thousands of dollars; a hefty chunk of these sums went to the North Korean government.

In 1998, a South Korean television network aired a documentary about a celebrity singer from the South, Hyon Mi, who was reunited with her sister from North Korea in the Chinese city of Changchung thanks to the services of one such private agency. The documentary was hugely popular, but it provoked bitter feelings from some viewers, such as a seventy-eight-year-old man quoted by the *Korea Herald*. His wife and children were lost in North Korea, he told the reporter. "Is is fair that only famous and well-to-do people are allowed to meet lost relatives?" he asked. "For many years, I have tried to find my family in the North. But now I wonder if a poor person like me can meet his family while still alive."[16]

Over coffee in Seoul one afternoon, Kim Duk-hong, a prominent defector from North Korea, described to me how he had operated a profitable family-reunification business in China in the 1990s. Kim Duk-hong arrived in South Korea in 1997 along with his boss Hwang Jong-yap, the highest ranking defector ever to leave the North. Family reunification was a side business for Kim Duk-hong, whose real job in China was running an institute dedicated to spreading North Korea's *juche* ideology. Pyongyang had ordered him to raise money to fund his institute, and as he cast around for ideas to carry out the orders, he saw a market opportunity in the family-reunification racket. South Korea and China had established diplomatic ties in 1992, making it easier for South Koreans to visit China. South Koreans would pay handsomely for the opportunity to meet long-lost relatives from North Korea, he reasoned.

Kim Duk-hong was a member of the powerful Central Committee of the Workers' Party. As such, as he delicately put it, "I could easily search the national registry" that contains information about every North Korean. "I would check the social security numbers and then find them," he said.[17]

At the request of a South Korean family, Kim Duk-hong's business would track down a missing relative in North Korea, arrange for him to receive an exit permit to visit China, and set up a meeting with his relatives from the South. The relatives would spend a week together before returning to their separate homes in North Korea and South Korea. "At the end they would be separated," Kim Duk-hong said, "but if the South Korean family wanted to send money, that could be arranged with my security office."

For North Korea, enforcing family separation has been an essential tactic in its strategy of isolating its citizens and forcing its will on them. In 2000, on the eve of Kim Dae-jung's summit in Pyongyang with Kim Jong Il, the Far Eastern Economic Review published an emotional essay by Don'o Kim, a Korean-Australian novelist who had been born in North Korea.

In 1950, when war broke out between North and South Korea, Don'o Kim was visiting his uncle in Seoul. He was ten years old. Kim never saw or heard from his mother again. At the time of the publication of his essay, he still did not know whether she was alive or dead. It would be a miracle, he wrote, if the summit paved the way for family reunifications. No group will welcome this more jubilantly than what he called the "38 People," Koreans like him who fled from North to South during the Korean War, crossing the 38th parallel.

The author criticized successive governments of South Korea for giving low priority to the issue of divided families, but he reserved his greatest scorn for the regime in Pyongyang. He wrote, "No government anywhere can claim to have incarcerated its people for so long and so successfully."[18]

Don'o Kim's words still hold true. North Korea remains a prison for most of its people. But not for all. The North Koreans who escape are helping to liberate their countrymen by means of the most lethal weapon their jailers have encountered: information.

PART VI

THE FUTURE

While the grand little army of abolitionists was waging its untiring warfare for freedom, prior to the rebellion, no agency encouraged them like the heroism of fugitives. The pulse of the four millions of slaves and their desire for freedom were better felt through 'The Underground Railroad' than through any other channel.

—WILLIAM STILL
PREFACE TO THE REVISED EDITION OF THE
UNDERGROUND RAILROAD RECORD
SEPTEMBER 1878

INVADING NORTH KOREA

An invasion of North Korea has already begun. No soldiers or tanks are involved, and not a single bullet will be fired. Rather, the weapons are cellphones, radios, flash drives, DVDs, and videotapes. It is an information invasion, not a military one, and the strategic objectives are far-reaching: Open the country to information from the outside world, nurture dissent, destroy the Kim family regime.

North Korea long has been the most closed nation on earth and its people the least informed about the world outside its borders. It is the world's worst media environment. As noted earlier, radio, television, cellphones, and the Internet are all tightly controlled by the state. Radios are fixed to state-run stations and must be registered with the government. Only government-approved shows are broadcast on television. Cellphones are configured so as to be limited to domestic calls, and a user would be safe to assume his line is tapped.

Computer users—about 15 percent of the population—may access only the government-run Intranet, and even then they must receive special clearance by the state. Access to the Web is reserved for a tiny super-elite.

The international media organization, Reporters Without Borders, routinely ranks North Korea at the bottom of its annual index of global press freedom, in the company of Sudan, Syria, Burma, Iran, Turkmenistan, and other totalitarian states. One report from Reporters Without Borders neatly describes the job of the North Korean journalist as "feeding the public mind-numbing propaganda." It characterizes the journalist's job as publicizing the greatness of Kim Il Sung and Kim Jong Il, demonstrating the superiority of North Korean socialism, and criticizing the imperialist actions of the United States, South Korea, and Japan. At least forty North Korean journalists have been sent to prison for crimes such as misspelling a senior official's name or questioning the official version of Korea's history.[1]

So controlled are the media that when the state-run television network broadcast the British-made soccer film *Bend It Like Beckham*, in December 2010, the event made international headlines. According to the British government, which arranged for the film to air in honor of the tenth anniversary of the establishment of diplomatic ties between London and Pyongyang, this was the first time that a Western movie had been shown on television in North Korea. Even so, the North Korean censors did not permit viewers to see the film in its entirety. The network broadcast a bowdlerized version, minus the bits on religion, interracial marriage, and homosexuality. These subjects are taboo in North Korea.

Much has been written about the liberating power of information technology. The world saw its effect in Beijing in 1989, when democracy activists used facsimile machines to tell the outside world what was happening in Tiananmen Square, an event that prompted the late American strategic thinker Albert Wohlstetter to quip, "the fax shall make you free." The Buddhist monks who led a push for freedom in Burma in 2007 communicated with each other and the outside world through text messaging. A few years later, the Tunisian, Egyptian, and Libyan rebels who overthrew their country's long-standing authoritarian leaders became friends on Facebook, micro-blogged on Twitter, and posted video and photographs on YouTube.

None of that could happen North Korea—yet. In information-technology terms, North Korea is locked in a time warp. It is Ground Hog's Day 1953 over and over again. Founder Kim Il Sung understood the power of information, and after the Korean War ended, he made sure that his regime had a monopoly on it. It was a lesson that the late Kim Jong Il also learned and that he appears to have handed down to his son and heir, Kim Jong Eun, who has taken steps to seal off the border with China. None of the modern technologies that connect us to each other and the world at large are available in North Korea. There is no text messaging, no email, no photo sharing, no social networking.

Even a low-tech form of information technology—the mail service—is highly restricted. North Korea is a member of the Universal Postal Union, but it has direct postal service with a limited number of countries. South Korea is not among them. Contrast this with East and West Germany. Throughout the Cold War, Germans in one part of the divided country could send letters to their relatives in the other part of the country. Koreans have not been able to do so for sixty years. If a South Korean wants to communicate with a North Korean, there are no institutional channels by which to do so.

But all this is changing, made possible by the North Koreans who have fled to China and, especially, by those who have gone on to South Korea or the West. North Koreans may be in exile, but they are determined to find ways to communicate with their families and friends at home. The leaders of the information invasion are North Koreans now in exile and intent on getting information into and out of their country.

In South Korea, the North Korean diaspora has established an array of nonprofit organizations aimed at prying open North Korea by providing its citizens with information banned there. Four independent radio stations, founded and staffed by refugees, broadcast from Seoul to North Korea. A Web magazine run by exiles is publishing information gathered by a stable of covert reporters operating in North Korea. A think tank is developing back-channel lines of communications with intellectuals and military officers in North Korea. These efforts are funded by private sources from South Korea and, in the United States, by the State Department and the National Endowment for Democracy, a nonprofit, bipartisan organization created by Congress in 1983 to strengthen democratic institutions around the world through nongovernmental efforts. In 2011, the National Endowment for Democracy spent $1.3 million on programs supporting human rights, development, and democracy in North Korea.

North Korean exiles perform three essential functions in opening up their homeland. Above all, they are conduits of information. Through calls on illegal Chinese cellphones, remittances, and other interactions, the refugees provide a window on the wider world to family members still locked inside North Korea. Word of mouth may be a pre-technology way of spreading information, but it is effective. When North Koreans hear a trusted relative describe his life in South Korea, his conversion to Christianity, or his new understanding of North Korea's history, they are likely to believe what he says, even when it contradicts Pyongyang's propaganda.

Second, North Koreans who settle in South Korea serve as a "bridge population," in the words of the president of the National Endowment of Democracy, Carl Gershman. The exiled North Koreans link their homeland with South Korea and the world at large. These people, Gershman said, are "giving voice to the voiceless society left behind."[2]

In this respect, the information invasion works two ways. First, it ferrries information about the outside world into North Korea. Second, it enables exiles to get information out of North Korea. In addition to educating their fellow citizens left behind in North Korea, the exiles are also finding success in interpreting their secretive country to the larger world. In recent years, a mini-surge of books, articles, documentaries, TV shows, and websites has presented refugees' stories about life in North Korea. These have given the world an unprecedented window on life in North Korea. It is harder than it ever was for anyone—especially South Koreans—to hide their heads in the sand and pretend they do not know the brutal realities of life in that country.

Third, as a population acculturated to the South but with roots in the North, the refugees are preparing for the eventual integration of North Korea into a united Korea. They will be a vital resource when that occurs. This is especially true of the under-thirty generation. As was the case in Eastern Europe after the collapse of Communism, young North Koreans are more intellectually malleable, more open to new ideas than their elders are. Gershman calls them the 1.5 generation. He says these young exiles are sucking up information about the Western world: "how people in South Korea and other countries respect and defend human rights and democracy, how political parties organize and campaign, how workers fight for their rights and entrepreneurs compete in the marketplace, how journalists report the news and NGOs educate, defend, and give voice to society."

Young North Korean exiles are also more receptive than their elders are to South Korea's culture of education and hard work. When the time comes for rebuilding North Korea, the corps of educated and highly motivated North Koreans in exile will be a valuable resource.

One of the generals in the information war is Kim Seong-min, a former propaganda officer in the Korean People's Army. He now runs Free North Korea Radio, a shortwave radio station in Seoul that broadcasts news into North Korea. Free North Korea Radio went on the air in December 2005 with the goal of breaking the regime's lock on information. It is one of four independent, refugee-run radio stations in Seoul that broadcast information into North Korea.

Kim Seong-min arrived in Seoul in 1999. His decision to leave North Korea was heavily influenced by what he had learned from illegally listening to Voice of America and the Korean Broadcasting System. He came to realize that much of what his government was telling him was a lie.[3]

He credits a song with opening his eyes. One day he paid a visit to a friend who played the guitar. The friend played a song he had heard on a forbidden radio broadcast from South Korea. The song began with the words, "Do you know how high I can fly?" Kim could not get the uplifting lyrics out of his head. What did they mean? What kind of society would encourage such personal aspirations? The next day he bought a radio.

He soon became addicted to the foreign broadcasts. Shows about news and history were his favorites. He especially liked a program called "True History," which debunked the false information taught in North Korean schoolbooks. He recalls his initial disbelief at hearing that Kim Jong Il was born in a village in the Soviet Union, not under a double rainbow on the sacred Mount Paektu, as North Korean propaganda taught. Or that the Korean War began when Kim Il Sung's forces invaded the South on June 25, 1950, not with an invasion of the North by American and South Korean forces. At first he didn't believe what he was hearing, but the more he listened, and the more evidence the show presented, the more he began to doubt the truthfulness of the North Korean textbooks.

He recalls, too, his astonishment at hearing a radio interview with a North Korean defector who had escaped to the South. Kim

Seong-min had believed the regime's propaganda that Seoul would execute any North Korean who fled to South Korea. Yet there was the defector, telling radio listeners about his job, his apartment, his new life in Seoul, courtesy of the South Korean government. The experience gave Kim Seong-min the courage to dream about going to South Korea. It also taught him about the power of information to change minds.

Kim Seong-min was risking his livelihood and perhaps his life by listening to foreign radio broadcasts. As a mechanical matter, it's relatively easy to unscrew the back of a radio and adjust the set so it can receive frequencies other than those of state-run stations. But tampering with a radio is a serious crime. Kim Seong-min knew people who had disappeared into the gulag for doing so. Radio owners are required to register the serial number of their set with the police, and refugees recount stories of officials conducting snap inspections of owners' homes to make sure the radios had not been adjusted. Police periodically searched Kim Song-min's military barracks, looking for radios that had been tampered with. He prepared an explanation in case police questioned him: Listening to the enemy was important in his work as a propaganda officer. In the event, he was never caught.

The South Korean broadcasts on KBS, the Korean Broadcasting System, stopped airing criticism of the North in the early 2000s, when President Kim Dae-jung deemed it unnecessarily provocative. Kim Seong-min, by then in Seoul, started Free North Korea Radio to fill that void. In a repressive society, he said, people need more than food aid. They need food that can stir their minds.

Walk into Free North Korea Radio's office in downtown Seoul, and its mission is immediately evident. A huge framed sign presides like a guardian angel over the newsroom. The cursive Korean letters, painted in a bold, black script, read: *"Toward freedom! Toward democracy! Toward reunification!"* These same words begin every broadcast.

Kim Seong-min is a fiery speaker with a vision of a free and unified Korea. In 2006, he met at the White House with President

George W. Bush. When the world's most powerful man asked him what he would do to help North Korea if he were president of the United States, Kim Seong-min's reply was unhesitating: "Accept the refugees in China, all of them." Welcoming North Korean refugees to the United States would send an important message to Kim Jong Il as well as to the people of North Korea, he told Bush. It would demonstrate to North Koreans that the government's anti-American propaganda was false. By doing to, it would help to destroy the regime from within. If the United States accepted more refugees fleeing North Korea, word would filter back, more people would leave, and the regime would eventually implode.

Like Kim Seong-min, most of the reporters and editors at Free North Korea Radio have escaped from North Korea. For security reasons, no one except Kim Seong-min uses his real name on the air. The other journalists keep their identities secret. While they are afraid that Pyongyang will seek retribution against family members still living in North Korea, they also are also concerned about their own personal safety in Seoul. Free North Korea Radio lost its lease on its first office when the landlord was spooked by the number of threats against it. It no longer publishes its address. Kim Seong-min, whose work has made him one of the most prominent North Koreans in South Korea, has received numerous death threats.

Free North Korea Radio hopes to play the same role in prying open North Korea as Western radio stations played in Eastern Europe during the Cold War. Lech Walesa, the first democratically elected leader of Poland, has said that "without Western broadcasting, totalitarian regimes would have survived much longer." In Russia, as Korea scholar Peter Beck has noted, at the height of the Cold War, one-quarter of the public was listening to jammed and banned broadcasts by the Voice of America, Radio Liberty, and Radio Free Europe. The radios knew this based on interviews at that time with Russian émigrés and travelers. Recently opened Soviet archives confirm this information.[4]

A survey of North Korean exiles confirms the impact of radio broadcasts to North Korea. It is impossible to conduct social research in North Korea. Refugees in China are, however, accessible. So in 2008, the National Endowment for Democracy commissioned a survey of refugees in China to try to learn more about their radio-listening habits when they lived in North Korea. The National Endowment for Democracy has funded émigré radio stations that broadcast to North Korea and northeast China, including Free North Korea Radio, and wanted to know more about its listeners.

The survey, conducted by the InterMedia Institute, found some refugees who said they had zero access to any type of media while in North Korea. But it also found that a high percentage of respondents had owned media devices when they lived in North Korea. Radios were the most commonplace, and a majority of respondents—57 percent—owned a radio. Thirty-five percent had a color TV, and 13 percent had a black-and-white TV. Sixteen percent owned video CD players, a now mostly obsolete technology that preceded DVD players. Fifteen percent of respondents owned VCR players, and 4 percent owned DVD players. InterMedia concluded, "The fact that some people owned these modern technologies in North Korea showed that the influence of the outside world is penetrating into North Korea."[5]

Of the two hundred North Koreans surveyed in China, InterMedia reported that seventy-four people had listened to foreign radio broadcasts in North Korea. Most of those who had listened to foreign radio broadcasts at least once continued to listen regularly, data that support anecdotal evidence that the information habit is addictive. Once people start to listen, they find it hard to stop. Recent arrivals—identified as those who left after 2006—were more likely to have listened to foreign radio broadcasts in North Korea, a finding that suggests that North Koreans increasingly are disregarding the law.

Almost all—98 percent—were aware of the harsh punishments meted out for listening to foreign radio broadcasts or watching foreign films. More than a third—35 percent—knew someone who had been punished for doing so. Yet that didn't seem to deter them. [6]

In the specific case of Free North Korea Radio, the survey showed that listeners in North Korea spent at least thirty minutes every time they tuned in to the station. Some spent up to an hour. The majority said they understood the Korean language spoken by the presenters, most of whom were from North Korea and spoke with North Korean accents. Most interesting of all, more than three-quarters of listeners found Free North Korea Radio "somewhat trustworthy" or "very trustworthy." Since the content of Free North Korea Radio and the other refugee-run radio stations often contradicts what North Koreans are taught, it is noteworthy that listeners placed so much confidence in the radio's reporting. Listeners reported similarly high degrees of confidence in the reporting of Radio Free Chosun and Open Radio North Korea. InterMedia concluded that all three radio stations have their niche in North Korea and complement each other.

There is a vacuum of news and information in North Korea, and the refugee-run radio stations play a critical role in opening up the country. They are feeding North Koreans' hunger for information.

Meanwhile, inside North Korea itself, it is courageous local journalists, armed with miniature cameras and flash drives, who are helping to set their country on the path to freedom. Incredible as it may seem in a country where journalism as it is practiced in modern democracies is punishable by a trip to the gulag or public execution, such reporters are a growing phenomenon. Armed with satellite phones, easy-to-hide miniature cameras, and USB drives, these brave journalists are getting videos, photographs, and written information out of North Korea.

Several news organizations support reporters working clandestinely in North Korea. One is *Rimjin-gang* magazine, a division of

AsiaPress International, based in Osaka. The founder and editor of *Rimjin-gang* is a Japanese journalist by the name of Jiro Ishimaru. *Rimjin-gang* is the Korean name for the Imjin River, which begins in North Korea and runs south across the demilitarized zone. The name is a metaphor for the magazine's mission of North Korean journalists sending information to the South. "I came to realize that outsiders attempting to shed light on North Korea hit a wall that is simply impossible to breach," Ishimaru said. "No one can report on a nation better than its own people."[7]

Ishimaru runs a staff of eight reporters. For security reasons, each reporter operates independently. They have no knowledge of one another's identity or the stories their colleagues are reporting. The reporters are men and women who want to do something meaningful with their lives. They are patriots who want to help their country, Ishimaru said. They believe that "if you don't do something, you are just a slave."

Ishimaru recruits *Rimjin-gang*'s reporters in the border regions of northeast China from among the refugees who have fled North Korea. He and colleagues from South Korea give the budding journalists a crash course in the basics of journalism and teach them how to use essential technology. The fledgling journalists then go back to North Korea with enough money to travel around the country, pay bribes if they get into trouble, and hire help when they are ready to return to China. In North Korea, they operate under cover of their "real" jobs—housewife, truck driver, factory worker, etc.—but secretly they are taking photographs or videos and compiling information they write up when they are back in China.

It is next to impossible for ordinary North Koreans to get close to military installations, the gulag, or the Kim family. So *Rimjin-gang*'s journalists have set more realistic reporting goals for themselves. They focus on three areas: day-to-day life in North Korea, especially the regime's complicity in the starvation of its people through the withholding of food; the illegal market economy; and everyday corruption. By the end of 2010, they had produced more than one hundred hours of video on these subjects. One tape showed bags of rice labeled "WFP"—for the United Nations World Food Program—being sold in a marketplace rather than distributed to the needy. Another showed uniformed soldiers using a military truck as a private bus service for paying customers. A haunting third video showed a gaunt, disoriented young woman rummaging through a barren field in search of something to eat. *Rimjin-gang* later reported that this woman died of starvation.

Free North Korea Radio also has underground reporters in North Korea. Its journalists employ similar methods to obtain information. Like the *Rimjin-gang* journalists, they cover stories, secretly take photos or video, and then transport the tapes and flash drives across the border to China. The information they gather is then broadcast back into North Korea. There is no dissident movement in North Korea, and better information is a necessary prerequisite. In late 2009, after the regime introduced monetary reforms that wiped out the value of many people's savings, Free North Korea Radio was one of the first news organizations to report on the popular discontent that ensued. North Koreans who tuned into Free North Korea Radio heard that many of their countrymen shared the dissatisfaction they felt. They learned they were not alone.

Free North Korea Radio also broadcasts guidance for North Koreans who are thinking of trying to escape. One such story advised North Koreans to beware of the man-traps that border guards had built along the banks of the Tumen River, hoping to snare people in the process of leaving. The traps were primitive but effective—deep holes in the ground covered with brush. If someone fell into the trap, he would be unable to climb out of it. An added cruelty was the sharp spikes in the trap that would pierce the captive as he fell. Free North Korea Radio broadcast warnings about the man-traps, and the reporter's video was posted on the radio's website, where North

Koreans living in China might see it and warn family and friends who were thinking of leaving.

Some of Free North Korea Radio's programming targets the North Korean refugee community in China, where access to radio and the Internet is relatively free and where the Korean-language radio stations have a wide listenership among refugees. It invites listeners to send in comments. It broadcasts a phone number and an email address that listeners who want to escape from China can call on for assistance. Callers are directed to someone who can help them find a way to reach the new underground railroad.

North Koreans' hunger for information has created a market that Chinese entrepreneurs are seizing. Their motive is profit, not propaganda. Traders cross the border into North Korea, where they sell cheap Chinese radios that are small enough to be hidden easily but powerful enough to be tuned to foreign broadcasts. The radios cost about three dollars on the local black market. Listeners can pick up signals that allow them to listen to Korean-language stations from China as well as broadcasts from Voice of America, Radio Free Asia, and the refugee-run radio stations out of Seoul.

Traders also peddle secondhand video cassette players and video CD players from China. In China, VCR players and VCD players mostly have been replaced by newer DVD technology. Enterprising merchants buy the discarded VCD and VCR devices from their Chinese owners and sell them across the border in North Korea. They also sell the video cassettes and video CDs to play on the devices. It's against North Korean law to possess an unregistered VCD or VCR player or to watch South Korean videos, but the law-enforcement system has broken down enough that more North Koreans are taking the risk, assuming that if they get caught they can bribe local officials to look the other way.

The latest episodes of popular South Korean soap operas turn up in North Korean markets within twenty-four hours of airing.

Entrepreneurs in northeast China put satellite dishes on their roofs so they can download the shows from Korean-language TV stations, make copies, and rush them across the border into North Korea. As one refugee said, yes, North Koreans are scared to risk watching South Korea TV shows, but "the temptation to see the video, the soap opera, is much bigger than the fear of punishment." Korean-speaking visitors to Pyongyang report that the widespread familiarity with the illegal South Korean soap operas has created a new fad in the capital: speaking in a Seoulite accent.

A time-honed method of sending information into North Korea is via balloon. Balloon propaganda dates back to the early 1950s, when the governments on both sides of the newly created DMZ launched giant balloons carrying propaganda leaflets that were dropped on the other side of the border. The balloon war raged until the early 2000s, when peacemaking efforts spearheaded by then President Kim Dae-jung put an end to the government-sponsored launches. Rough estimates put the number of leaflets dropped by balloon by both Koreas at two and a half billion.

Kim Dae-jung's balloon ban did not apply to nongovernment groups, and religious and civic activists kept up the barrage of balloons flying north across the DMZ. Today the balloons have gone high-tech. They are equipped with GPS-guidance devices that enable operators to drop the contents over targeted areas. They carry DVDs, CDs, and USB drives, as well as printed material and food. Dropped leaflets are typically printed on a waterproof plastic film to make for easier reading. It is a crime for North Koreans to pick up and read the leaflets or eat the food that falls out of the sky. But anecdotal evidence from refugees who have escaped suggests that some do. In 2008, Pyongyang threatened South Korea with military action if it didn't stop the private balloon launches—a sign that the balloon drops might be having the desired effect.

The balloon drops typically contain information about current events. In 2011, that included news of the poor state of Kim Jong Il's health and the Arab Spring democracy uprisings in the Middle East. After North Korea bombed a South Korean–held island near a disputed sea border in 2010, killing four people, the South Korean government resumed its official balloon drops. In early 2011, it reportedly sent balloons to North Korea carrying food, medicine, and leaflets with news of public protests in Libya against Moammar Gadhafi, the country's longtime dictator.

In contrast to the balloon drops, which reach North Koreans mostly at random, even when they are GPS-guided, a range of efforts involving new technologies and creative means of delivery is targeting information to a more elite segment of society. The aim is to reach what a free society might call the "opinion makers." In North Korea, that means government officials, academics, and professionals.

One effort to reach the elites is led by North Korean Intellectuals Solidarity. NKIS was founded in 2008 in Seoul by so-called defector intellectuals. Members are North Koreans with college and professional degrees who have escaped to South Korea. NKIS estimated that of the fifteen thousand North Koreans living in in the South in 2008, about six hundred had such credentials. The president is Kim Heung-gwang, who was a professor of computer science in North Korea before he escaped to South Korea in 2004.

NKIS targets its peers in North Korea. It seeks to inform them about what is happening in their own country and also provide news about the rest of the world. The target audience consists of professors, students, and other highly educated North Koreans. Such people are likely to have access to computers, although not to the Internet, whose use is reserved for a tiny minority of trusted super-elites. These educated North Koreans are intellectually curious and, it is hoped, likely to be receptive to new ideas.

Hyun In-ae, vice president of NKIS and a professor of philosophy when she lived in North Korea, explained the decision to focus on the professional classes: "In order to change North Korea, people should change. It's as simple as that. We want to trigger change in North Korea." All the democratic revolutions worldwide have been led by educated, middle-class citizens, she noted. "We're not actually expecting something like civil uprising in North Korea, toppling the regime, and that kind of thing. But our expectation is that when there are changes, if we keep doing this, maybe there will be a foundation or awareness of these things so that the public can respond correctly. That's our goal."[8]

NKIS uses a variety of delivery systems to send information to North Korea. One is USB drives, which have the advantage of being portable and easy to hide. On first use, the drives appear to be blank, but after the user opens them a certain number of times, they display material that the user did not know was there. That might be a slickly produced video biography of Kim Jong Il that counters the propaganda myths about his birth. Or it could be a copy of a South Korean news show. The same technique is employed for DVDs, which are doctored to play forbidden material partway through the movie or the TV show the owner thought he was buying. Sometimes a flash drive will also contain entertainment—a computer game or a music video of a popular North Korean folk song. The expectation is that North Koreans will find the material entertaining and will be motivated to share it with friends. NKIS wants it to get passed around. "Anything going into North Korea from the outside is illegal, but a lot of people are watching foreign movies and soap operas because it's fun," Hyun In-ae said. "So long as the material is fun, it will work."

NKIS avoids direct criticism of the Kim family, judging that people would be too afraid to watch it. Such criticism crosses a red line, NKIS believes, and would be counterproductive. Illegal material is widely available now, Hyun In-ae pointed out. Many North Koreans will take the risk of watching it so long as it doesn't attack their leaders.

NKIS is also trying to spread information about democracies. It has created what Hyun In-ae calls an eBook on democracy, containing information on the history and makeup of democracies around the world. The eBook presents the history of revolutions and the grassroots movements that gave birth to them. It discusses the institutions that sustain democracies, such as an impartial judicial system. "North Koreans' idea of democracy is just that you have the right to vote—that's all," Hyun In-ae said. "But democracy is much more than that."

NKIS uses several means to get its material into North Korea, most of which it won't discuss. Sometimes it relies on Chinese traders, who take in the USB drives or DVDs and sell them on the black market. The traders think the USB drives are blank, and they don't know that the DVDs carry extra material. Another technique is to pay a courier to drop off a stack of DVDs on a street corner, leaving them for curious passersby to pick up. NKIS is working on finding ways to get its material into colleges, universities, and "genius schools," the special schools for gifted children that exist in every province. Students at genius schools have access to computers, and some have them at home.

The North Korean regime is taking increasingly strong measures to halt the information invasion. In the wake of the Arab Spring democratic uprisings in the Middle East in 2011, there were numerous reports of a new crackdown on the illegal Chinese cellphones smuggled into the country. People living in the border areas were warned to hand over unlicensed cellphones or face severe punishment. A refugee-run radio station in Seoul reported that a North

Korean was executed by firing squad after he was caught with an illegal cellphone and confessed to supplying information to someone in South Korea. There were also accounts that the North Korean government ordered institutions and households to report on how many computers, USB drives, and MP3 players they owned.

The crackdown on cellphone use was confirmed by the Venerable Pomnyun Sunim, a respected Buddhist monk and humanitarian activist in South Korea who closely follows events in North Korea. His publication *North Korea Today* provides detailed, up-to-date information about conditions on the ground in North Korea based on reports from a wide range of in-country sources. *North Korea Today* is published weekly by the organization Good Friends for Peace, Human Rights, and Refugee Issues, of which the Venerable Pomnyun serves as chairman.

The Venerable Pomnyun said the crackdown on illegal cellphones has accelerated since the death of Kim Jong Il in December 2011 and the accession of his son, Kim Jong Eun, to the supreme leadership of North Korea. Kim Jong Eun is so determined to keep information out of the country, the monk said, that he even ordered the reinvestigation of people arrested in the past for illegal cellphone use. Also according to the Venerable Pomnyun, people selling South Korean–made or Chinese goods in local markets have been arrested, and Kim Jong Eun is so fearful about the contamination of foreign ideas that he also wants to eliminate all foreign products from domestic markets. In another extreme move to keep information out of the country, the young dictator has uprooted the families of North Koreans who have fled and forcibly moved them to interior locations away from the Chinese border, making it impossible for them to receive phone calls from their relatives in China or South Korea.[9]

In June 2011, the regime announced that it was closing universities and colleges for ten months for the purpose of sending students to work in factories, farms, and construction projects throughout the countryside. The regime presented the move as a way for students to help their country achieve its goal of becoming a "great, prosperous, and powerful nation" by April 15, 2012, which marked the one-hundredth anniversary of Kim Il Sung's birth. A more plausible explanation for dispersing the students was that then dictator Kim Jong Il wanted to staunch the flow of information about the Arab Spring. Revolutions can form intellectual roots on university campuses, and the regime wanted to eradicate the possibility that student demonstrators would demand freedoms.

The upheaval in Libya and the overthrow and death of dictator Moammar Gadhafi, a so-called Revolutionary Comrade of North Korea, were especially disturbing to the Kim family regime. In October 2011, American Defense Secretary Leon Panetta said that Pyongyang refused to let two hundred North Korean contract workers return home from Libya because it feared they would spread word about Gadhafi's fate. The regime believed that if the workers returned to North Korea, "word of Gadhafi's demise and news on what's happening throughout the Arab world might reach the North Korean people," Panetta said. He called it "another example of North Korean extreme behavior."[10] According to the South Korean press, Pyongyang also refused to permit North Koreans in Egypt to return home.

The North Korean regime's response to the information invasion reflects the fundamental insecurity at the heart of every totalitarian state. Like his father and grandfather before him, Kim Jong Eun understands the subversive potential of information. He realizes how compelling liberal ideas would be if a large segment of North Korea's population were exposed to them. Even something as ordinary in the rest of the world as making a phone call to a friend or relative in another country is a threat to the regime. It exposes the caller to the truth about his own country and the world at large.

North Koreans' eyes are beginning to open. It may take a while for them to act on the information they are receiving, but in the meantime, policy makers in Washington, D.C., Seoul, and the United Nations need to become more aggressive about ensuring that the liberating power of information is available to the North Korean people.

CONCLUSION:
ONE FREE KOREA

Not long after I began the research for this book, I interviewed Kim Seong-min, the defector and former military propagandist for the Korean People's Army who now runs Free North Korea Radio in Seoul. We met on a gloomy February afternoon at his broadcasting studio in a nondescript, gray office block on the outskirts of the city. The building was situated off one of the sinuous, urban alleyways that Seoulites navigate with ease but that bewilder visitors to the city. You'll never be able to find this place, Kim Seong-min told me when I set up the appointment. He offered to send his bodyguard-driver, along with an English-speaking student intern, to pick me up at my hotel. It was a kind gesture, and I appreciated it.

In addition to being one of the most prominent North Korean defectors in South Korea, Kim Seong-min is also an outspoken and involved backer of the new underground railroad. His radio station counts many listeners among the North Korean émigré community in China. Kim Seong-min knows that North Koreans hiding in China are usually desperate, and he believes that the radio's mission includes reaching out to them in tangible ways. Toward that end, the radio maintains a hotline that listeners can phone for assistance. Callers are linked up with people who will shelter them and, if they wish, help them get out of China on the new underground railroad. Four times every hour while on the air, Free North Korea Radio broadcasts the phone number of the hotline. When we met at his studio in Seoul, Kim Seung-min recited the number by heart: "02-2699-0977." Since its start-up in 2005, Free North Korea Radio has helped a thousand North Koreans connect with the underground, he said.

As the interview came to a close, I asked Kim Seong-min if he had any advice as I pursued my research into the new underground railroad. He replied in a voice so soft that the interpreter and I had to lean forward in our chairs to hear him. "Remember those who did not make it," he said.

Since its beginning in the late 1990s, the new underground railroad has carried thousands of North Koreans to safety in South Korea and a few other countries. The rescue operations that began in a small, haphazard way in the late 1990s have grown into the multi-faceted, efficient underground railroad of today.

But for every North Korean who succeeds in exiting China on the new underground railroad, there are many who fail to reach their destinations. They do not make it, to use Kim Seong-min's formulation. No one keeps records of the names or numbers of North Koreans who perish trying to get out of China. Or of those who are arrested and repatriated and disappear back into North Korea. Or of those still hiding in China, too frightened of being arrested and forcibly returned to North Korea to attempt an escape.

In some sense, every one of the twenty-four million people still locked in North Korea belongs in the category of those who did not make it. But there is hope for them, too. While the long-term effects of the new underground railroad are not yet known, it's already evident that it is having a profound impact in North Korea itself. Those who escape are beginning to transform North Koreans' understanding of their country and helping to open their eyes to the rest of the world. The transformative process works in reverse as well. The testimonies of the escapees are educating the world about the secretive country they fled.

As the stories in this book have demonstrated, the new underground railroad serves two important purposes. First, it delivers a measure of human decency and the prospect of freedom to people who otherwise are destitute and hopeless. North Koreans inside North Korea are mostly unreachable. Helping the North Koreans hiding in China and wherever else they flee is a concrete way of serving a small percentage of a captive people. It is a worthwhile endeavor as a purely humanitarian matter. For Americans, helping North Koreans achieve freedom, even the small number of them represented by the refugees in China, upholds our moral values as a nation.

Second, the new underground railroad is a wedge to pry open a nation that has been sealed from the outside world for more than half a century. The assistance that the new underground railroad provides one refugee is magnified many times over in the friends and family with whom he communicates back home. As Pastor Phillip Buck likes to say, help one North Korean refugee escape, and you are helping to save an entire people. You are educating a network of North Koreans about the reality of life outside their borders. For the Christians who operate in the underground in China, a well-known verse from the Gospel of John holds special meaning: "And ye shall know the truth, and the truth shall make you free."[1]

The world can point to few successes, if any, in negotiating with North Korea. The country's illegal nuclear program and global arms trade continue apace despite widespread international opprobrium and sanctions, and in defiance of the regime's myriad promises to shut them down. Its other illicit activities continue, too—drug running, counterfeiting, insurance fraud, computer hacking. The suffering of the North Korean people continues unabated, despite a mountain of authoritative reports on the regime's human rights abuses from the United Nations, the United States, South Korea, and a panoply of international organizations. The Kim family regime in Pyongyang remains impervious to the carrots and sticks that the international community employs.

There are, however, two things that the regime plainly fears: the outflow of its citizens and the inflow of information. Pyongyang's crackdown on citizens who try to leave reflects the essential insecurity at the core of every totalitarian regime. So, too, does its suppression of information coming from any source other than itself. It is the response of a government that understands just how subversive the truth can be if a significant segment of its population is exposed to it. The regime knows that information, if spread, threatens the very essence of its power. This gives it a powerful incentive to keep its citizens from encountering any and all unauthorized information.

Pyongyang is right to fear the new underground railroad and the information invasion that it has launched. An informed population is more likely to rise up against the regime and demand its ouster. The seeds of the collapse of the Kim family regime are being planted by those who flee.

The lessons for those who care about the suffering of the North Korean people should be clear: Expand the new underground railroad. Find ever better means of delivering information to those left behind.

The challenge for world policy makers is to tap the power of the new underground railroad, nourish the capacities of the North Korean diaspora, and formulate policies to speed along the process of liberation and reunification. This deserves to be a regional effort, involving the United States, China, Japan, South Korea, and Russia, the same countries that are part of the on-again, off-again nuclear negotiations with Pyongyang.

The main obstacle to action is China. Beijing understandably fears having a large, semipermanent refugee population on its border, with its potential for creating heavy social and economic burdens. That is no excuse for China's failure to live up to its legal and humanitarian responsibilities to protect the North Korean refugees within its borders, but it is an entirely reasonable concern. That said, there is no reason that China should have to bear this burden alone.

The solution is to bring the new underground railroad above ground.

What if China were merely a way station for North Korean refugees, a place where they stayed briefly before transferring to resettlement facilities in other countries? Instead of being forced to hide in China, North Koreans who crossed the river would have a better option. They could go to the Office of the United Nations High Commissioner for Refugees or another designated humanitarian organization and receive immediate protection. If the North Koreans were processed swiftly in China and then departed, Beijing would have little reason to fret about the financial or social costs of managing a large, illegal population on its border. Nor, in case of a crisis in North Korea, would it have to worry about struggling by itself with a flood of refugees.

The United Nations has many shortcomings, as it has proved many times over in its failure to restrain North Korea on WMD and nuclear proliferation and its inability to reduce the suffering of the North Korean people. But the international organization has demonstrated that it does one task well: caring for refugees. The Office of the High Commissioner for Refugees excels at that work. If Beijing allowed the U.N. agency to do its job and operate on the Sino-Korean border, the UNHCR's record elsewhere in the world demonstrates that it could be highly effective.

Unlike refugees who cross borders just about everywhere else in the world, North Koreans who reach Chinese soil already have a guaranteed home: South Korea. The United States, Japan, Canada, and European countries have taken in small numbers of North Korean refugees, and it would be desirable for them to accept more, if only to signal the importance those countries place on assisting the displaced North Koreans. But there is no need for them to accept large numbers of refugees. It's natural and appropriate that South Korea should be the destination for the overwhelming majority of North Korea's freedom seekers. For reasons of language, culture, family, and proximity to the North, almost all North Koreans who escape opt to live in South Korea. That is as it should be.

The logistical issues of bringing the underground railroad above ground are complex, but it's possible to address them. To minimize the length of their stay in China, the North Koreans who arrive in China could, with Beijing's approval, move on to temporary facilities in neighboring countries. There they would be interviewed and processed for resettlement in South Korea or wherever else they want to go. A dozen international humanitarian organizations, including such groups as Doctors Without Borders, have offered in the past to help establish refugee centers in neighboring countries to care for the North Koreans.[2] Mongolia, which has good relations with both Koreas, could be one such place. Its geographical location close to northeast China, where the overwhelming number of the refugees are located, is also a point in its favor.

Thailand already is acting as a de facto resettlement center for hundreds of North Koreans every year under a quiet arrangement with South Korea. North Koreans who reach Thailand are housed in a detention center in Bangkok, where they are interviewed and processed for resettlement by the South Korean government before leaving for Seoul. The whole process takes about a month. The South Korean government pays most of the costs of caring for them while they are in Thailand.

A resettlement model that could be instructive here is the successful rescue of two million Indochinese refugees in the late 1970s and '80s. In the aftermath of the Vietnam War, the United States accepted 1.2 million Indochinese refugees. Australia, Canada, and France each resettled more than one hundred thousand, and other countries took in significant numbers. Paul Wolfowitz observed this process firsthand as assistant secretary of state for East Asia from 1982 to 1986. According to Wolfowitz, a key to the success of the Indochinese resettlement program was the partnership between the first-asylum countries of Southeast Asia—Thailand, the Philippines, Malaysia, Indonesia, and Singapore—and the countries of final resettlement. Wolfowitz called the system "a great humanitarian achievement" and has urged that countries adopt a similar effort on behalf of the North Korean refugees in China. Under his proposal, "even relatively modest levels, for example, twenty-five thousand per year, could permit resettlement of a quarter of a million refugees over a ten-year period."[3]

Bringing the underground railroad above ground would provide another benefit for China. It would allow it to fulfill its obligations under the 1951 United Nations Refugee Convention and its 1967 protocol to care humanely for refugees within its borders. By doing so, China would signal the world that it is a responsible nation and prepared to stand by its word. Its current refusal to live up to these responsibilities puts it in the category of international scofflaw. It throws into doubt China's commitment to all the global treaties it has signed and ratified.

Showing compassion to the North Korean refugees would also signal the world that China has a heart. That is not always evident to those who follow its treatment of democratic activists, Tibetans, Uighurs, and other of its citizens who defy the government. Beijing's forcible repatriation of North Koreans has the effect of aligning China's behavior with the savagery of the Kim family regime, the world's worst abuser of human rights. It puts China in the category of the uncivilized nations, a designation it does not otherwise deserve. China's mistreatment of some of its citizens, appalling as it sometimes is, usually does not sink to Pyongyang's level.

Treating the North Koreans humanely ought to be an easy choice for Beijing. The North Korean refugees pose no threat to its authority, and Beijing would pay no domestic political price for treating them well. It would have the additional benefit of putting China in good stead with its top trading partners: the European Union, the United States, Japan, and South Korea.

To the extent that North Korean refugees impose a burden on China, a regional resettlement program of the sort suggested above could ameliorate the problem. But not all of the North Koreans hiding in China are a burden for that country. Some North Koreans there make a contribution to China even though they are there illegally. The United States, South Korea, and other countries in the Pacific Rim could help these refugees by encouraging Beijing to provide legal status for them.

North Korean women who voluntarily marry Chinese men, for example, can be a boon to the smooth operation of Chinese society, which has a shortage of women of marriageable age. Arresting and repatriating North Korean brides serves no good purpose. It breaks up families and alienates the women's Chinese husbands. The government sometimes seems to understand this. It often turns a blind eye to the presence of some of the North Korean brides, in effect allowing them to stay indefinitely. It would make better sense to legalize the women's immigration status.

The children of Chinese–North Korean unions already qualify for legal status under China's Nationality Law, which guarantees citizenship to the offspring of a Chinese national. Yet many local governments refuse to register such children, or their fathers fail to do so, forcing them into a kind of stateless limbo, as described earlier in my discussion of half-and-half children. Their unregistered status, which denies them education and other public benefits, will not benefit China as the children reach their teen years and adulthood and seek a productive place in China's modernizing economy. Tens of thousands of these children are growing up in China. It is in Beijing's interests to ensure that they are registered and permitted to take up their full rights as Chinese citizens.

Some of the children are de facto orphans, abandoned by Chinese fathers who cannot care for them and by North Korean mothers who have either fled or been repatriated. Their lack of official papers makes it impossible for foreigners to adopt them. Legislation has been introduced in the United States Congress calling on the State Department to develop a strategy that would enable Americans to adopt these half-and-half children.[4] China could facilitate that process by making sure the children receive the Chinese citizenship papers to which they are entitled.

China already tolerates the presence of North Korean traders, family visitors, and some kinds of workers, even when they arrive illegally. Immigration programs providing legal protection from repatriation to such categories of refugees would be humane and helpful. Along those lines, China could implement a guest-worker program that would allow North Korean laborers to stay in China legally.

Despite its long alliance with North Korea, China today is no whole-hearted fan of that country. It recognizes that Pyongyang is a dangerous, unpredictable ally over which it has insufficient control and that Pyongyang's bad behavior could escalate out of control. Yet Beijing persists in the alliance because it fears instability on the peninsula. The biggest challenge for Washington, Seoul, and Tokyo is persuading Beijing that a Korea unified under a democratic, capitalist system would not be a threat to China. To the contrary, it would be an advantage.

A collapse of North Korea would have huge implications for China: disruption of regional trade, refugees streaming across its border, even war. China would almost certainly intervene militarily to stem chaos in North Korea—and to keep refugees from flooding across the river. But doing so would be costly both economically and in terms of China's international prestige. At some point, China would face difficult choices: Does it go it alone and try to install a Beijing-friendly government that it might or might not be able to control better than it controls the Kim family regime? Or does it work together with Seoul and Washington to find a solution that would include reunification of the two Koreas and permanent stability?

U.S. policy should be to encourage China to see the wisdom of reunification. China is South Korea's largest trading partner, a fact that augurs well for Beijing's economic interests in a unified Korea. Two-way trade between China and South Korea reached $200 billion in 2011 and should hit $300 billion by 2020.[5] Contrast that with the growing dependence of North Korea's broken economy on Chinese aid. China provides most of North Korea's food and fuel and Sino-North Korean trade amounts to more than 70 percent of North Korea's total trade.[6] In addition, China's goal of developing the three Rust Belt provinces bordering North Korea would be advanced by a stable and economically viable neighbor. In any case, North Korea is an anachronism in a region that has undergone a spectacular transformation from poverty to prosperity in the past half century. The rest of East Asia has grown up around it. Today, 25 percent of the world's trade passes through Northeast Asia. China, Japan, and South Korea are near the top of the list of the world's largest and strongest economies.

As for security issues, surely the United States and South Korea could accommodate Chinese concerns about a unified peninsula. Once the North Korean military threat is gone, the need for an American military presence on the Korean Peninsula would decrease substantially and might disappear altogether. Washington, Beijing, and Seoul need to start talking about such issues now rather than waiting until a crisis makes them unavoidable. That would include developing a regional plan to address a potential refugee crisis in the event of political destabilization in North Korea.[7]

Kim Jong Il had a dream. In it, the late leader of North Korea saw himself being stoned to death. The first rocks were thrown by Americans. Then came a hail of stones from the Americans' South Korean lackeys. Finally the nightmare reached its terrifying crescendo as North Koreans themselves lined up to pummel their leader. It was every dictator's nightmare: being deposed by his own people, who rose up against him.

Kim Jong Il divulged his dream to Chung Jun-yung, the late founder of the Hyundai Group, the South Korean car maker, who was a frequent visitor to Pyongyang during the years of the Sunshine Policy. The tycoon's son, Chung Mong-joon, a South Korean politician and onetime presidential candidate, recounted that story on television in early 2011 after his father's death. "My father met Kim Jong Il many times and had lengthy conversations with him over meals," the younger Chung explained. "Kim once said, 'Many people come to greet me wherever I go, but I know that they don't like me.'"[8]

Call it the Ceausescu effect. Defectors who moved in Kim Jong Il's orbit before they fled North Korea express the view that the late dictator was terrified he would suffer the same fate as that of Nicolae Ceausescu, the longtime strongman of Communist Romania and, like the North Korean dictator, the subject of a bizarre personality cult. On Christmas Day in 1989, a few weeks after the collapse of the Berlin Wall, Romanians rose up against Ceausescu and his wife, Elena. The couple was arrested, tried, and convicted of a range of capital offenses, including genocide against their fellow Romanians. The death sentence was carried out immediately. Just as North Koreans lined up in Kim Jong Il's dream to stone him to death, hundreds of Romanians volunteered to take a spot on the firing squad that killed their detested dictator.

The collapse of Communism in Europe took place with dazzling speed. So, too, it could happen in North Korea, which in any case is moving toward a denouement after the death in December 2011 of Kim Jong Il. His son and heir, Kim Jong Eun, is green, untested, and widely distrusted. Like his father, Kim Jong Eun is said to fear that his own people will kill him. In the younger Kim's case, it is the example of what happened to Libya's Moammar Gadhafi that is the stuff of nightmares. Gadhafi died at the hands of Libyan rebels in the democratic uprising of 2011, a few months before Kim Jong Eun became North Korea's supreme leader. His bloody final moments were captured on a grainy cellphone video that sped around the Web, presumably even reaching the computer screen of Kim Jong Eun in Pyongyang. The Libyan strongman was pulled from his hiding place in a drainage pipe and battered by an angry mob before being shot by a young man wearing a Yankees cap.

The new underground railroad has set in motion forces that are transforming North Korea and that may ultimately prove politically destabilizing. As we saw in Eastern Europe twenty years ago and in North Africa and the Middle East during the Arab Spring of our own decade, oppressed people can rise up with incredible speed to challenge even seemingly entrenched dictatorships. South Korea needs to be ready to jump at the chance of reunification, and the rest of the world needs to be ready to help.

No one wants to exercise a military option with North Korea. War games show that the West would emerge victorious, but at great cost of human life on both sides of the DMZ. How much better it would be to adopt policies encouraging an outflow of North Koreans who can then educate their friends and family left behind. Working from outside, these émigrés can spur internal pressures for change.

In trying to restrain a belligerent North Korea, the world speaks of sanctions and even manages to enforce them once in a while—to

Possessing a Bible is a crime in North Korea. This New Testament, published in the early twentieth century, was smuggled out of North Korea by a Christian whose family had hidden it for more than half a century. (Courtesy of Open Doors USA)

North Korean dictator Kim Il Sung greets American evangelist Billy Graham during Graham's visit to Pyongyang in 1994. (Courtesy of the Billy Graham Evangelistic Association)

North Korean refugees worship secretly in China. (Courtesy of Open Doors USA)

Defense Secretary Donald Rumsfeld unveils a satellite photograph of the Korean Peninsula at night at a Pentagon news conference in 2006. (Robert Ward/ Department of Defense)

American Steve Kim (far right) and a group of North Korean refugees whom he sheltered in Guangdong Province in southern China. (Courtesy of 318 Partners Mission Foundation)

Mug shot of Steve Kim, taken by Chinese police after his arrest in 2003 for the crime of helping North Korean refugees. (Courtesy of 318 Partners Mission Foundation)

Steve Kim (circled) in formation in the yard of the Chinese prison where he spent four years. (Courtesy of 318 Partners Mission Foundation)

American missionary Tim Peters in China with children who are half North Korean and half Chinese. (Courtesy of Helping Hands Korea)

Pastor Phillip Buck of Seattle wins the Train Foundation's Civil Courage Prize for his work helping North Koreans escape from China. (Jonathan Barth/Courtesy of the Train Foundation)

The Korean Church Coalition rallies in support of freedom for North Korea in front of the U.S. Capitol in July 2011. (Courtesy of Maria Kim)

American activist Suzanne Scholte addresses the North Korea People's Liberation Front, a Seoul-based organization of more than one hundred former North Korean soldiers who vow to overthrow the Kim family regime and reunify the Korean Peninsula. Scholte was named an honorary general. (Henry Song/ Courtesy of Defense Forum Foundation)

Secretary of State Hillary Clinton and First Lady Michelle Obama stand with Dr. Lee Ae-ran, an escapee from North Korea who was honored with an International Woman of Courage Award by the U.S. State Department in 2010. (U.S. Department of State)

Three Liberty in North Korea campus spokesmen—Stefan Hutzfeld, Angel Chung Cutno, and Lindsay Capehart—stand in front of the van that took them up and down the Eastern Seaboard in the fall of 2010. (Courtesy of the author)

Kim Seong-min in the newsroom of Free North Korea Radio, under a sign that proclaims the radio's motto: "Toward freedom! Toward democracy! Toward reunification!" (Courtesy of the author)

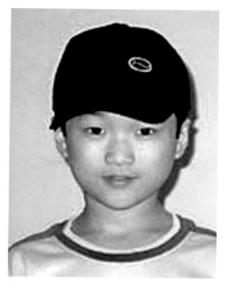

Yoo Chul-min, a ten-year-old North Korean boy who fled to China, died of exposure in the Gobi Desert in Mongolia after walking across the Chinese border. (Courtesy of Helping Hands Korea)

Yoo Chul-min's father, Yoo Sang-jun, prays at his son's grave in Mongolia. (Courtesy of Helping Hands Korea)

Youn Mi-rang, director-general of Hanawan, the resettlement center for North Korean refugees, meets with the author in Youn's office outside Seoul. (Courtesy of the author)

Kim Chun-ae, a pseudonym for a North Korean broadcaster, in the Seoul studio of Radio Free Asia. (Courtesy of Radio Free Asia)

little or no effect. Meanwhile an effective way to pressure the murderous Pyongyang regime is largely overlooked: its own people. As yet, there is no organized dissent in North Korea. But thanks to the new underground railroad, awareness is growing among ordinary North Koreans of the world outside their country's borders. They have an increasing skepticism, disdain even, of the regime that denies them the freedoms and prosperity that exist elsewhere.

Joseph Gwang-jin Kim, the boy who fled North Korea by walking across the frozen Tumen River on the eve of Kim Jong Il's birthday in 2005, spoke in Manhattan about his escape. He addressed a group of Americans funding the new underground railroad. Speaking in English, he thanked them for their support of him and his countrymen. "What you are doing changed my life," Joseph told his benefactors. Then he added, "and it will eventually change North Korea."

Kang Su-min, a North Korean woman now living in Seoul after years on the run in China, is similarly optimistic. She likes to say that most of her fellow exiles look to the future, not the past. They focus not on what their nation is today but what it may become tomorrow.

North Korea is the modern world's most repressive state. One day that will change. Meanwhile, the escape to freedom of a small number of its people is a rare good-news story that foretells a happier future for that sad country.

ACKNOWLEDGMENTS

This book could not have been written without the North Korean men, women, and children who shared their personal stories with me. They did so even when it brought back painful memories and awakened demons they would prefer to let sleep. Many spent long hours with me describing their decisions to flee, how they escaped, and their hopes for the country they left behind. I stand in awe of their courage and determination. I am profoundly grateful to them all.

I am also deeply indebted to the South Koreans, Americans, Chinese, and others who were willing to discuss their sensitive work helping North Koreans on the run. I owe a special debt to the Rev. Phillip Buck, Adrian Hong, Michael Horowitz, Steven Kim, Tim Peters, Suzanne Scholte, and Hannah Song, who went out of their way to help me navigate the story of the new underground railroad. I am thankful for their generous assistance and for their prayers.

In South Korea, I benefited from the wisdom of experts who provided information, introductions, and interesting perspectives. Park Syung-je's analysis of the Kim family regime was invaluable. Dan Southerland and Oh Joong-sok of Radio Free Europe shared their expertise and introduced me to the brave, articulate North Korean refugees who work with them in Seoul. Lee Keum-soon of the Korea Institute for National Unification and Youn Mi-rang of the Hanawon resettlement center offered perspectives based on their interviews with hundreds of North Koreans who had fled to South Korea. I am grateful, too, to Evan Ramstad, chief of the *Wall Street Journal*'s news bureau in Seoul. He and *Journal* reporter Jaeyeon Woo were exceptionally hospitable to their former colleague.

U.S. Army Colonel Kevin Madden, now retired, hosted me on my one visit to the Democratic People's Republic of Korea. From Seoul, he guided me to the South Korean side of the DMZ, where I entered the Joint Security Area that has been administered by the U.S.-led United Nations Command since the 1953 armistice that suspended the Korean War. There, in a conference room that straddles the border, I stepped into the surreal world of North Korea and had my picture snapped standing next to a DPRK soldier. Col. Madden is an astute and compassionate observer of North Korea, and he was generous in sharing knowledge gained from more than two decades studying that country and interacting with North Korean officials.

I thank U.S. special envoys Jay Lefkowitz and Robert King and United Nations special rapporteur Vitit Muntarbhorn for their overviews of human rights issues in North Korea. I also thank Minky Worden of Human Rights Watch, who provided introductions to North Korea– and China-watchers in Asia. I am grateful to Lenko Lenkov of the America for Bulgaria Foundation for his introduction to former Bulgarian diplomat Momchil Metodiev, who shared his research on the North Korean students who defected in Sofia in the 1960s. I benefited greatly from the expertise of Lieutenant-General

Michael M. Dunn (Ret.), who provided many fascinating insights about North Korea.

Several written sources were especially useful. I turned often to Bradley K. Martin's history of the Democratic People's Republic, *Under the Loving Care of the Fatherly Leader*; Stephan Haggard and Marcus Noland's book, *Witness to Transformation: Refugee Insights into North Korea*; numerous research papers published by the Washington-based Committee for Human Rights in North Korea; articles by Andrei Lankov of Kookmin University in Seoul; and the annual White Papers on Human Rights in North Korea published by the Korea Institute for National Unification in Seoul. I am grateful to Carl Herzig for permission to read his unpublished biography of Steven Kim.

I began to cover the new underground railroad when I worked at the *Wall Street Journal*, where I was a deputy editor of the editorial page. I thank editorial-page editor Paul A. Gigot for encouraging me to pursue the North Koreans' story and for his counsel in helping me think through the ethical issues involved in writing about vulnerable people for whom publicity might bring dire consequences. The *Journal* has the best editors in the newspaper business, and I was fortunate to work with many of them on my North Korea articles, including Howard Dickman, Erich Eichman, David Feith, Eric Gibson, Daniel P. Henninger, Michael Judge, Mary Kissel, Robert Pollock, Joseph A. Rago, Hugo Restall, Nancy deWolf Smith, and Bret Stephens, and as well as former editors Tunku Varadarajan, Bari Weiss, and Dana White. Marie Fortini and Carol Muller provided superb administrative and research assistance.

I owe a special debt to the Consulate General of the Republic of Korea in New York. Consul Park Jungyoul set up meetings for me with South Korean officials and provided helpful background material. I also thank the consul general in New York, Ambassador Kim Young-mok, as well as his predecessor, Ambassador Kim Kyungkeun. Both went out of their way to advise me.

I appreciate the assistance of the Consulate General of Japan in New York for helping me better understand North Korea's abduction of its citizens as well as Japan's policy on North Korea. I thank Yasuhisa Kawamura and Akira Sugiyama of the Japan Information Center and a former consul general, Ambassador Shinichi Nishimiya. I am grateful, too, to Kyoko Nakayama, formerly minister of state for the abduction issue.

This book benefited greatly from the research assistance of Dan Yong Chung. I was fortunate to have such a knowledgeable, careful, and dedicated researcher at my side. I am especially grateful to Dan for his sensitive recommendations on covering the issue of half-and-half children in China. I thank Maria Kim for attending a rally in Washington, D.C., for me and Barbara Scott for researching photos for the book. I also thank my interpreters and translators: Yoonjung Seo, Henry Song, Eunjung Park, Oh Min-jae, and Su Park.

I am grateful to the Smith Richardson Foundation, which provided financial support for travel, research assistance, acquisition of some photographs, and completion of my website. The foundation's Marin Strmecki and Allan Song have my sincere thanks. I also thank Kenneth R. Weinstein, president and CEO of the Hudson Institute, where I have found a congenial intellectual home as a senior fellow. I am grateful to John Raisian, David Brady, and Mandy MacCalla of the Hoover Institution at Stanford University, where I was a visiting media fellow in January 2010.

My friend Rick Hibberd, a graphic designer, was generous with his time and creativity. He advised me on the photographs included in this book and helped prepare them for publication. He also made first-rate suggestions about my website and publicity materials. John Kramer offered superb advice on promotion.

I appreciate the support of Roger Kimball, president and publisher of Encounter Books. I am grateful to my expert editor, Molly Powell, as well as to Heather Ohle, Sam Schneider, and Lauren Miklos of Encounter. I thank my adept agents, Glen Hartley and Lynn Chu, for finding a good home for *Escape from North Korea*.

Every writer needs a cheering squad, and mine was led, as always, by my mother, Virginia Kirkpatrick, who passed away as this book was entering production. I feel blessed to have had her encouragement, support, and confidence. I also thank my dear sisters, Holly Kirkpatrick Whiting and Robin Kirkpatrick Koves, along with my stepchildren, Jacqueline David, Nicole David Channing, and Zachary David. They were patient listeners, excellent sounding boards, and fountains of good cheer at difficult moments. In addition, Jacqueline helped me with online research, while Nicole read portions of the manuscript and offered smart, constructive criticisms.

Escape from North Korea is dedicated to my husband, Jack David, who played many invaluable roles during the two years I spent working on it. He was a gracious host to my sources, an intrepid fellow traveler to faraway places, and a master martini-maker at every milestone in the book's progress. He was the book's first reader and my toughest editor, keeping me on message and never letting me get away with sloppy thinking or imprecise language. I thank him with all my heart.

—Melanie Kirkpatrick
May 2012

HOW TO HELP

Committee for Human Rights in North Korea
http://hrnk.org/

Crossing Borders
http://crossingbordersnk.org

Defense Forum Foundation
http://www.defenseforum.org

Good Friends: Research Institute for North Korean Society
http://goodfriendsusa.blogspot.com

Helping Hands Korea
www.helpinghandskorea.org

Korean Church Coalition
http://www.kccnk.org

Liberty in North Korea
http://www.linkglobal.org

North Korean Refugee Services Mission
www.nkrsm.org

318 Partners Mission Foundation
http://318.iebee.com

NOTES

Epigraphs: The quotations that precede each section of this book are drawn from William Still's *Underground Railroad. A Record of Facts, Authentic Narratives, Letters, &c., Narrating the Hardships Hair-Breadth Escapes and Death Struggles of the Slaves in their efforts for Freedom, as Related by Themselves and Others, or Witnessed by the Author; Together with Sketches of Some of the Largest Stockholders, and Most Liberal Aiders and Advisors of, the Road* (Philadelphia: Porter & Coates, 1872), http://www.quinnipiac.edu/other/abl/etext/ugrr/ugrr.html.

INTRODUCTION

1. Still, *The Underground Railroad Record*, 51–54.

2. In 2011, the twenty-three countries with embassies in Pyongyang were Brazil, Bulgaria, Cambodia, China, Cuba, the Czech Republic, Egypt, Germany, India, Indonesia, Iran, Laos, Malaysia, Mongolia, Nigeria, Pakistan, Poland, Romania, Russia, Sweden, Syria,

the United Kingdom, and Vietnam. The Palestinian Authority also maintained an office in Pyongyang.

3. Interview with Kim Young-hwa, December 2009.

4. http://data.worldbank.org/country/korea-republic.

5. "North Korea Might Now Have The Bomb, but It Doesn't Have Much Electricity," *Daily Mail*, October 13, 2006, http://www .dailymail.co.uk/news/article-410158/North-Korea-The-Bomb-doesnt-electricity.html#.

6. Terry Miller and Kim R. Holmes, eds., Index of Economic Freedom, The Heritage Foundation and Wall Street Journal 2011, 245, http://www.heritage.org/index/.

7. *Freedom in the World 2011,* Freedom House, 2011, http://www .freedomhouse.org/template.cfm?page=363&year=2011.

8. *World Watch List: Where Faith Costs the Most,* Open Doors International, 2011, http://www.opendoorsusa.org/persecution/ world-watch-list.

9. "UN Expert Spotlights 'Abysmal' Human Rights Situation in DPR Korea," UN News Service, October 22, 2009, http://www .un.org/apps/news/story.asp?NewsID=32681&Cr=dprk&Cr1=&Kw1 =report&Kw2=vitit&Kw3=korea.

10. Lee Jong-heon, "North Korea's Gulags Hold 200,000 Political Prisoners," UPI, January 20, 2010.

11. Committee on Human Rights in North Korea, www.hrnk .org.

12. *North Korea: A Case to Answer, A Call to Act,* Christian Solidarity Worldwide, 2007, http://dynamic.csw.org.uk/article .asp?t=report&id=35.

13. Marcus Noland, deputy director, Peterson Institute for International Economics, in a presentation at the Korea Society, January 2010.

14. Press conference in Washington, D.C., December 2006.

15. Interview with Kang Su-min, February 2010.

16. Still, *The Underground Railroad Record*, 31.

17. http://www.nationalcenter.org/FugitiveSlaveAct.html.

18. Harriet Beecher Stowe, *Uncle Tom's Cabin or Life Among the Lowly*, ed. Elizabeth Ammons, 2nd ed. (New York: W.W. Norton & Company, 2010), 72.

19. Katherine Kane, executive director, Harriet Beecher Stowe Center, in a presentation at the center, September 2010.

20. Still, *The Underground Railroad Record*, 44.

21. *Weekly Report*, 318 Partners Mission Foundation, November 9, 2009.

CHAPTER 1: Crossing the River

1. Mary C. Pearl, "Natural Selections: Roaming Free in the DMZ," *Discover Magazine*, November 2006, http://discovermagazine.com/2006/nov/natural-selections-dmz-animals.

2. Stephan Haggard and Marcus Noland, eds., *The North Korean Refugee Crisis: Human Rights and International Response* (Washington, D.C.: Committee for Human Rights in North Korea, 2006) 20, http://www.hrnk.org/publications-2.

3. *2010 Human Rights Report*, U.S. Department of State, April 8, 2011, http://www.state.gov/g/drl/rls/hrrpt/2010/eap/154388.htm.

4. Interview with Joseph Gwang-jin Kim, October 2009. Adrian Hong, who led Joseph to the U.S. Consulate in Shenyang, and Sharon Rose, Joseph's foster mother, also provided information for this section.

5. *Progress for Children: A Report Card on Nutrition, No. 4*, UNICEF, May 2006, 20, http://www.unicef.org/progressforchildren/2006n4/.

6. Kongdan Oh, Testimony in the U.S. Senate Committee on Foreign Relations, Subcommittee on East Asian and Pacific Affairs, June 5, 2003.

7. Koo Bum-hoe, "Small-Scale Riots Break Out in North Korea Due to Famine," Yonhap News Agency, November 14, 1991; "Life

in North Korea Told by Yanbian Koreans (Parts 1 and 2)," Yonhap, November 15, 1991.

8. Yoonok Chang, Stephan Haggard, and Marcus Noland, "Migration Experiences of North Korean Refugees: Survey Evidence from China" (working paper, Peterson Institute for International Economics, March 2008) 10, http://www.iie.com/publications/interstitial .cfm?ResearchID=899.

9. Ibid., 5.

10. Andrei Lankov, "Lives of N. Korean Defectors," *Korea Times*, August 15, 2010.

11. Melanie Kirkpatrick, "Let Them Go," *Wall Street Journal*, October 14, 2006.

12. For a discussion on the number of North Korean refugees in China, see Stephan Haggard and Marcus Noland, *Witness to Transformation: Refugee Insights into North Korea* (Washington, D.C: Peterson Institute for International Economics: 2011), 2.

13. *2009 Human Rights Report,* U.S. Department of State, March 11, 2011, http://www.state.gov/g/drl/rls/hrrpt/2009/ eap/135995.htm.

14. Universal Declaration of Human Rights, Article 13, http:// www.un.org/en/documents/udhr/.

15. International Covenant on Civil and Political Rights, Article 12, http://www2.ohchr.org/english/law/ccpr.htm.

16. Constitution of the Democratic People's Republic of Korea, http://asiamatters.blogspot.com/2009/10/north-korean-constitution- april-2009.html.

17. For more details on North Korea's regulation of travel, see the "2009 White Paper on Human Rights in North Korea," Korea Institute for National Unification, 2009, 212–29.

18. Interview with Jiro Ishimaru, chief editor and publisher of Asia Press International, October 2010.

19. *North Korea Today: No. 114*, Research Institute for North Korean Society, Good Friends: Center for Peace, Human Rights and

Refugees, March 2008, http://goodfriendsusa.blogspot.com/2008/03/
north-korea-today-no-114.html.

20. The birthday of Kim Jong Il's son and heir, Kim Jong Eun, is
believed to be January 8. (The year of his birth is unknown, though it
is widely assumed to be in the mid-1980s.) In 2012, the day was not
declared an official holiday and there were no celebrations. It had been
less than a month since the death of Kim Jong Il, and the country
was still in mourning. A documentary about Kim Jong Eun was aired
on the state-run television network that day. In it, the country's new
leader was praised as "the genius among geniuses."

CHAPTER 2: Look for a Building with a Cross on It
    1. Interview with Hwang Gi-suk, February 2010.
    2. Interview with Eom Myong-hui, December 2009.
    3. Bradley K. Martin, *Under the Loving Care of the Fatherly Leader*
(New York: Thomas Dunne Books, 2004), 12.
    4. *Thank You, Father Kim Il Sung: Eyewitness Account of Severe
Violations of Freedom of Thought, Conscience, and Religion in North
Korea* (Washington, D.C.: United States Commission on International
Religious Freedom, 2005), 12–15. http://www.uscirf.gov/images/
stories/pdf/nkwitnesses.pdf.
    5. Ibid., 50–51
    6. Interviews with Tim Peters, Helping Hands Korea, between
2003 and 2011.
    7. Bill Powell, "Long Walk to Freedom," *Time Asia*, May 1, 2006.
    8. Tim Peters, Testimony to the U.S. House of Representatives,
Committee on International Relations, Subcommittee on Asia and the
Pacific, April 29, 2004.
    9. South Korean Ministry of Unification, http://www.unikorea
.go.kr/CmsWeb/viewPage.req?idx=PG0000000365.
    10. Mike Kim, *Escaping North Korea: Defiance and Hope in the
World's Most Repressive Country* (Lanham, Md.: Rowman & Littlefield,
2008), 187.

CHAPTER 3: Defectors

1. Interview with Youn Mi-rang, director general of Hanawon, the Settlement Support Center for North Korean Refugees, February 2010.

2. Interview with Evans Revere, president of the Korea Society, November 2009.

3 "The Man Who Bought Gadgets for Kim Jong-Il," BBC News, December 3, 2010; Sim Sim Wissgott, "NKorea Defector Tells of Business Deals in West," Agence France Presse, September 3, 2010.

4. Some of the details of the Changs' defections are related by press secretary James Rubin in the U.S. Department of State "Daily Press Briefing #122," August 26, 1997.

5. Interview with Momchil Metodiev, editor of the Bulgarian journal *Christianity and Culture*. Metodiev also provided a copy of his unpublished paper on the subject of the North Korean defectors to Bulgaria, May 2010.

6. Kim So-yeol, "Exchange Student Rebels Look Back," www.dailynk.com, June 11, 2010.

7. Interviews with Kim Cheol-woong in 2008, 2010, and 2011.

8. Dave Brubeck, as quoted in "Remembering Katyn," editorial, *Wall Street Journal*, December 1, 2010.

9. Chae-Jin Lee and Stephanie Hsieh, "China's Two-Korea Policy at Trial: The Hwang Chang Yop Crisis," *Pacific Affairs* 74, no. 3, Autumn 2001, 321–41; Don Oberdorfer, *The Two Koreas: A Contemporary History*, rev. ed. (New York: Basic Books, 2001) 399–401. Also, interviews with Hwang Jang-yop, October 2003; Kim Duk-hong, February 2011.

10. Rone Tempest, "China Grapples with Defection Dilemma," *Los Angeles Times*, Februrary 14, 1997.

11. Ban Ki-moon, who went on to become Secretary-General of the United Nations, was the South Korean government's secret emissary to Manila to persuade the Philippine government to permit Hwang and Kim to stay there for one month.

12. Email correspondence with Jae Ku, director of the U.S.-Korea Institute at Johns Hopkins University's School of Advanced International Studies, August 2011.

CHAPTER 4: Brides for Sale

1. Steven Kim's story is based on interviews, October 2009 and December 2009.

2. Article 318 of the Chinese criminal code says in part: "Whoever makes arrangements for another person to illegally cross the national border (frontier) shall be sentenced to fixed-term imprisonment of not less than two years but not more than seven years and shall also be fined," http://www.cecc.gov/pages/newLaws/criminalLawENG.php.

3. *World Population Prospects, the 2010 Revision*, United Nations, Department of Economic and Social Affairs, Population Division, http://esa.un.org/unpd/wpp/Excel-Data/fertility.htm.

4. Wei Xing Zhu, Li Lu, Therese Hesketh, "China's Excess Males, Sex Selective Abortion, and One Child Policy: Analysis of Data from 2005 National Intercensus Survey," *British Medical Journal*, April 9, 2009, http://www.bmj.com/content/338/bmj.b1211.full?sid=b22439fb-4766-4809-bd93-7f4c6d73b1d5.

5. Ibid.

6. "Gendercide: The Worldwide War on Baby Girls," *Economist*, March 6, 2010.

7. *Lives for Sale: Personal Accounts of Women Fleeing North Korea to China* (Washington, D.C.: Committee for Human Rights in North Korea, 2009), 9, http://www.hrnk.org/publications-2.

8. Zhu, Li, Hesketh, "China's Excess Males."

9. Steven V. Mosher, "When Gender Gaps: China's One-Child Policy and the Wholesale Elimination of Little Baby Girls," Weekly Briefing (blog), April 28, 2009, Population Research Institute, http://pop.org/content/april-28-when-gender-gaps-chinas-one-child-policy-and-the-wholesale-elimination-of-little-baby-girls-957.

10. Interview with "Naomi" (pseudonym), May 2006.

11. Interview with "Hannah" (pseudonym), May 2006.

12. Interview with Lee Keum-soon, senior researcher at the Korean Institute for National Unification, February 2010.

13. Lee Keum-soon, *The Border-Crossing North Koreans: Current Situations and Future Prospects*, Korean Institute for National Unification, 2006, 32.

14. *2009 Trafficking in Persons Report*, U.S. Department of State, 227, http://www.state.gov/documents/organization/123357.pdf.

15. *Lives for Sale*, 31.

16. Ibid., 32.

17. Ibid.

18. Press conference, North Korean Freedom Week, Washington, D.C., April 2009; video interview with Bang Mi-sun, http://www.youtube.com/watch?v=L3ZFRewLCi8.

19. Interview with Mark Lagon, director of the Office to Monitor and Combat Trafficking in Persons, U.S. Department of State from 2007 to 2009, March 2010.

20. *Weekly Report*, 318 Partners Mission Foundation, January 8, 2010.

CHAPTER 5: Half-and-Half Children

1. Interviews with "Mary and Jim" (pseudonyms), February 2010 and April 2010.

2. *Denied Status, Denied Education: Children of North Korean Women in China*, Human Rights Watch, April 2008, 2.

3. B.R. Myers, *The Cleanest Race: How North Koreans See Themselves—and Why It Matters* (Brooklyn: Melville House, 2010).

4. Interview with Mo Jongryn, professor at Yonsei University, January 2010.

5. "2009 White Paper on Human Rights in North Korea," Korea Institute for National Unification, 435–38.

6. Ibid., 435.

7. Ibid., 437.

8. Ibid., 436.

9. Ibid., 435.

CHAPTER 6: Siberia's Last Gulag

1. The *2011 Global Trafficking in Persons* report by the U.S. Department of State estimates the number of North Korean loggers in Russia to be "tens of thousands," www.state.gov/g/tip/tiprpt/2011/164232.htm. The Associated Press found Russian government figures that put the number of loggers at 32,600 in 2007. Kwang-tae Kim, "3rd North Korean Logger Attempts to Defect in Russia, Propelled by Dream of 'Freedom of Life,'" Associated Press, March 19, 2010.

2. Email correspondence with the Rev. Peter Jung, Justice for North Korea, August 2010.

3. The South Korean newspaper, *Chosun Ilbo*, reported in 2011 that there were three thousand North Koreans construction workers in Vladivostok, with three thousand more expected to arrive. It also reported that seven of the North Korean construction workers were sent back to North Korea, apparently after being caught watching South Korean movies on DVDs. "Vladivostok Teeming With N. Korean Laborers," www.chosun.com, August 18, 2011.

4. The history of North Korean loggers in Russia as related in this section comes from *Democratic People's Republic of Korea/Russian Federation: Pursuit, Intimidation and Abuse of North Korean Refugees and Workers,* Amnesty International, September 8, 1996.

5. Claudia Rosett, "Logging Time: Harsh Labor Camps in Siberia Still Exist in Democratic Russia—North Korea Operates Them to Harvest the Timber, Shares Profits With Host—Hunger, Cold and Worse," *Wall Street Journal*, April 11, 1994.

6. Claudia Rosett, "Freedom's Edge: Evil as Usual," www.forbes.com, March 11, 2010.

7. Rosett, "Logging Time."

8. This section is based on an interview with "Mr. Chang," a pseudonym for a former logger now living in South Korea, February 2010.

9. *Pursuit, Intimidation and Abuse*, Amnesty International, 20.

10. This section is based on an interview with the Rev. Phillip Buck, January 2010.

11. Rosett, "Logging Time."

12. Nicholas D. Kristof, "North Korea Delivers Warning in Sub Incident," *New York Times*, October 3, 1996; "Behind the Limelight, Forensic Lab Struggling," *JoongAng Daily*, November 17, 2006.

13. Andrei Lankov, "North Korean Loggers in Siberia," *Korea Times*, November 13, 2006.

14. *Pursuit, Intimidation and Abuse*, Amnesty International, 9.

15. Martin, *Under the Loving Care,* 407.

16. *2011 Global Trafficking in Persons,* U.S. Department of State.

17. Email correspondence with the Rev. Peter Jung, Justice for North Korea, August 2010.

18. Kwang-tae Kim, "3rd North Korean Logger Attempts to Defect in Russia, Propelled by Dream of 'Freedom of Life,'" Associated Press, March 19, 2010; email correspondence with the Rev. Peter Jung.

CHAPTER 7: Old Soldiers

1. The story of the rescue of South Korean POWs is based on interviews with "Mr. Jung" (a pseudonym); the man who served as the intermediary between Mr. Jung's team and the South Korean government; a former high-ranking official in President Kim Young-sam's administration; and a South Korean civilian who traveled frequently to the Sino-Korean border in the 1990s and was familiar with these events.

2. "2010 White Paper on Human Rights in North Korea," Korea Institute for National Unification, 2010, 480–85.

3. The Korean War Armistice Agreement, Article III, Arrangement Relating to Prisoners of War, July 27, 1953, http://news.findlaw.com/wp/docs/korea/kwarmagr072753.html.

4. "2010 White Paper on Human Rights in North Korea," 480.

5. "The Transfer of U.S. Korean War POWs to the Soviet Union," Joint Commission Support Branch, Research and Analysis Division, Defense Prisoner of War/Missing Personnel Office (DMPO), U.S. Department of Defense, August 26, 1993, http://www.dod.mil/pubs/foi/Personnel_and_Personnel_Readiness/POW_MIA/543.pdf.

6. An alternate Romanization of the general's name is "Kang Sang-ho."

7. The South Korean Defense Ministry says it has not been able to confirm the findings of the U.S. Department of Defense. See "2010 White Paper on Human Rights in North Korea," 482–83.

8. Zygmunt Nagorski Jr., "Unreported G.I.'s in Siberia," *Esquire*, May 1953.

9. Jon Herskovitz and Christine Kim, "War Still Raging for South Korean POWs in North," Reuters, April 5, 2010.

10. "POW Spent 43 Years in North Korea," *Dong-A Ilbo*, November 20, 2006.

11. http://commdocs.house.gov/committees/intlrel/hfa27228.000/hfa27228_0f.htm.

12. "We Want to Know It," Seoul Broadcasting System, October 1998

13. "Foreign Ministry Under Fire for Ignoring POW's Call for Help," *Chosun Ilbo*, November 24, 2006.

14. "2010 White Paper on Human Rights in North Korea," 481.

15. "S. Korea's Defense Minister Seeks Return of Korean War POWs in China," *Yonhap News*, July 14, 2011

CHAPTER 8: Hunted

1. The story of the Shenyang Six is based on interviews with Adrian Hong, co-founder of Liberty in North Korea; Jay Lefkowitz,

President George W. Bush's special envoy for human rights in North Korea; and background interviews with U.S. government officials.

2. Joseph Gwang-jin Kim, whose escape story is related in Chapters 1 and 2, was one of the three North Korean boys who were living in the U.S. Consulate in Shenyang at that time, waiting for exit permits from Beijing.

3. "2010 White Paper on Human Rights in North Korea," Korea Institute for National Unification, 69.

4. David Hawk, *The Hidden Gulag: Exposing North Korea's Prison Camps* (Washington, D.C.: Committee for Human Rights in North Korea, 2003), 58, http://www.hrnk.org/publications.htm.

5. Ibid., 59.

6. Interview with Seo Won-kyong, December 2009.

7. Mr. Seo's story has a tragic ending. In June 2011, he murdered his wife, stabbing her to death in their apartment in Rochester, N.Y. He then hanged himself. His motives for the murder-suicide were unknown.

8. Peter Martin and David Cohen, "Through Chinese Eyes: Zhu Feng," *The Interpreter*, Lowy Institute for International Policy, October 18, 2011.

9. Sophie Delaunay, regional coordinator for North Korea for Doctors Without Borders, testimony to the U.S. House of Representatives Committee on International Relations, Subcommittee on East Asia and the Pacific, May 2, 2002.

10. "Urgent Appeal for Protection of North Korean Refugees in China," press release, Doctors Without Borders, January 19, 2003.

11. Interview with Justin Wheeler, vice president of global awareness, Liberty in North Korea, February 2011.

12. "China: Protect North Korean Refugees," press release, Human Rights Watch, March 9, 2004.

13. http://www.unhcr.org/3b66c2aa10.html.

14. This section is based on an interview with Roberta Cohen, nonresident senior fellow, Brookings Institution, October 2010.

15. "Legal Grounds for Protection of North Korean Refugees," Roberta Cohen, Brookings Institution, October 4, 2010.

16. South Korea raised the issue of China's forced repatriation of North Korean refugees on February 27, 2012, at the U.N. Human Rights Council's meeting in Geneva. Rather than mentioning China by name, it referred instead to "all countries directly concerned."

17. www.savemyfriend.org.

18. *Taken! North Korea's Criminal Abduction of Citizens of Other Countries,* The Committee for Human Rights in North Korea, 2011.

19. Megumi's story is best told by her parents, Shigeru and Sakie Yokota, in a Japanese *manga,* or graphic book: *Megumi,* illustrated by Soichi Moto, published by the Headquarters for the Abduction Issue, Government of Japan, 2008.

20. Details of Kim Dong-shik's disappearance are in a civil lawsuit brought by his brother and son against North Korea in 2009 in the United States District Court for the District of Columbia, *Kim et al. v. Democratic People's Republic of Korea et al.* See especially a First Amended Complaint, November 23, 2009. Civ. No. 09-648 (RWR).

21. http://foreignaffairs.house.gov/110/33621.pdf.

22. Statement by Adrian Hong, hearing, U.S. House of Representatives, Committee on Foreign Affairs, Subcommittee on Asia, the Pacific, and the Global Environment, March 1, 2007, http://foreignaffairs.house.gov/110/33621.pdf.

CHAPTER 9: Jesus on the Border

1. Interview with the Rev. Eom Myong-hui, December 2009.

2. Rodney Stark, Byron Johnson, and Carson Mencken, "Counting China's Christians," First Things, May 2011.

3. Zhu Weiqun, a member of the central committee of the Chinese Communist Party, in comments published in a party journal, *Qiushi,* and reported by the official Xinhua News Agency. "China Party Official Warns Members Over Religion," Associated Press, December 19, 2011.

4. Years later, Pastor Eom's daughters followed her to China and then South Korea and the United States on the new underground railroad. Her husband stayed behind.

5. Interviews with Kang Su-jin, February 2010 and February 2011.

6. *International Religious Freedom Report 2010*, U.S. Department of State, November 17, 2010, http://www.state.gov/g/drl/rls/irf/2010/148874.htm.

7. Ibid.

8. Interview with Scott Flipse, deputy director of policy and research, United States Commission on International Religious Freedom, October 2010.

9. "North Korean Defector Killed for Going Back With 20 Bibles to Spread the Gospel," Associated Press, July 4, 2010.

10. Son Gyeong-ju's testimony at the Lausanne Congress is available at http://www.youtube.com/watch?v=0KEFbo2tJ_8.

11. Interview with Carl Moeller, president/CEO, Open Doors USA, April 2011.

12. http://www.seoulusa.org/ministries/underground-university/.

13. Matthew 10:23.

14. Melanie Kirkpatrick, "North Korea's Unlikely Messenger," *Wall Street Journal*, February 7, 1004.

CHAPTER 10: The Journey out of China

1. The story of the Rev. Phillip Buck (né John Yoon) is based on interviews with Pastor Buck in December 2006, October 2007, and January 2010. Grace Yoon Yi provided biographical information about her father. I also drew from interviews with Hwang Gi-suk, Kang Su-jin, and Choi Jung—North Koreans whom Pastor Buck sheltered in China and then led out of the country.

2. Fiona Terry, "The Deadly Secrets of North Korea," Doctors Without Borders, August 2, 2001.

CHAPTER 11: Let My People Go

1. Exodus 9:1.

2. Interview with Pastor Lee Heemoon, December 2009.

3. Interview with the Jo family, December 2009.

4. Jo Jin-hye, as quoted in Sohee Khim, "N. Korean Defector Talks for KASA," *The Daily Princetonian,* March 28, 2011.

5. Interview with the Seo family, December 2009.

6. Sharon Suh, *Being Buddhist in a Christian World: Gender and Community in a Korean American Temple* (Seattle: University of Washington Press, 2004), 3.

7. Interview with Donald Sung, June 2010.

8. Interviews with Michelle Park Steel and Shawn Steel, May 2011.

9. "House Passes Bill Requiring U.S. to Plan for Family Reunification for Korean Divided Families," news release, U.S. Representative Mark Kirk, Dec. 12, 2007.

10. Helie Lee, *In the Absence of Sun: A Korean American Woman's Promise to Reunite Three Lost Generations of Her Family* (New York: Three Rivers Press, 2002), 237.

11. www.kccnk.org.

12. Interview with Sam Kim, Korean Church Coalition, July 2010.

13. Interviews with Michael Horowitz, Hudson Institute, June, July and December 2010.

14. Interview with Representative Ed Royce, May 2011.

15. Interviews with Suzanne Scholte, Defense Forum Foundation, February 2010 and January 2011.

16. Gal Beckerman, *When They Come for Us, We'll be Gone: The Epic Struggle to Save Soviet Jewry,* (New York: Houghton Mifflin Harcourt, 2010) 46–49, 55–56.

CHAPTER 12: Be the Voice

1. Interviews with Angel Chung Cutno, volunteer for Liberty in North Korea, October 2010 and November 2010.

2. Interview with Kevin Park, student activist, January 2010.

3. Interview with Kim Ju-song (pseudonym), former North Korean military officer, November 2009.

4. See Chapter 8, "Hunted," for the story of LiNK's co-founder, Adrian Hong. Hong and two other LiNK workers were jailed in China for providing assistance to six North Koreans.

5. Interviews with Lindsay Capehart and Stefan Hutzfeld, LiNK volunteers, October 2010.

CHAPTER 13: Almost Safe

1. Interview with the defector, who wishes to remain unnamed, January 2011.

2. This section is based on email correspondence with Norbert Vollertsen in March 2011; interviews with Vollertsen and Tim Peters in the mid- to late 2000s; an interview with Kim Sang-hun in February 2010; and news reports from the time about the rushes on the embassies.

3. John Burton, "Protests Against China's Stance on North Koreans," *Financial Times*, July 1, 2001.

4. Migeddorg Batchimeg, "Mongolia's DPRK Policy: Engaging North Korea," *Asian Survey*, March–April 2006, 27597.

5. Ravdan Bold, Mongolia's ambassador to the United States, as quoted in "Mongolia Bars North Koreans," *Far Eastern Economic Review*, August 14, 2003, 8.

6. Interview with the Rev. Eom Myong-hui, December 2009.

7. Interview with Tim Peters, February 2011.

8. Norimitsu Onishi, "North Korea Denounces Seoul for Welcoming Defectors," *New York Times*, July 30, 2004.

9. http://wikileaks.org/cable/2009/12/09BANGKOK3145.html and also on a mirror site at http://cablesearch.org/cable/view.php?id=09BANGKOK3145&

10. Interview with Phil Robertson and Sunai Phasuk, both of Human Rights Watch, February 2011.

11. Immigration Bureau of the National Police Office of Thailand, as quoted in "Illegal North Korean Migrants on the Rise," *Bangkok Post*, May 6, 2011.

12. This section is based on interviews in February 2011 with Hannah Song, President/CEO of Liberty in North Korea; Sarah Yun, protection officer of LiNK's shelter in Southeast Asia; and Angeline Chong, LiNK's field director.

CHAPTER 14: Unification Dumplings

1. South Korean Ministry of Unification, http://www.unikorea .go.kr/CmsWeb/viewPage.req?idx=PG0000000365.

2. Jih-Un Kim and Dong-Jin Jang, "Aliens Among Brothers? The Status and Perception of North Korean Refugees in South Korea," *Asian Perspective* 31, no. 2, 2007, 5–13.

3. Kay Seok, "New Film Shows Struggles of North Koreans in South," Associated Press, April 17, 2011.

4. Interview with Patrick Cheh, a producer of the movie *Crossing*, June 2008.

5. Ashley Rowland and Hwang Hae-rym, "Facing Apathy and the Gulags: Ex-North Korean Inmates Struggle to Raise Concern in South," *Stars and Stripes*, February 9, 2010.

6. South Korea abstained from voting for the United Nations human rights resolution in 2005 and 2007. It voted for it in 2006, after North Korea conducted a nuclear test.

7. Cho Myung-chul was the North Korean defector who was named to a high-level government post. In the parliamentary elections of April 2012, Mr. Cho became the first North Korean to be elected to the National Assembly.

8. This section is based largely on an interview with Youn Mi-rang, director general of Hanawon, February 2010.

9. Background interview with Ministry of Unification official, February 2010.

10. Interviews with Choi Jung and three other North Korean women who do not want to be named, February 2010.

CHAPTER 15: Left Behind

1. "Political Humor From North Korea," *Radio Free Asia*, September 10, 2008.

2. Stephan Haggard and Marcus Noland, eds., *The North Korean Refugee Crisis: Human Rights and International Response*, (Washington, D.C.: Committee for Human Rights in North Korea, 2006), 25.

3. Cellphones actually were introduced to North Korea in November 2002 and gained as many as 20,000 subscribers. The regime banned their use in 2004 after the Ryongchon train explosion, as part of its effort to cover up the extent of the disaster. At the time, there were credible reports that word of the disaster was spreading fast, through the use of cellphones.

4. "*Internet Enemies: North Korea*," Reporters Without Borders, March 11, 2011, http://en.rsf.org/north-korea-11-03-2011,39755.html.

5. "Defectors Send $10 Million a Year to N. Korea," *Chosun Ilbo*, February 7, 2011.

6. Several North Korean refugees told me that brokers usually take a cut of 30 percent.

7. Survey in November 2010 by the Organization for One Korea, as reported in "Over 60% of N. Korean Defectors Send Resettlement Aid to North," www.arirangtv.com, February 23, 2011.

8. Song Sang-ho, "Remittance to N. Korea helps Enlighten About South Korea: Defector," *Korea Herald*, February 13, 2011.

9. Background interview with an official of South Korea's Ministry of Unification, February 2010.

10. Interview with "Ms. Lee" (a pseudonym), February 2011.

11. Interview with Youn Mi-rang, director general of Hanawon, February 2010.

12. Interview with Lee Keum-soon, Korean Institute for National Unification, February 2010.

13. Interviews with "Sun-mi" and "Bo-mi" (pseudonyms) in February 2011.

14. Lee Kyung-nam, former director of Donghwa Research Institute, as quoted in "Separated Families Skeptical About Reunions," *Korea Herald*, June 12, 2000.

15. http://wikileaks.org/cable/2009/09/09SEOUL1400.html or on a mirror site at http://cablesearch.org/cable/view .php?id=09SEOUL1400&hl=n.

16. Byun Eun-mi, "Reunion With Separated Family in North Korea Still Beyond Reach for Many," *Korea Herald*, April 17, 1998.

17. Interview with Kim Duk-hong, February 2011.

18. Don'o Kim, "Yearning to Go Home," *Far Eastern Economic Review*, June 15, 2000.

CHAPTER 16: Invading North Korea

1. "Journalism in the Service of a Totalitarian Dictatorship," Reporters Without Borders, October 22, 2004.

2. Interview with Carl Gershman, president, National Endowment for Democracy, October 2010.

3. Interviews with Kim Seong-min, founder, Free North Korea Radio, in 2007, 2008, and 2010.

4. Peter Beck, "North Korea's Radio Waves of Resistance," *Wall Street Journal,* April 16, 2010.

5. "International Broadcasting to North Korea: An Evaluation of Three South Korean Independent Radio Stations," InterMedia, September 2008.

6. "International Broadcasting to North Korea," InterMedia, March–August 2008. A 2012 Intermedia report finds access to media devices is now much higher.

7. Interview with Jiro Ishimaru, chief editor and publisher, *Rimjin-gang,* October 2011. See also *Rimjin-gang: Reports From Inside North Korea* (Osaka, Japan: Asia Press International, 2010).

8. Interview with Hyun In-ae, vice president of North Korea Intellectuals Solidarity, February 2011.

9. Venerable Pomnyun Sumin, chairman, Good Friends for the Peace, Human Rights and Refugee Issues and the Peace Foundation, in remarks at U.S.-Korea Institute at SAIS, Washington, D.C., February 1, 2012.

10. "N. Korea Bars Return of Workers From Libya: Panetta," Agence France Presse, October 27, 2011.

CHAPTER 17: Conclusion: One Free Korea

The title of this chapter is inspired by Joshua Stanton's excellent blog on North Korea, One Free Korea, at www.freekorea.us.

1. John 8:32.

2. Suzanne Scholte, as quoted in Mark W. David, *The Human Rights Crisis in North Korea: Challenges and Opportunities* (Stanford: Hoover Institution, 2005).

3. Paul Wolfowitz, "How to Help North Korea's Refugees," *Wall Street Journal,* June 16, 2009.

4. Representative Ed Royce introduced the North Korean Refugee Adoption Act in 2010 and 2011. The bill never made it to the floor of the House of Representatives for a vote.

5. Lee Chung-min, "Falling Out of Love With North Korea," *Wall Street Journal Asia,* December 28, 2011.

6. Ibid.

7. The Washington-based Committee on Human Rights in North Korea has made this recommendation.

8. "Kim Jong Il 'Has Nightmares of Being Stoned by His People,'" *Chosun Ilbo,* March 28, 2011.

INDEX

Ulan Bator

MONGOLIA

GOBI DESERT

DISCARD

CHINA

BHUTAN

INDIA

BANGLADESH

Kunming•

BURMA

VIETNAM
Hanoi

LAOS

Chiang Saen•

Chiang Mai
•

THAILAND